Looking at Philosophy

Text and Illustrations
by
Donald Palmer

Looking at Philosophy

The Unbearable Heaviness of
Philosophy Made Lighter

THIRD EDITION

Donald Palmer

Professor Emeritus at College of Marin
Visiting Assistant Professor at North Carolina State University

Boston   Burr Ridge, IL   Dubuque, IA   Madison, WI   New York
San Francisco   St. Louis   Bangkok   Bogotá   Caracas   Kuala Lumpur
Lisbon   London   Madrid   Mexico City   Milan   Montreal   New Delhi
Santiago   Seoul   Singapore   Sydney   Taipei   Toronto

For Katarina & Christian

McGraw-Hill Higher Education 🪐
*A Division of The **McGraw-Hill** Companies*

LOOKING AT PHILOSOPHY, THIRD EDITION

Published by McGraw-Hill, a business unit of The McGraw-Hill Companies, Inc., 1221 Avenue of the Americas, New York, NY, 10020. Copyright © 2001, 1994, 1988, by The McGraw-Hill Companies, Inc. All rights reserved. No part of this publication may be reproduced or distributed in any form or by any means, or stored in a database or retrieval system, without the prior written consent of The McGraw-Hill Companies, Inc., including, but not limited to, in any network or other electronic storage or transmission, or broadcast for distance learning.

Some ancillaries, including electronic and print components, may not be available to customers outside the United States.

This book is printed on acid-free paper. ·

    5 6 7 8 9 0   MAL/MAL   0 9 8 7 6 5 4 3

ISBN 0-7674-0596-X

Library of Congress Cataloging-in-Publication Data
Palmer, Donald.
    Looking at philosophy : the unbearable heaviness of philosophy made lighter / Donald Palmer.—3rd ed.
      p.   cm.
    Includes bibliographical references (p.) and index.
    ISBN 0-7674-0596-x
    1. Philosophy—History. 2. Philosophy—History—Caricatures and cartoons. 3. American wit and humor, Pictorial.   I. Title.
B74.P26 2000
190—dc21

                                00-031032

Sponsoring editor, Kenneth King; production editor, Julianna Scott Fein; manuscript editor, Karen Dorman; design manager and cover designer, Violeta Diaz; text designer and art editor, Robin Mouat; cover illustration, Donald Palmer; manufacturing manager, Randy Hurst. The text was set in 12/17 Tekton by TBH Typecast, Inc., and printed on acid-free 45# Highland Plus by Malloy Lithographing, Inc.

Text Credits: Page 391, from *The Random House Dictionary*, Unabridged, Second Edition, 1993. Reprinted with permission from Random House, Inc.

www.mhhe.com

Preface

Wittgenstein once said that a whole philosophy book could be written consisting of nothing but jokes. *This is not that book,* nor does this book treat the history of philosophy as a joke. This book takes philosophy seriously, but not gravely. As the subtitle indicates, the goal of the book is to lighten the load a bit. How to do this without simply throwing the cargo overboard? First, by presenting an overview of Western philosophy from the sixth century B.C.E. through three-quarters of the twentieth century in a way that introduces the central philosophical ideas of the West and their evolution in a concise, readable format without trivializing them, but at the same time, without pretending to have exhausted them nor to have plumbed their depths. Second, following a time-honored medieval tradition, by illuminating the margins of the text. Some of these illuminations, namely those that attempt to schematize difficult ideas, I hope will be literally illuminating. Most of them, however, are simply attempts in a lighter vein to interrupt the natural propensity of the philosophers to succumb to the pull of gravity. (Nietzsche said that only the grave lay in that direction.) But even these philosophical jokes, I hope, have a pedagogical function. They should serve to help the reader retain the ideas that are thereby gently mocked. Thirty years of teaching the subject, which I love—and which has provoked more than a few laughs on the part of my students—convinces me that this technique should work. I do not claim to have achieved Nietz-sche's "joyful wisdom," but I agree with him that there is such a thing and that we should strive for it.

Before turning you over to Thales and his metaphysical water (the first truly heavy water), I want to say a word about the women and their absence. Why are there so few women in a book of this nature? There are a number of possible explanations, including these:

1. Women really are deficient in the capacity for sublimation and hence are incapable of participating in higher culture (as Schopenhauer and Freud suggested).
2. Women have in fact contributed greatly to the history of philosophy, but their contributions have been denied or sup-pressed by the chauvinistic male writers of the histories of philosophy.
3. Women have been (intentionally or unintentionally) system-atically eliminated from the history of philosophy by political, social, religious, and psychological manipulations of power by a deeply entrenched, jealous, and fearful patriarchy.

I am certain that the first thesis does not merit our serious attention. I think there is some truth to the second thesis, and I may be partially guilty of suppressing that truth. For example, the names of at least seventy women philosophers in the late classical period alone have been recorded, foremost of which are Aspasia, Diotima, Aretê, and Hypatia. (Hypatia has been belatedly honored by having a journal of feminist philosophy recently named after her.) Jumping over centuries to our own age, we find a number of well-known women con-tributing to the history of philosophy in the first half of the current century, including Simone de Beauvoir, Susanne Langer, and L. Susan Stebbing.

However, no matter how original, deep, and thought-provoking were the ideas of these philosophers, I believe that, for a number of reasons (those reasons given in the second and third theses are probably most pertinent here), none of them has been as historically significant as the ideas of those philosophers who are discussed in this book. Fortunately, things have begun to change in the past few years. An adequate account of contemporary philosophy could not in good faith ignore the major contributions to the analytic tradition of philosophers Iris Murdoch, Philippa Foot, G. E. M. Anscombe, and Judith Jarvis Thompson, nor those contributions to the Continental tradition made by Gayatri Chakravorty Spivak, Monique Wittig, Luce Irigaray, and Julia Kristeva. Furthermore, a new wave of women philosophers is already beginning to have considerable impact on the content of contemporary philosophy and not merely on its style.

So, despite the risks, I defend the third thesis. I truly believe that if women had not been systematically excluded from major participation in the history of philosophy,[1] that history would be even richer, deeper, more compassionate, and more interesting (not to mention more joyful) than it already is. It is not for nothing that the book ends with a discussion of the work of a contemporary woman philosopher and with a question posed to philosophy herself, "Quo vadis?"—Whither goest thou?

The third edition has added considerably more material, especially concerning ancient Greek philosophy, medieval philosophy, the philosophy of the Renaissance, and Anglo-American analytic philosophy in the second half of the twentieth century. The Glossary has been expanded, and a section titled "Topics for Consideration" has been included at the end of each chapter.

Finally, I want to say that I have had some help with all three editions of this book. For assistance with the first edition, I am grateful to Kerry Walk and reviewers Job Clement, Daytona Beach Community College; Hans Hansen, Wayne State University; Yukio Shirahama, San Antonio College; and William Tinsley, Foothill College, who read parts of the manuscript and provided helpful suggestions. Donald Porter, College of San Mateo, read the whole thing. He clearly understood exactly what I was trying to achieve and gave me many good ideas for doing it better. For help with the second edition, I am indebted to Dasiea Cavers-Huff, Riverside Community College; Donald Porter, College of San Mateo; Matt Schulte, Montgomery College; and Robert White, Montgomery College. For reviewing the third edition,

I thank Timothy R. Allan, Trocaire College, Buffalo; Will Griffis, Maui Community College; Fred E. Heifner, Jr., Cumberland University; Joseph Huster, University of Utah; Brian Schroeder, Siena College; Samuel Thorpe, Ph.D., Oral Roberts University; James Tuttle, John Carroll University; Stevens F. Wandmacher, University of Michigan, Flint; and Andrew Ward, San Jose State University. I would also like to thank my colleague David Auerbach for having read and commented on parts of the manuscript. Jim Bull, my editor at Mayfield Publishing Company for the first two editions, had faith in this project from its inception. My editor at Mayfield for the third edition has been Ken King, whose insight and efficiency have helped make this edition an improvement over the first two. My thanks to Julianna Scott Fein and Robin Mouat of Mayfield's Production Department and copyeditor Karen Dorman for their expertise. My wife, Leila May, has been my most acute critic and my greatest source of inspiration. She kept me laughing during the dreariest stages of the production of the manuscript, often finding on its pages jokes that weren't meant to be there. I hope she managed to catch most of them. There probably are still a few pages that are funnier than I intended them to be.

Notes

1. See Mary Warnock, ed. *Women Philosophers* (London: J. M. Dent, 1996).

Contents

VII. Pragmatism, the Analytic Tradition, and the Phenomenological Tradition and Its Aftermath

The Twentieth Century   295

Introduction

The story of Western philosophy begins in Greece.

The Greek word "Logos" is the source of the English word "logic" as well as all the "-logies" in terms like "biology," "sociology," and "psychology, where "logos" means the theory, or study, or rationalization of something. "Logos" also means "word" in Greek, so it involves the act of speaking, or setting forth an idea in a clear manner. "Logos," therefore, designates a certain kind of thinking about the world, a kind of logical analysis that places things in the context of reason and explains them with the pure force of thought. Such an intellectual exercise was supposed to lead to wisdom (Sophia), and those who dedicated themselves to Logos were thought of as lovers of wisdom (love = philo), hence as philosophers.

What was there before philosophy, before Logos? There was *Mythos*—a certain way of thinking that placed the world in the context of its supernatural origins. Mythos explained worldly things by tracing them to exceptional, sometimes sacred, events that caused the world to be as it is now. In the case of the Greeks, Mythos meant tracing worldly things to the dramatic acts of the gods of Mount Olympus. The narratives describing these origins—myths—are not only explanatory but also morally exemplary and ritualistically instructive; that is, they provide the rules that, if followed by all, would create the foundation of a genuine community of togetherness— a "we" and an "us" instead of a mere conglomeration of individuals who could only say

Explaining Ancient Greek Customs

"I" and "me." Hence, myths are often conservative in nature. They seek to maintain the status quo by replicating origins: "So behaved the sacred ancestors, so must we behave." Myths had the advantage of creating a whole social world in which all acts had meaning. They had the disadvantage of creating static societies, of resisting innovation, and, many would say, of being false. Then, suddenly, philosophy happened—Logos broke upon the scene, at least according to the traditional account. (There are other accounts, however, accounts that suggest that Western Logos—philosophy and science—is just our version of myth.) But let us suppose that something different did take place in Greece about 700 B.C.E.[1] Let's suppose that the "first" philosopher's explanation of the flooding of the Nile River during the summer (most rivers tend to dry up in the summer) as being caused by desert winds (desert winds, not battles or love affairs among gods) really does constitute novelty. Natural phenomena are explained by other natural phenomena, not by supernatural events in "dream time"—the time of the ancient gods. In that case, Greece truly is the cradle of Western philosophy.

A Modern Myth?

Why Greece, and not, for example, Egypt or Judea? Well, let's be honest here. Nobody knows. Still, a number of historical facts are relevant to the explanation we seek. For one, there was a very productive contact between ancient Greece and the cultures of the eastern Mediterranean region—Persia,

Mesopotamia, Phoenicia, Cyprus, southern Italy, and Egypt, among others. The Greeks were a well-traveled group and were extremely adept at borrowing ideas, conventions, and artistic forms from the cultures they encountered and applying these elements creatively to their own needs. There is also a recent controversial theory that Greek culture derives greatly from African sources.[2] It is at least certain, as one historian of Greek ideas has recently said, that "the cultural achievements of archaic and classical Greece are unthinkable without Near Eastern resources to draw upon,"[3] and eastern North Africa fits into this map.

Also, unlike the case in some of the surrounding societies, there was no priestly class of censors in Greece. This observation does not mean that Greek thinkers had no restrictions on what they could say—we will see that several charges of impiety were brought against

some of them in the period under study—but that they were able nevertheless to get away with quite a bit that went against prevailing religious opinion.

Another historical fact is that the Greek imagination had always been fertile in its concern with intimate detail. For example, Homer's description of Achilles' shield takes up four pages of the Iliad. In addition, the many generations of Greek children who grew up on the poems of Homer and Hesiod[4]—two of the main vehicles that transmitted Greek religion—recognized in them their argumentative, intellectually combative, and questioning nature. The polemical nature of Greek drama and poetry would find a new home in Greek philosophy.

A final component of the world into which philosophy was born is the socioeconomic structure that produced a whole leisured class of people—mostly *male* people—with time on their hands that they could spend meditating on philosophical issues. It is always jolting to remember that during much of Greece's history, a major part of the economic foundation of its society was slave labor and booty from military conquests. This fact takes some of the luster from "the Glory that was Greece."

Still, for whatever reasons, the poetry and drama of the Greeks demonstrate an intense awareness of change, of the war of the opposites—summer to winter, hot to cold, light to dark, and that most dramatic change of all, life to death.

Indeed, this sensitivity to the transitory nature of all things sometimes led the Greeks to pessimism. The poets Homer, Mimnermus, and Simonides all expressed the idea "Generations of men fall like the leaves of the forest."[5]

But this sensitivity also led the Greeks to demand an explanation—

one that would be obtained and justified not by the authority of religious tradition but by the sheer power of human reason. Here we find an optimism behind the pessimism—the human mind operating on its own devices is able to discover ultimate truths about reality.

But let us not overemphasize the radicalness of the break made by the Greek philosophers with the earlier, mythical ways of thinking. It's not as if suddenly a bold new **atheism** emerged, rejecting all religious explanations or constraints. In fact, atheism as we understand it today was virtually unknown in the ancient world.[6] Rather, these early Greek philosophers reframed the perennial puzzles about reality in such a way as to emphasize the workings of nature rather than the work of the gods. For instance, they tended to demote **cosmogony** (theories about the *origins* of the world) and promote **cosmology** (theories about the *nature* of the world).

This new direction represents the beginnings of a way of thinking that the Greeks would soon call "philosophy"—the love of wisdom. We can discern in these early efforts what we now take to be the main fields of the discipline that we too call philosophy: ontology (theory of being); epistemology (theory of knowledge); **axiology** (theory of value), which includes ethics, or **moral philosophy** (theory of right behavior), and aesthetics (theory of beauty, or theory of art); and **logic** (theory of correct inference).

In fact, the theories put forth in ancient Greece could be called the origins of Western science with as much justification as they can be called the origins of Western philosophy, even though at that early period, no such distinctions could be made. Roughly, I would say that science deals with problems that can be addressed experimentally by subsuming the observable events that puzzle us under the dominion of natural laws and by showing how these laws are related causally to those events. *Philosophy*, on the other hand, deals with problems that require a speculative rather than an experimental approach. Such problems often require **conceptual analysis** (the logical scrutiny of general ideas) rather than observation or data gathering. Consider these questions, paying special attention to the italicized words:

Can we *know* why on rare occasions the sun darkens at midday?
Is it *true* that the moon's passing between the earth and the sun *causes* such events?
Can there be successful experiments that *explain* this phenomenon?

These questions are scientific questions. Now compare these questions to the following ones, paying attention again to the words in italics:

What is *knowledge?*
What is *truth?*
What is *causality?*
What is *value?*
What is *explanation?*

These questions invite conceptual analysis, which is part of philosophy.

But we are moving too fast and looking too far ahead. As I said, such distinctions had not yet been clearly drawn in the ancient world.

The thinkers there were satisfied to have asked the kinds of questions that were foundational both to philosophy and to science.

Topics for Consideration

1. Pick some observable phenomenon, such as what we now call the eclipse of the sun, and explain it from the perspective of science, and then again from some system of myth. (You may have to visit the library for this exercise.) Then use these two "stories" to demonstrate the difference between Logos and Mythos.

2. Think about your own patterns of belief. Are there any of them that you would acknowledge as Mythos rather than Logos? Here are two examples: (A) If you have religious beliefs, how would you characterize them in terms of this distinction? (B) What would it mean to assert that science itself is simply an instance of Western Mythos?

Notes

1. I have chosen to use the new dating coordinates B.C.E. (Before the Common Era) and C.E. (Common Era) rather than the older B.C. (Before Christ) and A.D. (Anno Domini, or The Year of Our Lord) because the attempt to gauge the whole of human history from the perspective of a particular religious tradition no longer seems tenable. But let's face it: this new system is a bit artificial. Probably there is something arbitrary about all attempts to date historical events. At least I am not following the lead of the nineteenth-century philosopher Friedrich Nietzsche, who proclaimed, "History begins with my birth." (We'll study Nietzsche later.)

2. Martin Bernal, *Black Athena: The Afroasiatic Roots of Classical Civilization*, vol. 1, *The Fabrication of Ancient Greece 1785–1985* (New Brunswick, N.J.: Rutgers University Press, 1987).

3. Robin Osborne, "The Polis and Its Culture," in *Routledge History of Philosophy*, vol. 1, *From the Beginning to Plato*, ed. C. C. W. Taylor (London and New York: Routledge, 1997), 14.

4. Homer, *The Iliad*, trans. Michael Reck (New York: IconEditions, 1994); Homer, *The Odyssey*, trans. Robert Fitzgerald (New York: Farrar, Straus & Giroux, 1998); Hesiod, *Theogony: Works and Days*, trans. Dorothea Wender (Harmondsworth, England: Penguin, 1976).

5. This sentiment can be found in the poems published in *Greek Lyric: An Anthology in Translation*, ed. and trans. Andrew M. Miller (Indianapolis and Cambridge: Hackett Publishing, 1996), 27, 117, 118.

6. See Catherine Osborne, "Heraclitus," in *From the Beginning to Plato*, 90.

1
The Pre-Socratic Philosophers

Sixth and Fifth Centuries B.C.E.

The thinkers who were active in Greece between the end of the seventh century B.C.E. and the middle of the fourth century B.C.E. are known today as the pre-Socratic philosophers, even though the last of the group so designated were actually contemporaries of Socrates.

(Socrates was born in 469 and died in 399 B.C.E. We look at his thought in the next chapter.) What all the pre-Socratic philosophers have in common is their attempt to create general theories of the cosmos (kosmos is the Greek term for "world") not simply by repeating the tales of how the gods had created everything, but by using observation and reason to construct general theories that would explain to the unprejudiced and curious mind the secrets behind the appearances in the world. Another commonality was that all the pre-Socratic philosophers stemmed from the outlying borders of the Greek world: islands in the Ionian Sea or Greek colonies in Italy or along the coast of Persia (in today's Turkey). Knowledge of these thinkers is tremendously important not only for understanding the Greek world of their time, but—as I have argued in the Introduction—for grasping the origins of Western philosophy and science.

The problem is that in fact very little is known about the pre-Socratic philosophers. Most of the books that they wrote had already disappeared by the time that the philosopher Aristotle (384–322 B.C.E.) tried to catalog and criticize their views. Today's understanding of the pre-Socratics is based mostly on summaries of their ideas by Aristotle and by later Greek writers who had heard of their views only by word of mouth. Many of these accounts are surely inaccurate because of distortions caused by repetition over several generations by numerous individuals. (Have you ever played the game called Telephone, in which a complicated message is whispered to a player, who then whispers it to the next player, and so on, until the message—or what's left of it—is announced to the whole group by the last player in the circle?) Also, these summaries often contained anachronistic ideas, that is, ideas from the later time projected back into the earlier views. Only fragments of the original works remain in most cases today, and even those few existing passages do not always agree with one another. Remember, these "books" were all written by hand on papyrus (a fragile early paper made from the crushed and dried pulp of an Egyptian water plant), and all editions of these books were copied manually by professional scribes. Furthermore, the

Telephone

meaning of many of the fragments is debatable, both because of the "fragmentary" nature of the scraps—key words are missing or illegible—and because of the obscure language in which many of these works were written. Nevertheless, a tradition concerning the meaning of the pre-Socratics had already developed by Aristotle's time, and it is that version of their story that influenced later philosophers and scientists. Therefore, that is the tradition that I report here, realizing that it is flawed and distorted in many ways.[1]

Thales

Philosophy makes its first self-presentation in three consecutive generations of thinkers from the little colony of Miletus on the coast of Asia Minor—today's Turkey—in the sixth century B.C.E. The first recorded philosopher is Thales of Miletus (ca. 580 B.C.E.). Here is what he seems to have written about in his long-lost book.

GRASS → TO → MILK

What substance must underlie grass
to allow it to be transformed to milk?

If there is change, there must be some *thing* that changes, yet
does not change. There must be a unity behind the apparent plurality
of things, a Oneness disguised by the superficial plurality of the
world. Otherwise the world would not be a *world*; rather, it would be a
disjointed grouping of unrelated fragments.

So what is the nature of this unifying, ultimately unchanging
substance that is disguised from us by the *appearance* of constant
change?

Like the myth makers before him, Thales was familiar with the
four elements: air, fire, water, and earth. He assumed that all things
must ultimately be reducible to one of these four—but which one?

Of all the elements, water is the most obvious in its transformations: Rivers turn into deltas, water turns into ice and then back into water, which in turn can be changed into steam, which becomes air, and air, in the form of wind, fans fire.

Then water it is!
All things are composed of water.

Thales' actual words were: "The first principle and basic nature of all things is water."[2]

This obviously false conclusion is valued today not for its content but for its form (it is not a great leap between the claim "All things are composed of water" and the claim "All things are com-

posed of atoms") and for the presupposition behind it (that there is an ultimate stuff behind appearances that explains change while remaining itself unchanged). Viewed this way, Thales can be seen as the first philosopher to introduce the project of **reductionism.** Reductionism is a method of explanation that takes an object that confronts us on the surface as being one kind of thing and shows that the object can be reduced to a more basic kind of thing at a deeper but less obvious level of analysis. This project is usually seen as a major function of modern science.

Anaximander

Still, not all of Thales' contemporaries accepted his formulation. For one, his student Anaximander (ca. 610–ca. 546 B.C.E.), also from the city of Miletus, said that if all things were water, then long ago everything would have returned to water. Anaximander asked how water could become its deadly enemy, fire—how a quality could give rise to its opposite. That is, if observable objects were really just water in various states of agitation—as are ice and steam—then eventually all things would have settled back into their primordial liquid state. Aristotle paraphrases

him this way: If ultimate reality "were something specific like water, the other elements would be annihilated by it. For the different elements have contrariety with one another. . . . If one of them were unlimited the others would have ceased to exist by now."[3] (Notice that if this view can be accurately attributed to Anaximander, then he subscribed to an early view of the principle of **entropy,** according to which all things have a tendency to seek a state of equilibrium.)

For Anaximander, the ultimate stuff behind the four elements could not itself be one of the elements. It would have to be an unobservable, unspecific, indeterminate something-or-other, which he called the Boundless, or the Unlimited (*apeiron* in Greek). It would have to be boundless, unlimited, and unspecific because anything specific is opposed to all the other specific things in existence. (Water is not fire, which in turn is not air, and so on.) Yet the Boundless is opposed to nothing, because everything is *it*.

Anaximander seems to have imagined the Boundless as originally moving effortlessly in a great cosmic vortex that was interrupted by some disaster (a Big Bang?), which caused the four elements to separate off from the vortex. In the only passage remaining to us from the book he wrote, Anaximander says:

> And from what source things arise, to that they return of necessity when they are destroyed, for they suffer punishment and make reparation to one another for their injustice according to the order of time.[4]

There are many possible interpretations of this amazing passage. According to the most dramatic interpretation, the whole world as you and I know it is the result of a cosmic error. Creation is an act

of injustice. But justice will be done; the world will eventually be destroyed, and "things" will return to their boundless source and revolve eternally in a vortex. This interpretation, which contains at least as much Mythos as Logos, exhibits a bizarre kind of optimism about the triumph of justice.

A less radical and less mythical interpretation would be this: Once the four elements were created, they became related to one another in antagonistic ways, but their opposition to one another balances out in an ecological harmony. If one element dominates at one period (say, water in a time of flood), it will later be compensated by the domination of another element at another period (say, fire in a drought). So the original unity of the Boundless is preserved in the apparent war of the opposites. In any case, the apeiron for Anaximander is immortal and indestructible, qualities usually associated with gods, as Aristotle points out.[5] Again, we see that pre-Socratic philosophy has not completely divorced itself from its religious origins.

Anaximenes

Some of Anaximander's followers asked, "How much better is an 'unspecific, indeterminate something-or-other' than nothing at all?" They decided that it was no better, that in fact it was the same as nothing at all, and knowing that *ex nihilo nihil* (from nothing comes nothing), they went on searching for the mysterious ultimate stuff.

The next philosopher,
Anaximenes (ca. 545 B.C.E.), thought it was *air*.

The air that we experience ("commonsense air") is a halfway house between all the other forms into which "primordial air" can be transformed through condensation and rarefaction.

With the idea of condensation and rarefaction, Anaximenes continued the project of reductionism. He introduced the important claim that all differences in quality are really differences in quantity (just more or less stuff packed into a specific space), an idea with which many scientists would agree today.

These first three philosophers, Thales, Anaximander, and Anaximenes, are known as the Milesians because they all came from the Greek colony of Miletus on the Persian coast and because they constitute the first *school* of philosophy. Despite the differences among them, they shared a number of characteristics, some of which would eventually become part of the Western scientific tradition: a desire for simple explanations, a reliance on observation to support their theories, a commitment to **naturalism** (the view that natural phenomena should be explained in terms of other natural phenomena) and **monism** (the view that ultimately there is only one kind of "stuff").

Rarefaction

fire
smoke
steam
AIR
mist
water
mud
dirt
stone

Condensation

The School of Miletus ended when the tenuous peace between the Greek outpost and Persia collapsed and the Persians overran the city.

Pythagoras

The Milesians' successor, Pythagoras (ca. 572–ca. 500 B.C.E.), from the island of Samos, near Miletus, did not seek ultimacy in some material element, as his predecessors had done. Rather, he held the curious view that all things are numbers. Literally understood, this view seems absurd, but Pythagoras meant, among other things, that a correct description of reality must be expressed in terms of mathematical formulas. From our science classes we are familiar with a great number of laws of nature, all of which can be written out in mathematical formulas (for example, the law of gravitation, the three

laws of motion, the three laws of thermodynamics, the law of reflection, Bernoulli's law, Mendel's three laws). Pythagoras is the great-great-grandfather of the view that the totality of reality can be expressed in terms of mathematical laws.

Very little is known about Pythagoras himself. Nothing he wrote has survived. It is almost impossible to sort out Pythagoras's own views from those of his followers, who created various Pythagorean monastic colonies throughout the Greek world during the next several hundred years. He seems to have been not primarily a mathematician but a **numerologist;** that is, he was interested in the mystical significance of numbers. For instance, because the Pythagoreans thought that the number 10 was divine, they concluded that what we would today call the solar system had ten members. This theory turns out to be roughly correct—the sun and nine planets—but not for Pythagoras's reasons.

Nevertheless, he anticipated the bulk of Euclid's writings on geometry and discovered the ratios of concord between musical sound and number. From this discovery he deduced a mathematical harmony throughout the universe, a view that led to the doctrine of "the music of the spheres." The ten celestial bodies move, and all motion produces sound. Therefore, the motion of the ten celestial bodies—being divine—produces divine sounds. Their music is the eternal background sound against which all sound in the world is contrasted. Normally, we hear only the "sound in the world" and are unable to hear the background harmony. But a certain mystical stance allows us to ignore the sound of the world and to hear only the divine music of the spheres.

The influence of Pythagoras was so great that the School of Pythagoreans lasted almost 400 years. The spell he cast on Plato alone would be enough to guarantee Pythagoras a permanent place in the history of philosophy. (We shall see that Plato turns out to be the most important philosopher of the Greek period and that he was a fine mathematician as well.) With hindsight, we can now look at Pythagoras's work and see those features of it that mark him and his followers as true philosophers. Nevertheless, it is only artificially that we distinguish that portion of Pythagorean thought that we declare to be philosophical. We should not ignore the less scientific aspect of Pythagoras's teachings, which to him were all part of a seamless whole. He was the leader of a religious cult whose members had to obey a strict number of esoteric rules based on asceticism, numerology, and vegetarianism.

Despite their vegetarianism, Pythagoreans had to forswear eating beans because eating beans is a form of cannibalism. A close look at the inside of a bean reveals that each one contains a small, embryonic human being (or human bean, as the case may be).

Heraclitus

The next philosopher, Heraclitus (ca. 470 B.C.E.) of Ephesus, only a few miles from Miletus, had a new perspective:

The basic stuff is *fire!*

Heraclitus wrote, "There is an exchange of all things for fire and of fire for all things,"[6] though he seems to have understood this idea more in a symbolic than in a literal sense.

There is something about the nature of fire that gives insight into both the appearance of stability (the flame's form is stable) and the fact of change (in the flame, everything changes).

Heraclitus drew some striking conclusions from this vision.

Reality is composed not of a number of things but of a process of continual creation and destruction.

"War is father and king of all."

"Conflict is justice."

These passages too should probably be understood symbolically and not literally.[7]

"You cannot step into the same river twice."[8]

Heraclitus explained this idea, saying, "Everything flows and nothing abides; everything gives way and nothing stays fixed."[9] In fact, for Heraclitus, the only thing that does not change is change itself.

Heraclitus was called the Dark One, or the Obscure One. Despite the survival of more than one hundred passages from Heraclitus's book and despite his having written in prose rather than in poetry, he is one of the most difficult of all the pre-Socratic philosophers. Heraclitus is hard to understand not only because he wrote in aphorisms—short, pithy sentences meant to summarize a universal truth—but also because he seems to have intentionally disguised the truth he was communicating. Justifiably or not, his ideas were interpreted pessimistically by later Greeks, and this understanding was handed down to posterity. According to this interpretation, his ideas create more than merely a philosophy—they constitute a mood, almost a worldview of nostalgia and loss:

> You can't go home again. Your childhood is lost.
> The friends of your youth are gone.
> Your present is slipping away from you.
> Nothing is ever the same.

Nevertheless, there was something positive in the Heraclitean philosophy. There existed an unobservable Logos—a logic—governing change that made change a rational phenomenon rather than the chaotic, arbitrary one it appeared to be. Heraclitus wrote: "Logos is always so."[10] This Logos doctrine deeply impressed Plato and eventually became the basis of the notion of the laws of nature. It is also directly related to a doctrine claimed by Christianity. Both God and Christ are equated with Logos in the Gospel of John: "In the beginning was the Word [Logos], and the Word [Logos] was with God and the Word [Logos] was God" (John 1:1); "And the Word [Logos] was made flesh, and dwelt among us" (John 1:14).

Parmenides

Heraclitus's successor Parmenides (ca. 515–ca. 440 B.C.E.) went a step further than his predecessor.

In effect, he said that you can't step in the same river once.

Parmenides begins with what he takes to be a self-evident truth: IT IS. This claim is not empirical—not one derived from observation; rather it is a truth of Reason. It cannot even be denied without self-contradiction. If you say, "It is not" (i.e., nothing exists), then you've proved that "It is," for if nothing exists, it's not nothing; rather it is something.

Parmenides believed that Being is rational, that only what can be thought can exist. Since "nothing" cannot be thought (without thinking of it as something), there is no nothing, there is only Being. From the mere idea of Being it follows that Being is uncreated, indestructible, eternal, and indivisible. Furthermore, Being is spherical, because only a sphere is equally real in all directions. (Maybe this notion is related to the idea of the twentieth-century physicist Albert Einstein, who claimed that space is curved?) Being has no holes (no vacuum) because, if Being is, there can't be any place where Being is not.

You Cannot Step in the Same River Once

From this argument it follows that motion is impossible because motion would involve Being going from where Being is to where being isn't (but there can't be any such place as the place where Being isn't).

In fact, for Parmenides the very idea of empty space was an impossible idea. Either space is a thing, in which case it is something and not nothing, or it is nothing, in which case it does not exist. Because all thought must have an object and because nothing is not an object, the idea of nothing is a self-contradictory idea.

It must be obvious to you that Parmenides has strayed a long way from common sense and from the facts that are revealed to us by the senses of sight, touch, hearing, smell, and taste—and primary among those facts is that motion exists and that things change. But if people laughed at Parmenides, they didn't laugh for long, for he soon had a powerful ally.

Zeno

The sly old fox Zeno of Elea (ca. 490 B.C.E.—?) wrote a now-famous series of paradoxes in which he defended Parmenides' outrageous views by "proving" the impossibility of motion using a method known as reductio ad absurdum.

In this form of argument, you begin by accepting your opponent's conclusions, and you demonstrate that they lead logically to an absurdity or a contradiction.

Zeno argued that, even granting motion, you could never arrive anywhere, not even to such a simple goal as a door. Before you can

get to the door, you must go halfway, but before you can go halfway, you must go halfway of the remaining halfway, but before you can do that, you must go halfway of halfway, but before you can go halfway, you must go halfway. When does this argument end? Never! It goes on to infinity. Therefore, motion would be impossible even if it were possible.

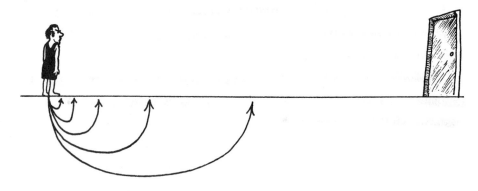

In yet another of his paradoxes, Zeno demonstrated that in a race between Achilles and a tortoise, if Achilles gave the tortoise a head start (as would only be fair), the swift runner could never overtake the lumbering reptile. This is because, before Achilles can pass the tortoise, he must arrive at the point where the tortoise used to be; but given the hypothesis of motion, the tortoise will never still be there. He will have moved on. This paradox will forever be the case. When Achilles arrives at a point where the tortoise was, the tortoise will have progressed. Achilles can never catch him.

The conclusions of these paradoxical arguments of Zeno defending the views of his master, Parmenides, may seem absurd to you, but they are actually derived from the mathematical notion of the infinite divisibility of all numbers and, indeed, of all matter. Zeno's arguments are still studied in postgraduate courses on the foundations of mathematics. Zeno is forcing us to choose between mathematics and sensory information. It is well known that the senses often deceive us, so we should choose the certainty of mathematics. With that suggestion Parmenides and Zeno caused a crisis in Greek philosophy. They radicalized the distinction between information based on the five senses and that based on pure reason (a distinction that would later develop into two schools of philosophy: **empiricism** and **rationalism**). Furthermore, they forced a reevaluation of the monistic

Is Reality One Thing?

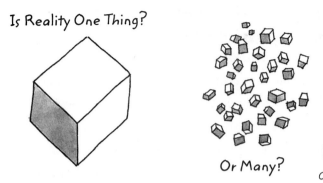

Or Many?

presupposition accepted by all Greeks heretofore (namely, the view that reality is composed of one thing), because thinkers came to realize that such a view led directly to Parmenides' conclusions. It appeared that philosophers either would have to accept Parmenides' shocking arguments or they would have to give up monism. In fact, they gave up monism.

Empedocles

The next group of philosophers are known as pluralists, precisely because they were unable to accept the monolithic stillness of Parmenides' Being. Therefore, they were forced to believe that ultimate reality is composed of a plurality of things rather than of only one kind of thing.

The first of this group was Empedocles (?–ca. 440 B.C.E.), a citizen of the Greek colony of Acragas on the island of Sicily, who believed that everything was composed of the simplest parts of the four elements: fire, air, earth, and water. He called these elements the "four roots."

But in the face of Zeno's critique of motion, Empedocles believed he needed to posit two forces to explain change and movement. These forces he called Love and Strife. Love is the force of unity, bringing together unrelated items to produce new creations, and Strife is the force of destruction, breaking down old unities into fragments.

(A curious version of Empedocles' theory was later to be accepted by the twentieth-century psycho-analyst Sigmund Freud, who named the two forces Eros and Thanatos [the life instinct and the death instinct]. Freud agreed with Empedocles that these forces formed the bases of all organic matter.)

The first theory of **evolution** developed out of Empedocles' system. Love brings together certain kinds of monsters. "Many heads grew up without necks, and arms were wandering about naked, bereft of shoulders, and eyes roamed about alone with no foreheads. Many

creatures arose with double faces and double breasts, offspring of oxen with human faces, and again there sprang up children of men with oxen's heads."[11]

And those that could survive, did survive.

(Aristotle later criticized this view as "leaving too much to chance.")

Anaxagoras

The next pluralist, Anaxagoras (ca. 500–ca. 428 B.C.E.) of Clazomenae, near Miletus, found Empedocles' theory too simplistic. He replaced the "four roots" with "infinite seeds." Each of these seeds is something like an element in today's chemistry; so in some ways, this theory sounds very modern. Every object in the world contains seeds of all elements, and in each object, the seeds of one element predominate.

"In all things, there is a portion of everything . . . For how could hair come from what is not hair? Or flesh from what is not flesh?"[12]

Anaxagoras agreed with Empedocles that some force explaining motion and change was required, but he replaced Empedocles' all too mythical figures of Love and Strife with one force, a mental one, which he called Nous, or Mind. This assumption means that the universe is organized according to an intelligent, rational order. Anaxagoras's Nous is almost like a god who creates objects out of the seeds, or elements.

Furthermore, there is a distinction between the animate and the inanimate world in that the organic world contains Nous within it as

a self-ordering principle, whereas the inorganic world is ordered externally by Nous. Nous itself is qualitatively identical everywhere, but its abilities are determined by the nature of the body that contains it. Humans aren't any smarter than carrots, but they can *do* more than carrots because they have tongues, opposable thumbs, and legs. (You wouldn't act very smart either if you were shaped like a carrot.)

Notice that Anaxagoras's theory is the first time that a philosopher distinguished clearly between living substance and "dead" matter. The anthropomorphic concept Nous looked promising to two of the most important later Greek philosophers, Socrates and Aristotle, but eventually it disappointed them. Socrates said that at first he found it an exciting idea, but it ended up meaning nothing at all, and Aristotle said that Anaxagoras stood out "like a sober man in the midst of loose talkers."[13] Later Aristotle was disillusioned by Anaxagoras, who used "reason as a **deux ex machina** for the making

of the world, and when he is at a loss to tell from what cause something necessarily is, then he drags reason in, but in all other cases
ascribes events to anything rather than reason."[14]

Leucippus and Democritus

400 bc   *460 - 370*

Precisely because Anaxagoras's view was anthropomorphic, it was
still too mythical for Anaxagoras's successors, a group of philosophers, led by Leucippus (ca. 460 B.C.E.–?) and Democritus
(ca. 460–ca. 370 B.C.E.), known as the
atomists.

They saw the world as
composed of material
bodies, which them-
selves are composed
of groups of "atoms."
The Greek word
ατομον (atomon)
means "indivisible,"
that which cannot be split.

Democritus made each atom a little piece of Parmenidean Being
(uncreated, indestructible, eternal, indivisible, containing no "holes")
and set them moving through empty space traversing absolutely

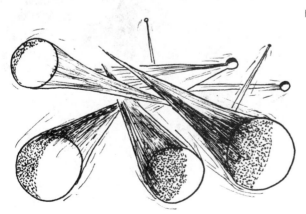

necessary paths that
are determined by
rigid natural laws.
So, contrary to
Parmenides' view,
both empty space
and motion are
real. Moreover, like
atoms themselves,
motion and space

are natural and basic, admitting of no further analysis. It is the appearance of *inertia* and not that of motion that needs explaining, and Democritus's explanation, like that of Heraclitus, is that inertia is an illusion. That is to say, it is explained away. Thus, by the year 370 B.C.E., Greek philosophy had been led to a thoroughgoing **materialism** and a rigorous **determinism.** There was nothing in the world but material bodies in motion and there was no freedom, only necessity.

What had the pre-Socratic philosophers achieved? In them, a special kind of thinking had broken free from its mythical and religious ancestors, developing its own

methods and content—a kind of thinking that would soon evolve into what today we know as science and philosophy. Looking back at the pre-Socratics, we see a direct lineage between them and the great thinkers of our own time: The dichotomy between reason and the senses that the German philosopher Immanuel Kant was to

resolve in the eighteenth century was first made clear by the pre-
Socratics; the first attempt to formulate a theory of evolution was
made by them; and the first effort to solve the riddle of how mathematical numbers hold sway over the flux of reality—all this we see as
a more or less unbroken genealogy from their time to ours.

But to the Greeks of the fifth century, the pre-Socratic philosophers had left a legacy of confusion.

The only thing the philosophers had succeeded in doing was to
undermine the traditional religious and moral values, leaving nothing
substantial in their place. (As the Greek dramatist Aristophanes

said, "When Zeus is toppled, chaos succeeds him, and whirlwind rules.")

Besides, "the times they were a' changin'," socially and politically as well as intellectually. The old aristocracy, dedicated to the noble values of the Homeric legends, was losing ground to a new mercantile class, which was no longer interested in the virtues of Honor, Courage, and Fidelity but in Power and Success. How was the new class to achieve these virtues in an incipient democracy? Through politics. And the access to political power was then, as it is today, through the study of rhetoric (read "law")—the art of swaying the masses with eloquent, though not necessarily truthful, argumentation.

Topics for Consideration

1. What is the problem of "the One and the Many" that presented itself to the early Greek philosophers? Pick three pre-Socratics with very different solutions to this problem and contrast their views.

2. Apply the distinction you learned in the Introduction between Mythos and Logos to the Milesian philosophers Thales, Anaximander, and Anaximenes. Which camp are they in?

3. If you lived in the Greek world during the sixth century B.C.E. and knew only what could be known at that period, which of the basic substances or entities would you choose as the foundation of reality, based on your own observations? Why? (Before you start, read the next topic.)

a. Water (Thales)

b. Air (Anaximenes)

c. Fire (roughly, Heraclitus)

d. Earth (*very roughly*, Democritus)

e. An indeterminate "stuff" (Anaximander)

f. Numbers (roughly, Pythagoras)

4. Same question as the previous topic, with this qualification: Based on what you *now* know at the beginning of the twenty-first century, but still limited to the categories a through f, which letter or combination of letters would you choose?

5. Contrast as dramatically as you can the theses of Heraclitus and Parmenides. What do you think would be the practical consequences, if any, of seriously accepting the philosophical claim of Heraclitus? of Parmenides?

6. Explain why Zeno's paradoxes provoked such a deep crisis in the intellectual environment of ancient Greece. Show how philosophical progress after Zeno required some compromise between the views of the Parmenidean camp and those of the pre-Parmenidean camp.

Notes

1. A readable account of recent scholarship on this topic can be found in *Routledge History of Philosophy*, vol. 1, *From the Beginning to Plato* (ed. C. C. W. Taylor [London and New York: Routledge, 1997]), Chapter 2, "The Ionians," by Malcolm Schofield; Chapter 3, "Heraclitus," by Catherine Osborne; Chapter 4, "Pythagoreans and Eleatics," by Edward Hussey; Chapter 5, "Empedocles," by M. R. Wright; and Chapter 6, "Anaxagoras and the Atomists," by C. C. W. Taylor. These investigations support large parts of the traditional views of the pre-Socratics as they are reported here, but also give good reasons for skepticism concerning the accuracy of other aspects of those views.

2. Philip Wheelwright, ed., *The Presocratics* (New York: Odyssey Press, 1966), 44. This sentence is one of only four remaining from Thales' book.

3. Ibid., 55.

4. Milton C. Nahm, ed., *Selections from Early Greek Philosophy* (New York: Appleton-Century-Crofts, 1962), 62.

5. "The unlimited is equivalent to the Divine, since it is deathless and indestructible" (Wheelwright, 55).

6. Ibid., 71.

7. Merrill Ring, *Beginning with the Pre-Socratics*, 2d ed. (Mountain View, Calif.: Mayfield Publishing, 2000), 70.

8. Ibid., 66.

9. Wheelwright, 70.

10. Ring, 62.

11. Nahm, 136.

12. Ibid., 150, 152.

13. Wheelwright, 168.

14. Aristotle, *Metaphysics*, trans. W. D. Ross, in *The Basic Works of Aristotle*, ed. Richard McKeon (New York: Random House, 1941), 697.

2

The Athenian Period

Fifth and Fourth Centuries B.C.E.

The Sophists

No surprise, then, that the next group of philosophers were not really philosophers as such but rhetoricians who became known as Sophists ("wise guys"). They traveled from city to city, charging admission to their lectures—lectures not on the nature of reality or truth but on the nature of power and persuasion. Plato and Aristotle wrote a lot about the Sophists, and according to the picture that they handed down to us, not just **skepticism** but cynicism became the rule of the day.

Protagoras

Perhaps the most famous (and least cynical) of the Sophists was Protagoras (ca. 490–ca. 422 B.C.E.). He taught that the way to achieve success is through a careful and prudent acceptance of traditional customs—not because they are true, but because an understanding and manipulation of them is expedient. For Protagoras all customs were relative, not absolute. In fact, *everything* is relative to human subjectivity. Protagoras's famous claim is *homo mensura—* man is the measure.

Man is the measure of all things, of things that are, that they are, and of things that are not, that they are not.[1]

Protagoras's emphasis on subjectivity, **relativism,** and expediency is the backbone of all **sophism.** According to some stories, Protagoras was indicted for blasphemy, and his book on the gods was burned publicly in Athens—yet one of the few remaining fragments of his writings concerning religion states, "As for the gods, I have no way of knowing either that they exist or that they do not exist."[2]

Gorgias

Another famous Sophist was Gorgias (ca. 483–375 B.C.E.). He seems to have wanted to dethrone philosophy and replace it with rhetoric. In his lectures and in a book he wrote, he "proved" the following theses:

1. There is nothing.
2. If there were anything, no one could know it.
3. If anyone did know it, no one could communicate it.

The point, of course, is that if you can "prove" these absurdities, you can "prove" anything. Gorgias is not teaching us some astounding truth about reality; he is teaching us how to win arguments, no matter how ridiculous our thesis may be.

Thrasymachus

Yet another Sophist was Thrasymachus, who is known for the claim "Justice is in the interest of the stronger." That is to say, *might makes right.* According to him, all disputation about morality is empty, except insofar as it is reducible to a struggle for power.

Callicles and Critias

According to the accounts handed down to us, two of the most cynical Sophists were Callicles and Critias.

Callicles claimed that traditional morality is just a clever way for the weak masses to shackle the strong individual. He taught that the strong should throw off these shackles and that doing so would be somehow "naturally right." What matters is *power*, not justice. But why is power good? Because it is conducive to *survival*. And why is survival good? Because it allows us to seek *pleasure*—pleasure in food, drink, and sex. Pleasure is what the enlightened person aims for, qualitatively and quantitatively. The traditional Greek virtue of *moderation* is for the simple and the feeble.

Critias (who was to become the cruelest of the Thirty Tyrants, the men who overturned the democracy and temporarily established an oligarchical dictatorship) taught that the clever ruler controls subjects by encouraging their fear of nonexistent gods.

So we see that the essence of sophism comprises **subjectivism,** skepticism, and **nihilism.** Everything the pre-Socratics stood for is devalued. There is no objective reality, and if there were, the human mind could not fathom it. What matters is not truth but manipulation and expediency. No wonder Socrates was so offended by sophism.

Yet we must say a few kind words about sophism despite its negativism. First, many of the Sophists were skilled politicians who actually contributed to the history of democracy. Second, history's animosity toward them is based mostly on reports we have of them

from Socrates and Plato, who were enemies of the Sophists. Third, and most important, sophism had the positive effect of making human beings aware not of the cosmos, but of themselves as objects of interest. In pre-Socratic philosophy, there was no special consideration of the human. Suddenly, with Protagoras's "man is the measure," humans became interested in themselves.

Socrates

The Sophists, who were professional teachers, met their match in a man who was possibly the greatest teacher of all time, Socrates (469–399 B.C.E.). Despite his overall disagreement with them, Socrates followed the Sophists' lead in turning away from the study of the cosmos and concentrating on the case of the human. But unlike the way the Sophists discoursed about the human being, Socrates wanted to base all argumentation on objectively valid definitions. To say "man is the measure" is saying very little if one does not know what "man" is. In the *Theatetus*, Socrates says:

Socrates' discourse moved in two directions—outward, to objective definitions, and inward, to discover the inner person, the soul, which, for Socrates, was the source of all truth. Such a search is not to be conducted at a weekend lecture but is the quest of a lifetime.

Truth (trōō_th_):
verity, conformity
with fact. Honesty,
integrity.

Socrates was hardly ever able to answer the questions he asked. Nevertheless, the query had to continue, for, as we know from his famous dictum,

"The unexamined life is not worth living."[3]

Socrates spent much of his time in the streets and marketplace of Athens, querying every man he met about whether that man knew anything. Socrates said that, if there was an afterlife, he would pose the same question to the shades in Hades.

Ironically, Socrates himself professed to know nothing. The oracle at Delphi said that *therefore* Socrates was the wisest of all men. Socrates at least *knew* that he knew nothing, whereas the others falsely believed themselves to know something.

Socrates himself wrote no books, but his conversations were remembered by his disciple Plato and later published by him as dialogues. Very often these Socratic dialogues will emphasize a specific philosophical question, such as "What is piety?" (in the dialogue titled *Euthyphro*), "What is justice?" (in *Republic*), "What is virtue?" (in *Meno*), "What is meaning?"(in *Sophist*), "What is love?" (in *Symposium*). The typical Socratic dialogue has three divisions:

1. A question is posed (e.g., the question of what virtue is, or justice, or truth, or beauty); Socrates becomes excited and enthusiastic to find someone who claims to know something.

2. Socrates finds "minor flaws" in his companion's definition and slowly begins to unravel it, forcing his partner to admit ignorance. (In one dialogue, Socrates' target actually ends up in tears.)

3. An agreement is reached by the two admittedly ignorant companions to pursue the truth seriously. Almost all the dialogues end inconclusively. Of course, they must do so. Socrates cannot give his disciples the truth. Each of us must find it out for ourselves.

In his quest for truth, Socrates managed to offend many of the powerful and pompous fig-

ures of Athens. (In fairness to his accusers, it should be mentioned that some citizens suspected Socrates of preferring the values of Sparta to those of his native Athens. Sparta was Athens's enemy in

the Peloponnesian War.) Socrates' enemies conspired against him, getting him indicted for teaching false doctrines, for impiety, and for corrupting the youth. They brought him to trial hoping to humiliate him by forcing him to grovel and beg for mercy.

Far from groveling, at his trial Socrates maligned his prosecutors and angered the unruly jury of 500 by lecturing to them about their ignorance. Furthermore, when asked to suggest his own punishment, Socrates recommended that the Athenians give him free board and lodging in the town hall. The enraged jury condemned him to death by a vote of 280 to 220.

Ashamed of their act and embarrassed that they were about to put to death their most eminent citizen, the Athenians were prepared to look the other way when Socrates' prison guard was bribed to allow Socrates to escape.

Despite the pleas of his friends, Socrates refused to do so, saying that if he broke the law by escaping, he would be declaring himself an enemy of all laws. So he drank the hemlock and philosophized with his friends to the last moment. In death, he became the universal symbol of martyrdom for the Truth.

The Death of Socrates
(Vaguely after Jacques-Louis David, 1787)

Plato

born into (noble family)

The most important of Socrates' young disciples was Plato (427–347 B.C.E.), who was one of the most powerful thinkers in history. He is also the founder of the first university, the Academy, where students read as exercises the Socratic dialogues that Plato had written.

Because of his authorship, it is often difficult to distinguish between the thought of Socrates and that of Plato. In general, we can say that Plato's philosophy was more metaphysical, more systematic, and more other-worldly than Socrates' philosophy was.

The essence of Plato's philosophy is depicted allegorically in the Myth of the Cave, which appears in his most important work, the Republic. In this myth Plato has Socrates conceive the following vision: Imagine prisoners

Plato

chained in such a way that they face the back wall of a cave. There they have been for life and can see nothing of themselves or of each other. They see only shadows on the wall of the cave.

These shadows are cast by a fire that burns on a ledge above and behind them. Between the fire and the prisoners is a wall-lined path along which people walk carrying vases, statues, and other artifacts on their heads. The prisoners hear the echoes of voices and see the shadows of the arti- facts, and they mistake

these echoes and shadows for reality.

Plato has Socrates imagine that one prisoner is unchained, turned around, and forced to look at the true source of the shadows. But the fire pains his eyes. He prefers the pleasant deception of the shadows.

Behind and above the fire is the mouth of the cave, and outside in the bright sunlight (only a little of which trickles into the cave) are trees, rivers, mountains, and sky.

Now the former prisoner is forced up the "steep and rugged ascent"[4] (Plato's allegory of education) and brought to the sunlit exterior world. But the light blinds him. He must first look at the shadows of the trees (he is used to shadows), then at the trees and

mountains. Finally he is able to see the sun itself (the allegory of enlightenment).

Plato suggests that if this enlightened man were to return to the cave, he would appear ridicu-lous because he would see sunspots everywhere and not be able to penetrate the darkness.

And if he tried to liber-ate his fellow prisoners, they would be so angry at him for disturbing their illusions that they would set upon him and kill him—a clear allu-sion to the death of Socrates.

The allegory of the liberation of the slave from darkness, deceit, and untruth and the slave's hard journey into the light and warmth of the Truth has inspired many philosophers and social leaders. But Plato meant it as more than just a poetic vision. He also gave it a precise technical application, seen in his Simile of the Line, also found in the *Republic*.[5] On the left side of the Line we have an **epistemology** (theory of knowledge); on the right side, an **ontology** (theory of being). In addition, we have an implicit **ethics** (moral theory) and **aesthetics** (theory of beauty). The totality constitutes Plato's **metaphysics** (general worldview).

The Line reveals the hierarchical nature of the objects of all these disciplines. Reality is a hierarchy of being, of knowledge, and of value, with objects that are most real, most certain, and most valuable at the top. A descending ontological, epistemological, moral, and aesthetic scale cascades down from the highest level in the guise of a mathematically organized series of originals and copies. The whole of the visible world is a copy of the whole of the intelligible

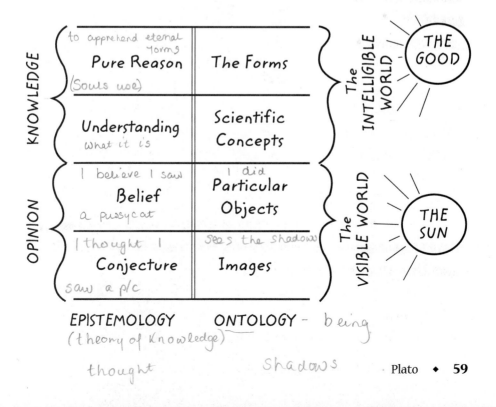

EPISTEMOLOGY   ONTOLOGY - being
(theory of knowledge)

thought   Shadows

world, yet each of these worlds is also divided into originals and copies.

For each state of being (right side of the Line), there is a corresponding state of awareness (left side). The lowest state of awareness is that of Conjecture, which has as its object Images, such as shadows and reflections (or images on the TV screen and video games).

The person in a state of conjecture mistakes an image for reality. This level on the Line corresponds to the situation of the cave-bound prisoners watching the shadows.

The next level, that of Belief, has as its object a particular thing— say, a particular horse or a particular act of justice. Like Conjecture, Belief still does not comprise knowledge but remains in the sphere of Opinion, still grounded in the uncertainties of sense perception. It is not yet "conceptual." It is not yet directed by theory (hypothemenoi), or by a definition in terms of **necessary** and **sufficient conditions**. (The person in a state of belief is like a prisoner who sees the artifact held above the wall inside the cave.)

Opinion and the objects of which it is aware are all sustained by the sun. Without the sun, there could be no horse and no image of a horse, nor could we be aware of them in the absence of light.

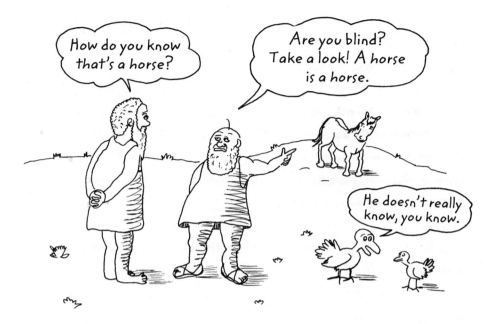

For Opinion to become Knowledge, the particular object must be raised to the level of theory. (This stage, Understanding, corresponds to the status of the released prisoner looking at the shadows of the trees in the world above the cave.)

But according to Plato, theories and definitions are not empirical generalizations dependent on particular cases and abstracted from them. To the contrary, rather than coming from below on the Line, theories are themselves images of something higher—what Plato calls the **Forms.** (In the same way that shadows and reflections are merely images of particular things, so theories or concepts are the shadows of the Forms.) When one beholds the Forms, one exercises Pure Reason, and one is like the liberated prisoner who gazed upon the trees and mountains in the sunlit upper world.

Plato's conception of the Forms is very complicated, but I can simplify it by saying that Forms are the eternal truths that are the source of all Reality. Consider, for example, the concept of beauty. Things in the sensible world are beautiful to the extent that they imitate or participate in Beauty. However, these beautiful things will break, grow old, or die. But Beauty itself (the Form) is eternal. It will

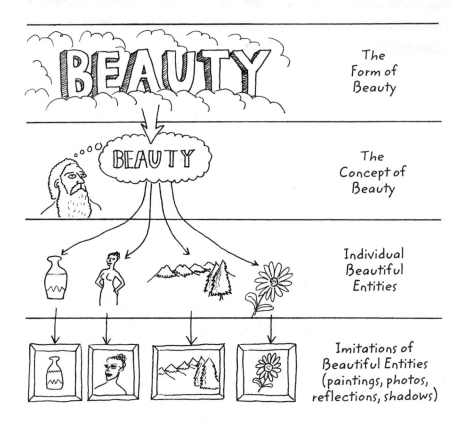

The
Form of
Beauty

The
Concept of
Beauty

Individual
Beautiful
Entities

Imitations of
Beautiful Entities
(paintings, photos,
reflections, shadows)

always be. The same can be said of Truth and Justice. (Also, more embarrassingly, of Horseness or of Toothpickness.)

Furthermore, just as the sensible world and awareness of it are dependent on the sun, so are the Forms and knowledge of them dependent on the Good, which is a Superform, or the Form of all Forms. The state of beholding the Good is represented in the Myth of the Cave by the released prisoner beholding the sun itself. Plato's theory is such that the whole of Reality is founded upon the Good, which is Reality's source of being. And all Knowledge is ultimately knowledge of the Good.

If you are puzzled by Plato's conception of the Good, you are in "good" company. Philosophers have debated its meaning for centuries. Clearly it plays a role very much like that of God in certain theological systems. For example, referring to the Simile of the Line, Plato calls the sun a "god" and claims that it is "the offspring of the Good."[6] The Good is the source of being, knowledge, and truth, but is something even "more beautiful"[7] than these. It is not surprising that many religiously oriented philosophers in the Middle Ages and the Renaissance—two periods in which Plato's influence was powerful—treated the Good as a **mystical** category. Something that is beyond being and knowledge is something that might be grasped only by a state of mind that transcends rationality. More orthodox religious thinkers treated the Good as identical to God. It was along these lines that Plato deeply influenced the development of Christianity, Judaism, and Islam. It would be a bad pun (and an anachronistic one, since the English language did not yet exist in Plato's time), but an illuminating one, to say that early Christianity dropped one "o" from "Good" and changed the "u" to an "o" in "sun" to create an icon of the relation between God and Christ.

Whatever Plato means by "the Good," he optimistically holds that if one ever comes to know the Good, one becomes good. Ignorance is the only error. No one would willingly do wrong.

How can we learn the Truth? Where can we find the Forms, and

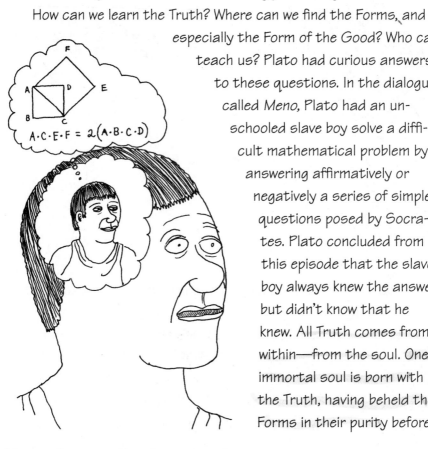

$$A \cdot C \cdot E \cdot F = 2(A \cdot B \cdot C \cdot D)$$

especially the Form of the Good? Who can teach us? Plato had curious answers to these questions. In the dialogue called Meno, Plato had an unschooled slave boy solve a difficult mathematical problem by answering affirmatively or negatively a series of simple questions posed by Socrates. Plato concluded from this episode that the slave boy always knew the answer but didn't know that he knew. All Truth comes from within—from the soul. One's immortal soul is born with the Truth, having beheld the Forms in their purity before its embodiment. Birth, or the embodiment of the soul, is so traumatic that one forgets what one knows and must spend the rest of life plumbing the depths of the soul to recover what one already knows—hence, Plato's strange doctrine that all Knowledge is recollection. Now we see Socrates' role as that of helping his student to remember, just as the psychoanalyst does with his or her patient today. (A modern version of Plato's doctrine of recollection is Freud's theory of unconscious memories.)

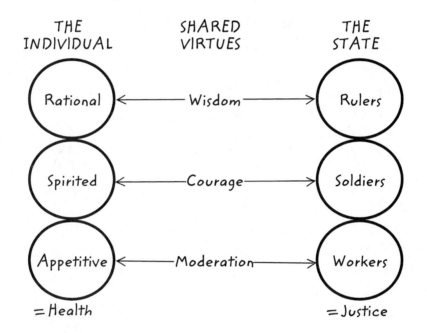

The *Republic* is well known not only for its epistemology but also for its social philosophy. The latter for Plato is a combination of psychology and political science. He said that the City (the "Republic") is the individual writ large. Just as the individual's psyche has three aspects—the appetitive, animal side; the spirited source of action; and the rational aspect—so does the ideal City have three classes —the workers and the artisans; the soldiers; and the rulers. In the psyche, the rational part must convince the spirited part to help it control the appetitive. Otherwise, there will be an unbalanced soul, and neurosis will ensue.

Similarly, in the City, the rulers must be philosophers who have beheld the Forms and therefore know what is good. They must train the military caste to help control the naturally unruly peasants. The latter will be allowed to use money, own property, and wear decorations in moderation, but the members of the top two classes, who understand the corrupting effect of greed, will live in an austere, absolute communism, sleeping and eating together, owning no property, receiving no salary, and having sexual relations on a prearranged schedule with partners shared by all. These rules will guarantee that the City will not be frenzied and anarchic—a strange beginning for the discipline of political science (one from which it has still not recovered)!

The members of the ideal City will be allowed to play simple lyres and pipes and sing patriotic, uplifting songs, but most artists will be drummed out of the Republic. This maltreatment has four reasons: (1) ontological—Because art deals with images (the lowest rung in the Simile of the Line), art is an imitation of an imitation. (Art is "three removes from the throne.");[8] (2) epistemological—The artist, at the conjectural stage,

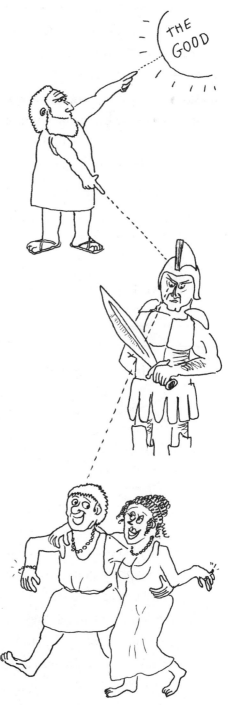

knows nothing but *claims* to know some- thing; (3) aesthetical—Art expresses itself in sensual images; hence, it distracts us from Beauty itself, which is purely intellectual; (4) moral—Art is created by and appeals to the appetite side of the soul (Freud's id). Art is either erotic or violent or both; hence, it is an incitement to anarchy. Even Homer must be censored, for he too is guilty of the artist's crimes: fraudulence, ignorance, and immorality.

(The whole enterprise of the *Republic* can be viewed as a plea that philosophy take over the role that art had hitherto played in Greek culture.)

Plato did not live to see the inauguration of his ideal state nor to see the installation of a Philosopher King who would know the Good, but the legacy that Plato left is still very much with us, for better or for worse. The eminent British-American philosopher Alfred North Whitehead once said that the history of philosophy is merely a series of footnotes to the *Republic*.

Plato's Simile of the Line would, to a great extent, lay out the framework of Western metaphysical thought from his time to ours. Many of the philosophers mentioned in this book were influenced deeply by Plato (Aristotle, the Stoics, the Neoplatonists, Saint Augustine, Saint Anselm, Saint Thomas Aquinas, Descartes, Spinoza, Kant, Hegel, Schopenhauer, Kierkegaard, Marx, Russell, and Whitehead, among others). Even those philosophers who hated Plato's philosophy, such as Nietzsche, often admired his intellectual power—a power that even Nietzsche could not escape.

Aristotle

Plato's influence is clearly seen in the thought of one of his best students, Aristotle (384–322 B.C.E.). Aristotle, born in Stagira, spent twenty years at Plato's academy. Soon after the death of the master, Aristotle left the school because of disagreements with its new chiefs, and he founded an academy of his own, the Lyceum. In Aristotle's school, Platonic philosophy was taught, but it was also criticized.

Aristotle

The main thrust of Aristotle's dispute with his mentor concerned the latter's other-worldliness. For Plato, there were two worlds: the unspeakably lofty world of Forms, and the world of mere

Mere Dog Copies

"things," which is but a poor imitation of the former. Aristotle contradicted this view, asserting that there is only *one* world and that we are right smack in the middle of it. In criticizing Plato, Aristotle asked: If Forms are essences of things, how can they exist separated from things? If they are the *cause* of things, how can they exist in a different world? And a most telling criticism has to do with the problem of *change* and *motion*, which the early Greeks had tried to solve.

They thought either that stability was an illusion (the view of Heraclitus, for example) or that motion was an illusion (the view of Parmenides). Plato had tried to resolve the dilemma by acknowledging the insights of both Heraclitus and Parmenides. The former's world is the unstable and transient realm of the visible. The latter's world

Parmenidean Permanence

Heraclitean Hustle

is the immutable realm of the intelligible composed of the eternally unchanging Forms, which themselves are poorly reflected in the transitory world of the visible. But did Plato's compromise really solve the problem of motion and change? Is it really comprehensible to explain "changing things" by saying that they are bad imitations of unchanging things?

Aristotle thought not. In offering his own solution to the problem, Aristotle employed some of the same terminology as Plato. He said that a distinction must be drawn between *form* and *matter*, but that these two features of reality can be distinguished only in thought, not in fact. Forms are not separate entities. They are embedded in particular things. They are *in* the world. To think otherwise is an intellectual confusion. A particular object, to count as an object at all, must have both form and matter. Form, as Plato had said, is universal, in the sense that many particulars can have the same form. Aristotle called an object's form its "whatness." That is, when you say *what*

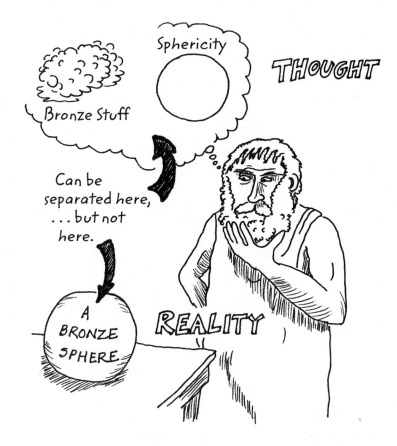

something is (it's a tree, it's a book), you are naming its form. The form is a thing's essence, or nature. It is related to the thing's function (a wheel, a knife, a brick, etc.).

An object's matter is what is unique to that object. Aristotle called it the object's "thisness." All wheels or trees have the same form (or function), but no two have the same matter. Matter is "the principle of individuation." An object with both form and matter is what Aristotle called a **substance.**

Each substance contains an essence, which is roughly equivalent to its form, as in Plato's writings; but unlike in Plato's account, in Aristotle's theory the essence cannot be separated from the substance in question. However, it is possible to perform the purely intellectual act of *abstracting* the essence from the substance. Indeed, part of the philosopher's job is to discover and catalog the different substances in terms of their essences and their **accidents,** that is, in terms of those features of the substance that are essential to it, and those that are not essential. (To be human, one must be rational, so rationality is part of the human essence; but although every human either has

hair or is bald, neither hairiness nor baldness is essential to human nature.) With this kind of analysis Aristotle initiated a philosophical method that would be pursued well into the modern period.

Aristotle's anti-Platonic metaphysics holds that reality is composed of a plurality of substances. It is not composed of an upper tier of eternal Forms and a lower tier of matter that unsuccessfully attempts to imitate those Forms. This theory represents Aristotle's **pluralism** as opposed to Plato's **dualism** (a dualism that verges on **idealism** because, for Plato, the most "real" tier of reality is the non-material). How does Aristotle's pluralism solve the problem of motion and change, a problem that was unsuccessfully addressed by his predecessors? It does so by reinterpreting matter and form as *potentiality* and *actuality,* and by turning these concepts into a theory of change. Any object in the world can be analyzed in terms of these categories. Aristotle's famous example is that of an acorn. The

acorn's matter contains the potentiality of becoming an oak tree, which is the acorn's actuality. The acorn *is* the potentiality of there being an oak tree. The oak tree is the actuality of the acorn. So, for Aristotle, form is an operating cause. Each individual substance is a self-contained **teleological** (i.e., goal-oriented) system. Notice that a substance's essence does not change, but its accidents do.

In fact, Aristotle analyzed all substances in terms of four causes. The *material cause* is the stuff out of which something is made (e.g., a chunk of marble that is to become a statue). The *formal cause* is the form, or essence, of the statue, that which it strives to be. (This form exists both in the mind of the artist and potentially in the marble itself.) The *efficient cause* is the actual force that brings about the change (the sculptor's chipping the block of stone). The *final cause* is the ultimate purpose of the object (e.g., to beautify the Parthenon).

Nature, then, is a teleological system in which each substance is striving for self-actualization and for whatever perfection is possible within

the limitations allowed it by its particular essence. In Aristotle's theory, as in Plato's theory, *everything is striving unconsciously toward the Good.* Aristotle believed that for such a system to work, some concrete perfection must actually exist as the *telos* (or goal) toward which all things are striving.

This entity Aristotle called the Prime Mover. It serves as a kind of god in Aristotle's metaphysics, but unlike the traditional gods of Greece and unlike the *God of West-ern religion,* the Prime Mover is almost com-pletely nonanthropomor-phic. It is the cause of the universe, not in the Judeo-Christian sense of creating it out of nothing, but in the sense of a Final Cause; everything moves toward it in the way a runner moves toward a goal. The Prime Mover is the only thing in the universe with no potentiality

because, being perfect, it cannot change. It is pure actuality, which is to say, pure activity. What activity?

The activity of pure thought. And what does it think about? Perfection! That is to say, about itself. The Prime Mover's knowledge is immediate, complete self-consciousness.

What we seem to have here is an absolutely divine case of narcissism. (In Greek mythology, Narcissus was an extraordinarily handsome youth who became transfixed by the reflection of his own beauty and remained staring at it until he died.)

Aristotle's moral philosophy, as it appears in his manuscript now called *The Nicomachean Ethics,* reflects his teleological metaphysics. The notion of *goal,* or *purpose,* is the overriding one in his moral theory. Aristotle noted that every act is performed for some *purpose,* which he defined as the "good" of that act. (We perform an act because we find its purpose to be worthwhile.) *Either* the totality of our acts is an infinitely circular series (we get up in order to eat breakfast, we eat breakfast in order to go to work, we go to work in order to get money, we get money so we can buy food in order to be able to eat breakfast, etc., etc., etc.)—in which case life would be a pretty meaningless endeavor— *or* there is some ultimate good toward which the purposes of all acts are directed. If there is such a good, we should try to come to know it so that we can adjust all our acts toward it in order to avoid that saddest of all tragedies—the wasted life.

According to Aristotle, there is general verbal agreement that the end toward which all human acts are directed is *happiness;*[9] therefore, happiness is the human good because we seek happiness for its own sake, not for the sake of something else. But unless we philosophize about happiness and get to know exactly what it is and

how to achieve it, it will be platitudinous simply to say that happiness is the ultimate good. To determine the nature of happiness, Aristotle turned to his metaphysical schema and asked, "What is the function of the human?" (in the same way he would ask about the function of a knife or an acorn). He came to the conclusion that a human's function is to engage in "an activity of the soul which is in accordance with virtue" and which "is in conformity with reason."[10] Before grasping this complicated definition, we must determine what "virtue" is and what kinds of virtues there are. But first, as an aside, I must mention that Aristotle believed that certain material conditions must hold before happiness can be achieved.

This list of material conditions reveals Aristotle's elitism: We need good friends, riches, and political power. We need a good birth, good children, and good looks ("A man is not likely to be happy if he is very ugly.")[11] We must not be very short. Furthermore, we must be free from the need of performing manual labor. ("No man can practice virtue who is living the life of a mechanic or laborer.")[12] I should note that Aristotle's moral theory would be left substantially intact if his elitist bias were deleted.

Let us now inspect Aristotle's idea of virtue. The Greek word is *areté*. It could equally well be translated as "excellence." Areté is that quality of any act, endeavor, or object that makes them successful acts, endeavors, or objects. It is, therefore, a *functional excellence*. For Aristotle, there are two kinds of virtue: intellectual and moral. Intellectual virtues are acquired through a combination of inheritance

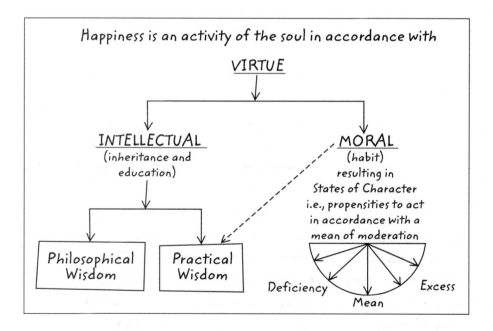

and education, and moral virtues through imitation, practice, and habit. The habits that we develop result in states of character, that is, in dispositions to act certain ways, and these states of character are virtuous for Aristotle if they result in acts that are in accordance with a golden mean of moderation. For example, when it comes to facing danger, one can act with excess, that is, show too much fear (cowardice). Or one can act deficiently by showing too little fear (foolhardiness). Or one can act with moderation, and hence virtuously, by showing the right amount of fear (courage). Aristotle realized that the choices we must make if we are to learn moral virtue cannot be made mathematically; rather, they are always context-bound and must be approached through trial and error.

Returning to the intellectual virtues of practical and philosophical wisdom, the former is the wisdom necessary to make judgments consistent with one's understanding of the good life. It is therefore related to moral virtue (as in the diagram). Philosophical wisdom is scientific, disinterested, and contemplative. It is associated with pure reason, and for Aristotle, the capacity for reason is that which is most human; therefore, philosophical wisdom is the highest virtue. So, when Aristotle defined happiness as "an activity of the soul in accordance with virtue," the activity referred to is philosophical activity. The human being can be happy only by leading a contemplative life, but not a monastic one. We are not only philosophical animals but also social ones. We are engaged in a world where decisions concerning practical matters are forced upon us constantly. Happiness (hence the good life) requires excellence in both spheres.

Aristotle's political views follow from his moral views. Just as happiness (*eudaimonia*) is the function or goal of the human individual, so is it the function of the state. Aristotle agrees with Plato that humans are endowed with social instincts. The state (*polis*) is a natural human organization whose goal is to maximize happiness for its citizens. In fact, the state is more natural than the family because only in the social climate produced by community can human nature be fully self-actualized. We see that in political theory, as everywhere in Aristotle's philosophy, teleology reigns supreme.

According to Aristotle, the distinction between nature and convention so touted by the Sophists is somewhat artificial. Law is natural to humans. Just as humans are naturally social, so is their desire to participate in the political body an innate disposition. But

Aristotle recognizes that different constitutional bases produce different kinds of states. As long as the constitution is designed for the common well-being (*eudaimonia*) of all its citizens, it is a just state. There are three possible legitimate forms of the state: governance by one person (a monarchy), governance by an elite group (aristocracy), and governance by the body of citizens itself (a polity—a limited form of democracy). In certain circumstances, Aristotle preferred a monarchy—where a strong individual with excellent political skills steps forward to impose conditions that will be conducive to the well-being of all citizens. But in practice, Aristotle favored a polity, even if many of the citizens are not excellent individuals. "For the many, of whom each individual is but an ordinary person, when they meet together may very likely be better than the few good, if regarded not individually but collectively."[13]

A Few Good Men

For each of the three sound forms of government, there is a possible perversion. A perverse government is one that has at heart not the interest of the whole of the citizenry, but only the interest of the rulers at the expense of the citizens. The perversion of monarchy is tyranny; the perversion of aristocracy is oligarchy; and the perversion of polity is democracy. Aristotle understood democracy as a government by the majority in a *polis* in which the bulk of its citizens are poor, and the poor look out exclusively for their own interests by taking the wealth of the rich for their own advantage. "If the poor, for example, because they are more in number, divide among themselves the prosperity of the rich—is this not unjust? . . . If this is not unjust, pray, what is?"[14] For Aristotle, this form of mob rule is as unjust as its opposite, the rich robbing and plundering the poor.

Despite Aristotle's predilection for what we would today call a modified democracy, his division of labor within the state was as harsh as Plato's. A great number of the inhabitants of the state— perhaps the majority—would be slaves. Aristotle provided a tortured argument trying to prove that some individuals are natural slaves and hence to be treated as mere property and as animate tools. Even those individuals who are citizens but are artisans or laborers are debarred from full participation in the advantages of citizenship. Furthermore, freedom is severely restricted for all members of the polis. At least this restriction is not as oppressive as Plato's was; Aristotle admonished Plato for outlawing private property and mar- riage in the ruling class. Aristotle believed that the desire to accumu- late wealth is based on a natural instinct and should be allowed expression, though the state should control the excesses produced by giving free rein to that instinct.

Aristotle's support for a modified form of democracy makes his political views more attractive to the modern mentality than is Plato's propensity toward totalitarianism, but this advantage is diminished by Aristotle's assumption that the wealth of the state will be based on slave labor, by his disfranchisement of female citi- zens, by his debasing the class of blue-collar (blue-toga?) workers in his republic.

Just as Aristotle's political philosophy was written in response to Plato's, so was his philosophy of art. Let us recall Plato's objec- tions to most art:

1. Ontological objection: Art is in the realm of images; hence, it has the lowest ontological status in the Simile of the Line. Artistic images are copies of copies of copies.

2. Epistemological objection: The artist is ignorant, but he purports to know Truth and to instruct it; therefore the artist is a *dangerous* ignoramus.

3. Aesthetic objection: Beauty (the Form) transcends the physical world, but art always reduces beauty to images, hence, to its lowest common denominator.

4. Moral objection: Art appeals not to the intellect—as does philosophy—but to the passions, which it stirs up, justifies, and loosens on an already chaotic (i.e., unphilosophical) public. Here too the artist is dangerous.

I am not just IGNORANT;
I am DANGEROUSLY ignorant

Homer

Aristotle agreed with Plato that the function of art is *mimesis*, "imitation" (or, as we would probably say today, "representation"). But he disagreed with Plato concerning the status of the *objects* represented in art. Rather than imitating mere things or individuals, art represents higher truths; hence, art, when successful, is a form of philosophy. Aristotle wrote:

> the poet's function is to describe, not the thing that has happened, but a kind of thing that might happen, i.e., what is possible as being probable or necessary. . . . Hence poetry is something more philosophical and of graver import than history, since its statements are of the nature rather of universals, whereas those of history are singulars.[15]

This philosophy, if correct, eliminates the first three of Plato's objections to representative art. As for the fourth objection, Aristotle argued that, far from provoking the passions, great art can *purge* from the viewers the passions that have built up in them. Aristotle says of the art of tragedy (and remember, it is generally agreed that some of the greatest tragedy ever written was from the Golden Age of Greece) that it achieves its effect "in a dramatic, not in a narrative form; with incidents arousing pity and fear, wherewith to accomplish its **catharsis** of such emotions."[16]

Not only did Aristotle make major contributions to metaphysics, ethics, aesthetics, and politics, but in addition, he single-handedly founded the science of logic, that is, the science of valid inference. Symbolic logic has developed a long way since Aristotle's time, but it is indebted to him as its founder, and it has made more additions than corrections to his work.

Some of Aristotle's empirical claims about the world leave something to be desired (for instance, his claim that falling rocks accelerate because they are happy to be getting home, or his claim that snakes have no testicles because they have no legs). Nevertheless, Aristotle's metaphysics, his ethics, his logic, and his aesthetics remain permanent monuments to the greatness of human thought.

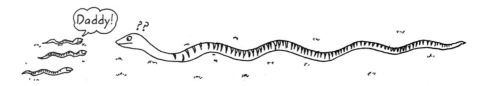

Topics for Consideration

1. It is claimed in this chapter that subjectivism, skepticism, relativism, and nihilism are at the heart of the project of sophism. Contrast these ideas with those seen in the philosophies of the pre-Socratics, and again with those in the philosophy of Plato.

2. Based on the few pages about Socrates that you have read here, write an essay speculating on what Socrates might have meant when he said, "The unexamined life is not worth living."

3. Make an alignment between Plato's Simile of the Line and his Myth of the Cave. Show that for each category or entity in the Simile, there is a corresponding category or entity in the myth.

4. In the Simile of the Line the sun—the ultimate source of light—is designated by Plato as "the lord of the visible world." That is, everything in the physical world is dependent on the sun, and all visual awareness of the physical world is because of the presence of light. The sun, in turn, is a copy of the Good, which is the "lord of the intelligible world." What does this analogy between the sun and the Good tell us about the objects and the relationships in the intelligible world and about our knowledge of this world?

5. William Wordsworth's poem "Ode: Intimations of Immortality from Recollections of Early Childhood" and John Keats's poem "Ode on a Grecian Urn" are sometimes called Platonic poems. Go to the library and locate them, and write an essay on one or both of them, interpreting them in the light of Plato's metaphysics. Also comment on the irony involved in the very idea of "Platonic poetry."

6. In Plato's *Republic* the healthy city is explained in terms of the same model as that of the healthy individual. Explain this congruity.

7. In the debate between Plato and Aristotle over the status of art, with which philosopher do you tend to agree? Defend your position.

8. Explain what it means to say that in the disagreement between Heraclitus and Parmenides, Plato credits both positions, but ultimately he sides with Parmenides.

9. Demonstrate the role played by teleology in the different aspects of Aristotle's philosophy.

10. In the text, the examples of an acorn and of a statue are used to illustrate Aristotle's theory of the four causes. Choose two other examples—one from nature and one from human manufacturing—and see if you can work each example through Aristotle's four causal categories.

11. First explain what Aristotle meant by describing moral action in terms of the golden mean, then show why engaging in moral action is a necessary condition but not a sufficient condition to achieve happiness, or the "good life."

12. Write an essay discussing the question of whether, in your opinion, the American constitutional system has addressed the objections that Aristotle directs toward the idea of democracy.

Notes

1. Philip Wheelwright, ed., *The Presocratics* (New York: Odyssey Press, 1966), 239.

2. Ibid., 240.

3. Plato, *Apology*, in *Plato on the Trial and Death of Socrates*, trans. Lane Cooper (Ithaca, N.Y.: Cornell University Press, 1941), 73.

4. Plato, *Republic*, in *The Dialogues of Plato*, vol. 1, trans. Benjamin Jowett (New York: Random House, 1937), 775.

5. There has been much scholarly debate concerning the best English translation of the Greek terms Plato uses in the Simile of the Line. Here is a transcription of the Greek words in question:

   1. *noesis*   2. *eide*
   3. *dianoia*   4. *hypothemenoi and ta mathematica*
   5. *pistis*   6. *ta horomeva*
   7. *eikasia*   8. *eikones*

   In designating *noesis* as "reason" and *dianoia* as "understanding," I am following the translations of both W. H. D. Rouse and Leo Rauch. But it should be mentioned that *noesis* has also been rendered as "understanding" (by G. M. A. Grube), as "knowledge" (by G. L. Abernathy and T. L. Langford), and as "intellection" (by Allan Bloom). *Dianoia* has been translated as "reasoning" (by Grube), as "thinking" (by Abernathy and Langford), and as "thought" (by Bloom). I have opted for Rouse's and Rauch's translation of *noesis* as "reason" because doing so best reveals the continuity between Plato and the later Western metaphysical tradition through Hegel and Kant. (We study Kant in Chapter 5 and Hegel in Chapter 6.) I have chosen to call the fourth square "scientific concepts." Plato gives us two Greek terms for that slot, *hypothemenoi* and *ta mathematica*. Many interpreters choose the second phrase, "mathematical objects," as the key phrase here—and it is true that Socrates used examples from arithmetic and geometry to explain this concept. I have selected "scientific concepts" because this category includes mathematical ideas but in fact encompasses more. I believe Plato did not mean to restrict *hypothemenoi* (literally "assumptions" or "postulates") to mathematical ideas. M. E. Taylor warns us against being misled by Plato's mathematical language here. He says that Plato "had before him no other examples of systematic and organized knowledge" than "the various branches of mathematics as recognized in the fifth century" (M. E. Taylor, *Plato: The Man and His Work* [New York: Meridian Books, 1960], 289). Plato is referring to organized conceptual knowledge, that is, roughly what today we would call scientific concepts. According to Plato, scientific concepts are inferior to Forms both because they are copies (imitations, shadows, reflections) of the Forms, and because the individual thinkers still depend on visual imagery when they operate at this level. In this sense the Forms, not the concepts, are mathematical, because they are image-free.

6. Plato, *Republic*, in *Great Dialogues of Plato*, ed. Eric H. Warmington and Philip G. Rouse, trans. W. H. D. Rouse (New York: New American Library, 1956), 305, 307.

7. Ibid., 308.

8. Ibid., 399.

9. The Greek word is *eudaimonia*. Some translators have preferred "well-being" over "happiness."

10. Aristotle, *Nicomachean Ethics*, in *A Guided Tour of Selections from Aristotle's "Nicomachean Ethics,"* ed. Christopher Biffle, trans. F. H. Peter (Mountain View, Calif.: Mayfield Publishing, 1991), 26.

11. Ibid., 30.

12. Aristotle, *Politics*, trans. Benjamin Jowett, in *The Basic Works of Aristotle*, ed. Richard McKeon (New York: Random House, 1941), 1183.

13. Ibid., 1190.

14. Ibid., 1189.

15. Aristotle, *Poetics*, trans. Benjamin Jowett, in *The Basic Works of Aristotle*, 1463–64.

16. Ibid., 1460.

3

The Hellenistic and Roman Periods

Fourth Century B.C.E. through Fourth Century C.E.

After the death of Aristotle, Greek civilization entered what historians call the Hellenistic era, a period of cultural decline. The Greek city-states, unable to solve the problem of political disunity, were decimated by the Peloponnesian War and ravaged by the plague. First they fell under Macedonian rule; then, after the death of Alexander the Great, they eventually were absorbed into the newly emerging Roman Empire. Many of the philosophies of this "decadent" period began in Greece but received their greatest exposure in Rome, including the two major philosophies of the period, Epicureanism and stoicism.

Epicureanism

Absense of pain — *Pleasure = Higher good.*

The philosophy of Epicurus (341–270 B.C.E.) is known (not surprisingly) as Epicureanism. If today the term hints of gluttony, debauchery, and bacchanalian orgies, that is not Epicurus's fault but the fault of some of his Roman interpreters. Epicurus himself led a life of sobriety and simplicity: eating bread, cheese, and olives; drinking a bit of wine; napping in his hammock; and enjoying conversation with his friends while

87

strolling through his garden. He died with dignity and courage after a painful, protracted disease.

Epicureanism was grounded in the atomic theory of Democritus, but, in fact, Epicurus, like all post-Alexandrian philosophers, does not seem to have been really interested in science but in finding out about the good life. However, since Aristotle's time, the

The Individual in the Roman Empire

notion of the "good life" had suffered a setback. It no longer made sense to advocate being active, influential, political, and responsible as a way of self-improvement. Reality seemed to be unmoved by personal initiative, and the individual developed a feeling of powerlessness as he or she was about to be absorbed into the massive, impersonal bureaucracy of the Roman Empire. Like Aristotle, Epicurus believed that the goal of life was happiness, but happiness he equated simply with *pleasure*. No act should be undertaken except for the pleasure in which it results, and no act should be rejected except for the pain that it produces. This belief provoked Epicurus to analyze the different kinds of pleasure. There are two kinds of desires, hence, two kinds of pleasure as a result of gratifying those desires: natural desire (which has two subclasses) and vain desire:

✱   I. Natural desire
    A. Necessary (e.g., desire for food and sleep)
    B. Unnecessary (e.g., desire for sex)
  II. Vain desire (e.g., desire for decorative clothing or exotic food)

The Pursuit of Vain Pleasure

Natural necessary desires must be satisfied and are usually easy to satisfy. They result in a good deal of pleasure and in very few painful consequences. Vain desires do not need to be satisfied and are not easy to satisfy. Because there are no natural limits to them, they tend to become obsessive and lead to very painful consequences.

The desire for sex is natural but usually can be overcome; and when it can be, it should be, because satisfaction of the sexual drive gives intense pleasure, and all intense emotional states are dangerous. Also, the desire for sex puts people in relationships that are usually ultimately more painful than pleasant and that are often extremely painful.

One of the natural and necessary desires to which Epicurus pays a great deal of attention is the desire for repose. This term is to be understood both physically and psychically. The truly good person (i.e., the one who experiences the most pleasure) is the one who, having overcome all unnecessary desires, gratifies necessary desires in the most moderate

way possible, leaves plenty of time for physical and mental repose, and is free from worry.

Notice that Epicurus's definition of pleasure is *negative*; that is, pleasure is the absence of pain. It is this negative definition that prevents Epicurus from falling into a crass sensualism. The trouble with this definition is that, taken to its logical extremity, the absence of life is better

than any life at all (a conclusion Freud also came to in his text *Beyond the Pleasure Principle*, where he claimed that behind the "pleasure principle" is Thanatos, the death instinct).

Beyond the Pleasure Principle

This deduction is a bit ironic because Epicurus himself claimed that his philosophy dispelled the fear of death. Democritus's atomism led Epicurus to believe that death was merely the absence of sensation and consciousness; therefore, there could be no sensation or consciousness of death to fear. "So long as we exist, death is not with us; but when death comes, then we do not exist."[1]

Some of Epicurus's Roman followers interpreted "pleasure" quite differently, defining it as a positive titillation. It is because of these extremists that today Epicureanism is often associated with sensualistic **hedonism**. Sickly Epicurus, swinging in his hammock, would have disapproved. (Though not too harshly. Polemics cause agitation, which is painful.) Epicurus's theory never constituted a major philosophical movement, but he had disciples in both Greece and Rome for a number of centuries. His most famous follower was the Roman Lucretius, who, in the first century B.C.E., wrote a long poem, *On the Nature of Things*, expounding the philosophy of his master. It is through Lucretius's poem that many readers have been introduced to the thoughts of Epicurus.

Stoicism — influenced developing christian religion.

Stoicism was another important Hellenistic philosophy that was transported to Rome. Stoicism was founded in Greece by Zeno of Cyprus (334–262 B.C.E.), who used to preach to his students from a portico, or stoa (hence the term "stoicism," literally, "porchism"). Like

Zeno of Citium
334 - 262 bce
Cyprus

Zeno at the Stoa

Epicureanism, stoicism had its roots in pre-Socratic materialism, but stoicism too, especially in its Roman form, became less interested in physics and more particularly concerned with the problem of human conduct. The three most interesting of the Roman stoics were Seneca (4–65 C.E.), a dramatist and high-ranking statesman; Epictetus (late first century C.E.), a slave who earned his freedom; and Marcus Aurelius (121–180 C.E.), a Roman emperor. (It's quite striking that a slave and an emperor could share the same philosophy of resignation, though probably this philosophy was easier for the emperor than for the slave!) The stoics accepted the Socratic equation that virtue equals knowledge. There exists a cognitive state

that, once achieved, expresses itself as a disposition to behave in a certain dispassionate manner, and in turn it guarantees complete well-being. One should strive throughout one's life to acquire this wisdom. Human excellence is attained instantaneously once one has gained the enlightenment.

The duration of such a life of perfection is indifferent (which fact leads to the stoic advocacy of suicide under certain circumstances). To achieve this state of blessedness, one must free oneself from all worldly demands, particularly those of the emotions and of pleasure seeking. The stoic wise person is an **ascete** who has transcended the passions that create a disorderly condition in the soul. The stoic has no interest in all those objects that in normal human beings excite the passions of grief, joy, hope, or fear.

What is the content of stoic wisdom? It is similar to the Aristotelian notion that the good consists of acting in accordance with one's nature. The stoic addition to this idea is that to so act requires acting in accordance with nature itself, that is, with the totality of reality (which the stoics take to be divine). Considered as a whole, reality is perfect. Humans will also become perfect if they learn to live in accordance with the divine plan of reality. This accomplishment requires that one make one's desires identical with the overall providential plan for the universe. In fact, a person can do *nothing but* conform to the grand design, and stoic wisdom consists in recognizing this truth. Fools are those who try to impose their own selfish desires on reality. This attempt results in unhappiness and unfreedom. If **freedom** is the unity of will and ability (i.e., being able to do what one wants), then the only way to be free is to want what the universe wants. We shouldn't wish that we could get what we desire; rather, we should desire what we get. If we could learn to equate what we want with what's the case, then we would always

Don't Try to Get What You Want—Rather, Want What You Get

be free and happy, because we'd always get just what we want. This is stoic wisdom.

The stoics realized that if one ever achieved this lofty state, the apparent harshness of reality might jeopardize one's inner equilibrium, and one might backslide into pain and anxiety. For this reason, and because the stoics believed that the amount of time one spent in the enlightened state was indifferent, the stoics advocated suicide in certain circumstances. If extreme conditions forced themselves upon one and if one realized that these conditions would destabilize the equilibrium of one's stoic soul and plunge one into unacceptable emotional agitation, one had every right to escape those conditions through suicide. Epictetus said of suicide, "If the smoke is moderate I will stay: if excessive, I go out. . . . The door is always open."[2] Marcus Aurelius used identical imagery: "The house is smoky, and I quit it."[3] Seneca said, "If [the wise man] encounters many vexations which disturb his tranquillity, he will release himself. . . . To die well is to escape the danger of living ill."[4] In fact, on the advice of the emperor Nero, Seneca did step into the bath and open his veins.

During the period when stoicism was exercising its greatest influence, a new social and religious form of thought was coming to the fore: Christianity. Although Christians were still a minority in the Empire, their religion had found an ever-growing number of adherents because its promises resonated with the needs of people at all levels of society. It bestowed meaning on even the most wearisome features of life; it offered a direct and personal connection to divinity through the person of Jesus, the son of a carpenter; its communal basis offered an identity that was much more concrete than that obtained by mere residence in the Roman Empire; and it offered salvation and eternal life. Although the Christians had not learned to defend their new religion with a systematic philosophy as they would in the Middle Ages, their doctrine was in competition with the philosophies of the day for the hearts and minds of men and women. All such thought systems were responding to the same problems, so it is no surprise that there are some similarities between Christianity and a philosophy like stoicism; for example, both philosophies share the doctrine of resignation, the disdain for attachment to earthly things, and the concern with conforming to the will of divine Providence. The differences cannot be overlooked, however, such as the discrepancy between stoic and Christian teachings on suicide. Whereas the stoic believed that suicide was justified to prevent oneself from going against the divine plan of the world, Christians believed that the act of suicide was prohibited by that same divine plan. Also, stoicism was inclined to be quietistic and acquiescent to political authority, whereas in its inception Christianity tended to be activistic and resistant to political domination.

Epictetus said, "Refuse altogether to take an oath, if it is possible; if it is not, refuse as far as you are able."[5] This attitude contrasts greatly with that of many Christians who refused to swear an oath on the divinity of the emperor and were martyred for that refusal.

Neoplatonism

After the death of the stoic Marcus Aurelius ("the last good emperor"), a long period of upheaval and disorder ensued. The helplessness that people felt in the face of the decadence of the crumbling empire was responded to by a religious revival. The most prominent philosophical religious competitor with Christianity during the third century C.E. was a mystical form of Platonism known today as Neoplatonism, espoused by Plotinus (204–270). We have already seen a deep-seated propensity toward other-worldliness in Plato, which Aristotle had criticized. Plato's claim of superiority for the other world fit in well with the world-weariness of the third century.

For Plotinus, as for Plato before him, absolute truth and certainty cannot be found in this world. Plato had taught a purely rational method for transcending the flux of the world and achieving truth and certainty, but Plotinus preached that such a vision can only be achieved extra-rationally, through a kind of ecstatic union with the One. The One was for Plotinus the Absolute, or God. Nothing can be truly known about the One in any rational sense, nor can any characterization of the One be strictly correct. If we review Plato's Simile of the Line from a Plotinian perspective, we see that language, and therefore thought, functions by drawing *distinctions* (we say "this is a pen,"

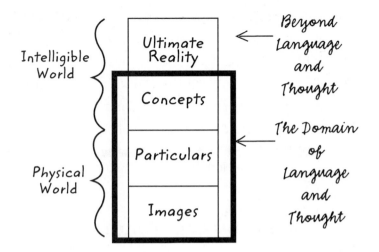

Intelligible World

Ultimate Reality — Beyond Language and Thought

Concepts

Particulars — The Domain of Language and Thought

Physical World

Images

meaning it is *not* the desk). But in the One, no distinctions exist; hence, nothing can be thought or said about it. A person can know the One only by uniting with it. That union can be achieved in this life in moments of mystical rapture, but in the long run the goal can only be achieved in death.

One can prepare for the ultimate union through an ascetic program of virtuous living. Plotinus's own version of the Line is based on his idea that God, or the Absolute, does not perform acts of creation (that would sully God's unchangeableness); rather, God "emanates." That is, God is reflected onto lower planes, and these reflections represent kinds of imitations of God's perfection in descending degrees of fragmentation. (What we have here is a kind of "gooey" Simile of the Line.) This metaphysics borders on **pantheism**—the view that reality and God are the same.

Because the philosophy of Plotinus and his followers was the last philosophy of the classical period, his version of Platonism was the one that was

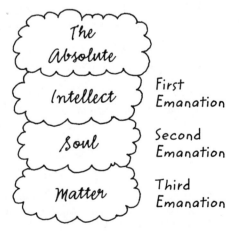

The Absolute

Intellect — First Emanation

Soul — Second Emanation

Matter — Third Emanation

handed down to the medieval world. Because of this fact, we will see that the problem of pantheism cropped up again in the Middle Ages, this time to haunt not the death scene of classicism but the birth scene of Christian philosophy. When the early Christian thinkers faced the task of unifying and systematizing the Christian worldview, they turned to the prevailing Platonic metaphysical scheme as a framework, and the Platonism they found was already heavily influenced by Plotinus's thought.

Topics for Consideration

1. Show why Epicurus's decision to define pleasure negatively (in terms of a lack of agitation) produces a very different philosophy from the Roman version of Epicureanism based on a positive definition of pleasure (in terms of the experience of titillation).

2. It is often believed that desires for food and sex are based on natural (i.e., biological) needs. Epicurus too calls them "natural" but claims that the fulfillment of the desire for food is "necessary," while the fulfillment of the desire for sex is "unnecessary." Explain what he means; explain what effect acting on his philosophy would have on one's life.

3. Write a short essay defending or attacking the view that *repose* is a key element of the "good life."

4. Are you convinced that both an emperor and a slave could follow the principles of stoicism? Explain your position.

5. Stoic philosophers claimed that we are happy only if we are free. What did they mean by "happiness" and "freedom"? Why, if freedom is such an important virtue, did they not agonize over choices that faced them?

6. Compare and contrast stoicism with Epicureanism as practiced by Epicurus, and then again with the later followers of Epicurus in Rome.

7. Compare and contrast Plato's version of the Simile of the Line (in Chapter 2) with Plotinus's version of it.

Notes

1. Epicurus, "Letter to Menoeceus," trans. C. Bailey, in *The Stoic and Epicurean Philosophers: Epicurus, Epictetus, Lucretius, Marcus Aurelius*, ed. Whitney J. Oats (New York: Modern Library, 1940), 31.

2. Epictetus, "Discourses of Epictetus," trans. P. E. Matheson, in *The Stoic and Epicurean Philosophers*, 267.

3. Marcus Aurelius, "Meditations," trans. G. Long, in *The Stoic and Epicurean Philosophers*, 523.

4. Seneca, *The Stoic Philosophy of Seneca*, ed. and trans. Moses Hadas (Garden City, N.Y.: Doubleday Anchor, 1958), 202–3.

5. Epictetus, "The Encheiridion," in *The Discourses of Epictetus*, ed. and trans. George Land (Mount Vernon, Va.: Peter Pauper Press, n.d.), 22.

4

Medieval and Renaissance Philosophy
Fifth through Fifteenth Centuries

All three of the main Western religions—Judaism, Christianity, and Islam—had their birth in the land that was home to the ancient Mediterranean desert cultures, in today's Egypt, Israel, Palestine, Jordan, and Saudi Arabia. By the beginning of the period now known as the Middle Ages, Islam had not yet appeared on the scene (I will speak more of Islam shortly), and Christianity was barely four hundred years old. But the main books of the Hebrew Bible on which Judaism was based already dated back 1,200 years. Judaism itself developed out of earlier, tribal **polytheistic** religions from which Judaism distinguished itself when it proclaimed that there was but one God, Jehovah, who had chosen the natives of ancient Judea—the Jews—with whom to

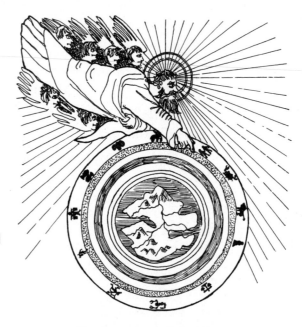

The Creation of the World
(After an Anonymous Medieval Painting)

establish a special covenant. This covenant was the basis of a law that not only lays moral strictures (the Ten Commandments), but also provides rituals governing dietary habits, marriage and funerary rites, prayers, sacrifices, and alms giving. The Jewish Bible, or Torah (later called the Old Testament by Christians), describes God's creation of the world, assigns humans a place in it, contains God's commandments, expresses his will, and relates a history of the Jews. It explains both the triumphs and the many sufferings of the Jews, whose homeland unfortunately lay on one of the major military cross-roads of the world; therefore, Judea suffered numerous invasions and brutal conquests. These holy writings also contain the fiery words of great prophets who are said to have recorded divinely inspired visions of God's will and of the future. Among other prophecies, one foretells the coming of a messiah (or "anointed one") who will liberate the Jews from their oppressors and establish a kingdom of Glory.

Christianity derived from precisely this Jewish prophetic tra-dition, when an initially small band of Jews—then later increasing numbers of non-Jews—claimed to recognize an individual named Jesus of Nazareth (ca. 4–39 C.E.) as the "Christ," a Greek transla-tion of the Hebrew word "messiah." The story of Jesus is told in four gospels (proclamations of good news): Matthew, Mark, Luke, and John. These books tell of the annunciation by angels to Jesus' virgin mother, Mary; of her pregnancy; of Jesus' humble birth in a stable; of his family's flight to Egypt to escape the wrath of the jealous King Herod; and of the miracles and cures Jesus performed. The gospels also tell of his teachings, which involve a reinterpretation of the Jewish law that de-emphasizes those features governing ritualistic practices and dietary habits and instead underscores an interior-ization of the law. This reinterpretation produces a doctrine of com-passion and aid for one's fellow human being, particularly for the downtrodden, despairing, and disadvantaged. Jesus' teachings also contain a strong element of **eschatological** prophecy that urges people to prepare for the Kingdom of God, which is at hand. Further-more, these Gospels tell the story of Jesus' betrayal by one of his

The Annunciation
(After Fra Angelico)

disciples, of his arrest by the Roman authorities—who forcibly included a rebellious Judea in their empire—of Jesus' trial and condemnation by the Jewish court, of his crucifixion by the Roman soldiers, of his burial and miraculous resurrection, and of the ascension to heaven of the living Christ. All these events were viewed by Jesus' followers, and by the Christian Scriptures themselves, as fulfillment of the prophecies of the Old Testament and therefore as proof that, indeed, Jesus was the Christ, the messiah foretold by the ancient prophets.

The Christian communities in Palestine immediately after Jesus' execution were composed mostly of Jews who saw Jesus' message as directed primarily toward Jews, but at the same time the doctrine was spreading to the broader Greek-speaking and Latin-speaking world. Indeed, after the first four gospels, the bulk of the rest of the New Testament is dominated by the letters of Christian leaders to communities of believers in the Greek-speaking parts of the Mediterranean world. Foremost among these writings are the letters of Saint Paul, Christianity's greatest missionary and organizer. In these letters he developed and clarified the doctrines of love and servitude and the spritualization and interiorization of the Hebrew law; he emphasized Jesus' suffering and death as an atonement for the sins of the whole human race and as a guarantee that this atonement meant an eternal life for those who believe in Jesus as the Christ and who live according to his teachings.

The New Testament concludes with an apocalyptic vision of the end of the world based on the writings of a Christian prophet called Saint John the Divine, not to be confused with Saint John, the author of the Fourth Gospel. John the Divine was indeed confused with Saint John during the first part of the Middle Ages, and this misunderstanding bestowed great authority on John the Divine's writing, known as the Book of Revelation. In his vision John sees a great battle between the forces of God and those of the devil, Satan, that results in the return of Christ, the Final Judgment of the living and the dead, the admission of the blessed into the New Jerusalem (heaven), and the consignment of the damned to hell.

During the three hundred years after Jesus' death, Christianity spread throughout the Roman Empire, but tumultuously so, because of the sometimes bloody repression of it by the Roman authorities and because of internal debates among its leaders concerning the correct form that Christian **dogma** should take. Its **canon** did not take form until the fourth century after the birth of Jesus.

**The Damned Dragged Down
to Hell by Demons
(After Luca Signorelli)**

Saint Augustine

In the year 313 C.E. an important event occurred. The Roman emperor Constantine was converted to Christianity, and even though only one in ten citizens of the Empire was a Christian, Christianity became the official religion of the realm. During the next couple of centuries, the early Church fathers turned to the prevailing Neoplatonic philosophical tradition in their search for intellectual foundations for their still relatively new religion. The first truly important philosopher in this Christian Platonic tradition was Augustine of Hippo (354–430). He had one foot squarely planted in the classical world and one in the medieval world, and he straddled the abyss that separated these two worlds.

As a young student of rhetoric in Rome, acutely aware of his own sensual nature, Augustine was concerned with the problem of good and evil. He became attracted to **Manicheanism** (founded by Mani of Persia in the third century), which was a philosophy that combined certain Christian and Persian elements and that understood reality in terms of an eternal struggle between the principle of light (Good) and the principle of darkness (Evil). The strife between these two principles manifested itself as the world. The soul represented the good and the body represented evil. As a Manichee, Augustine could attribute his many sins to a principle somehow outside himself.

But Augustine soon became dissatisfied with this "solution" to the problem of evil, and he became attracted to Neoplatonism and

its conception of an *immaterial reality*. It was from Neoplatonism that Augustine got his idea of evil not as a real feature of reality, but as a lack, an incompleteness, a privation. (Recall the Simile of the Line: the more goodness a thing has, the more real it is. Conversely, the less reality it has, the worse it is. Just as a dental cavity is a *lack* of calcium [a hole is not a thing, it is an absence of being], so is a sin not a thing, but an absence of goodness.) In 388, after a minor mystical experience,

Evil as the Absence of Being

Augustine converted to Christianity and never again vacillated in his intellectual commitment. Though Augustine returned to the religion of his mother (she was eventually designated by the Catholic Church as a saint, Saint Monica), his understanding of Christianity remained influenced by Neoplatonic ideas. But he would now admit that sin was not simply a privation of goodness, but the result of excessive self-love on the part of the sinner and the lack of sufficient love for God. In 391 Augustine was ordained a priest and in 396 became the Bishop of Hippo, on the North African coast. During this period, Christianity was still seeking to achieve focus on its own identity, and Augustine spent an enormous amount of energy combating a series of heresies: **Donatism, Priscillianism, Arianism,** and, of course, that of his former persuasion, Manicheanism. But at the same time, he had to combat a new and especially difficult heresy, that of **Pelagianism.** Pelagius's heresy was that of overaccentuating the role of free will in salvation and minimizing the role of God's grace. Much to Augustine's embarrassment, Pelagius had been using Augustine's book on free will to defend his own view.

So Augustine found himself walking a tightrope. He had to attack the Manichees for minimizing free will and attack the Pelagians for overemphasizing it. This problem occupied him in some very subtle philosophical reasoning.

The problem: If God is all-wise (omniscient), then he knows the future. If he knows the future, then the future must unfold exactly in accordance with his knowledge (otherwise, he does not know the future). If the events in the future must occur according to God's foreknowledge of them, then they are necessary, and there is no freedom. If there is no freedom, then humans are not responsible for their acts, in which case it would be immoral to punish people for their sins. (If God knew millions of years before Judas was born that he would betray Jesus, how could God send Judas to hell for his betrayal?) So the conclusion seems to be: Either God is omniscient but immoral, or he is benevolent but ignorant. How can Augustine avoid this unpalatable dilemma? He does so with a number of sophisticated arguments.

Does God's Foreknowledge Determine Our Actions?

One is that, for God, there is no past or future, only an eternal present. For him, everything exists in an eternal moment. To say "God knew millions of years before Judas's birth that he would betray Jesus" is to make the *human* error of believing that God is *in* time. In fact, God is outside of time. (That's what it means to say that God is eternal.) Another tack of Augustine's is to admit that God's knowledge of the world entails **necessity,** but to deny that necessity is incompatible with freedom. Like the stoics, Augustine believed that freedom is the capacity to do what one wants, and one can do what one wants even if God (or anyone else) already knows what that person wants. Augustine pointed out that God's foreknowledge of a decision doesn't cause the decision, any more than my own acts are caused by my knowledge of what I'm going to do.

I never had a chance!

Judas

I have just presented a sample of Augustinian thought. His philosophy is a profound meditation on the relation between God and the human being. It was addressed to a troubled and expiring world. The old order was crumbling. In fact, on the same day Augustine succumbed to the infirmities of old age in the cathedral at Hippo, the barbaric Vandals were burning the city. Even though they left the cathedral standing out of respect for him, the fires that consumed Hippo were the same ones that consumed the Roman Empire. The classical period was over, and that long night, which some call the Dark Ages, had commenced.

At the death of Augustine, Western philosophy fell into a state of deterioration that was to last for 400

God Is Not in Time

years. This period, the advent of the medieval world, truly was the dark night of the Western soul. The Roman legions could no longer control the frontiers of the Empire, and the Teutonic tribes from the eastern forest swarmed over the old Empire.

Rome was sacked twice within a thirty-five-year period. The new "barbarian" emperors no longer bore Latin names but Germanic ones. They were not interested in culture as it had been known in classical times. Philosophy as the Greeks and Romans had understood it was in danger of perishing.

The Encyclopediasts

During this long dark night, philosophy flickered only as individual candle flames at distant corners of the old, dead empire. Certain isolated monasteries in Italy, Spain, and Britain and on the rocky crags of islands in the Irish Sea produced what are known as the encyclopediasts, who systematically compiled and conserved whatever remnants of classical wisdom they could lay their hands on. The three salient figures in this tradition are Boethius (480–525) in Italy,

Isidore (570–636) in Spain, and The Venerable Bede (674–735) in England. (St. Isidore's encyclopedia is particularly revealing. Under the letter "A" can be found both an entry on the atomic theory and an entry on the Antipodes, a people who were supposed to inhabit the rocky plains of southern Africa and who, Isidore believed, had their big toes on the outside of the feet, thereby allowing them more maneuverability among the rocky fields where they dwelt!) Isidore's hodgepodge is emblematic of the state of philosophy during the Dark Ages.

An Antipode Showing Off in Rocky Terrain

John Scotus Eriugena

Suddenly, after four centuries of relative silence, philosophy blossomed forth in the work of the first great metaphysical system builder of the Middle Ages, the redundantly named John Scotus Eriugena ("John the Irishman, the Irishman" [ca. 810–ca. 877]). John had been called from Ireland to the Palatine School of King Charles the Bald to translate the Greek document known today as the Pseudo-Dionysius (a work falsely believed to have been written by St. Paul's Christian convert St. Dionysius but believed today to have been written by a Neoplatonic philosopher sympathetic to Christianity). John's own book, *On the Divisions of Nature*, was greatly influenced by his reading of the Pseudo-Dionysius and is a confusing combination of Christian dogma and Neoplatonic pantheism. Through his book and his influential translation, Platonism gained an even greater foothold in Christianity.

John's goal was the categorization and understanding of the totality of reality (what he calls "Nature"). The first categorical distinction he drew was between

THINGS THAT ARE   and   THINGS THAT ARE NOT

John Scotus Divides Up Nature

This distinction involves the Platonic supposition that there is a hierarchy of being, that some things are more real than other things. "Things that are not" are those entities that on a Neoplatonic scale contain a lesser degree of reality. For example, a particular tree or horse contains less being than the form "tree" or the form "horse"; hence, particulars are subsumed under this negative category. So are all "lacks" or "deprivations," such as sinful acts or acts of forgetting. The most surprising thing we find in this category is what John called "super-reality"—that which cannot be grasped by the human intellect, that which on the Neoplatonic scale is "beyond being." Apparently, John was talking about God.

What is left? What can be called the "things that are"? Only those entities that can be comprehended by pure human intellect, namely, the Platonic Forms! All else is beyond being.

So we find this Christian scholar in the apparently awkward position of claiming that God is among those things classified as nonexistent—in the same class where we would expect to find centaurs, griffins, round squares, and mountains made of gold. Why doesn't John's writing end all discussion of God once and for all? Because John's method of the "vias affirmativa and negativa" (borrowed from the Pseudo-Dionysius) allowed him to make sense of the nothingness of a being beyond being.

VIA AFFIRMATIVA	VIA NEGATIVA
We affirm:	We deny the affirmation:
"God is wise."	"God is not wise."
↑	↑
This affirmation is true only as metaphor. "Wisdom" is a word that gets its meaning from *human discourse*. We can apply it to God only **analogically** to give us a hint of his nature.	This negation is literal. Because "wisdom" gets its meaning from human discourse, it cannot literally apply to God.

This affirmation and its negation do not lead to a self-contradiction; rather, they serve as thesis and antithesis and are **dialectically** reconciled in a (Hegelian-like) synthesis that will lead us to realize that God is somehow superwise. The same method will show us why John said that God does not exist but that he [super] exists.

There is yet another way in which John Scotus Eriugena divided Nature:

1. Nature that creates and is uncreated (i.e., God)
2. Nature that creates and is created (i.e., the Platonic Forms)
3. Nature that is created and does not create (i.e., the physical world)
4. Nature that is not created and does not create (i.e., God)

(Remember, in this Neoplatonic schema, to say that something "X" creates is to say that there is something below X in the hierarchy of reality that is dependent upon X. Conversely, to say that something "Y" is created is to say that Y is dependent on something above it for its existence.)

In this system, God is both Alpha and Omega, Beginning and End, Creator and Goal of Creation. God issues out into the world and comes back to himself. John's philosophy looks suspiciously like Plotinus's pantheistic system of emanations, and though many attempts were made to defend *On the Divisions of Nature* against the charge of heresy, eventually it was condemned as heterodoxical, in 1225 by Pope Honorius III.

Alpha and Omega

Saint Anselm

After John Scotus Eriugena, there were no great system makers for the next 350 years. From the ninth to the thirteenth centuries, philosophy would be done in a more piecemeal manner than it had been done by Augustine or John Scotus, or than it would be done in the thirteenth century by Thomas Aquinas. It was confined to a kind of philosophical grammar of theological terms. A piecemeal approach, however, does not mean that philosophy was always unimpressive. One of the most striking pieces of philosophical logic produced in the medieval period is the demonstration of God's existence created by Anselm of Canterbury (1033–1109), later Saint Anselm. Today this demonstration is known as the **ontological argument** because it is derived not from observation but from the very idea of being ("ontology" equals "theory of being").

Anselm's argument began with a reference to the fool (of Psalms 53:1) who "says in his heart, 'There is no God.'" But, said Anselm, even the fool

is convinced that something exists in the understanding at least, than which nothing greater can be conceived. For when he hears of this he understands it. . . . And assuredly that than which nothing greater can be conceived, cannot exist in the understanding alone. For

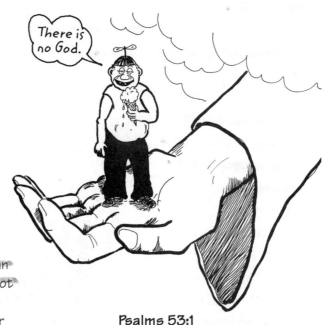

There is no God.

Psalms 53:1

suppose it exists in the understanding alone: then it can be conceived to exist in reality, which is greater. . . . Hence, there is no doubt that there exists a being than which nothing greater can be conceived, and it exists both in the understanding and in reality . . . and this being thou art, O Lord, our God.[1]

Try out Anselm's argument. Conceive in your mind the most perfect being you can think of. (Anselm believed it will look very much like the conception of the traditional Christian God—a being who is all-good, all-knowing, all-powerful, eternal, and unchangeable.) Now ask yourself, does the entity you conceived exist *only* in your mind? If it is even possible that it exists only there, then it is *not* the most perfect entity conceivable because such an entity who existed both in your mind and extramentally would be even more perfect. Therefore, if it's possible even to conceive of a most perfect being, such a being necessarily exists.

One that exists only here is less perfect than One

who exists out here.

This argument is a slippery one, and it immediately found detractors. A contemporary of Anselm's, Gaunilon, a monk by profession, made the following objections on behalf of the fool.

1. It is, in fact, impossible to conceive of "a being than which nothing greater can be conceived." The very project boggles the mind.

2. If Anselm's argument were valid, then it would follow that the mere ability to conceive of a perfect tropical island would logically entail the existence of such an island.

Gaunilon's Objections

Anselm's response was as simple as Gaunilon's rebuttle:

1. If you understand the phrase "most perfect being," then you already have conceived of such a being.

2. There is nothing in the definition of a tropical island that entails perfection, but the very definition of God entails that he be all-perfect, so it is impossible to conceive of God as lacking a perfection; and since it is obviously more perfect to be than not to be, the bare conception of God entails his existence.

This argument is both more difficult and more ingenious than it may appear to you. It is, in fact, a very good argument (which is not to say that it is flawless). Its genius is its demonstration that the sentence "God does not exist" is a self-contradictory sentence. That is why only a fool could utter it.

Take note of how very Platonic Anselm's argument is. First, it is purely **a priori**—that is, it makes no appeal whatsoever to sensorial observation; it appeals exclusively to pure reason. Second, it makes explicit the Platonic view that the "most perfect" equals "the most real." (Recall the Simile of the Line.)

The ontological proof has had a long and checkered history. We shall see it again more than once before this narration ends. Many philosophers think that Immanuel Kant finally put it to rest in the eighteenth century (by showing that the flaw in the argument was not one of logic but of *grammar*); but even today, 900 years after it was written, the argument has astute defenders.

Muslim and Jewish Philosophies

During the eleventh and twelfth centuries the growing influx into Europe of Latin translations from Arabic and Hebrew manuscripts had a dramatic effect on the directions that philosophy would take. Many of these works entered the Christian monastic world by way of Spain. From the ninth through the twelfth centuries the courts of the Muslim caliphs of Spain were the most cultured in Europe. The "Moors" (Arab, Berber, and other Muslim groups) had invaded Christian Spain in the year 711 C.E. as part of the militant expansion of Islam. Islam is the third of the three dominant Western religions, all of which derive from roughly the same area of the Middle East. The key figure in Islam is Muhammad, who was born at Mecca in today's Saudi Arabia in 570 and died in Medina in 632 C.E. According to the tradition, when he was forty years old he received a direct revelation from the angel Gabriel while meditating in a cave on a desert mountain. Over the next twenty years Muhammad continued to receive revelations that designated him as the latest in a long line of prophets of God that were to be accepted by the new religion, including all the great prophets from the Jewish Bible, but also Jesus of Nazareth. Muhammad copied the words that were revealed to him, and they became the Qur'an (or Koran), the holy book of the Islamic religion. The main idea in this religion is monotheism, just as it is in Judaism and Christianity (though Jews and Muslims often see the Christian **doctrine of the Trinity** as a backsliding into polytheism). Even more than Judaism or Christianity, Islam preaches the power of God (Allah) over the world and in everyday life. The words "Islam" and "Muslim" both derive from the Arabic word for "submission" or "surrender." Like the other two religions—but unlike the tribal religions of Muhammad's native Arabia—Islam forbids the use of idols. Like Judaism and Christianity it sees its patriarch in the biblical figure of Abraham. Islam preaches the brotherhood of all believers, and it requires charity to the poor. In addition, it stresses prayer (five times daily), purification, and fasting during holy days (Ramadan), and it enjoins the faithful to make a holy pilgrimage to Mecca at least once during one's lifetime.

Islam had tremendous appeal because of its theological simplicity, its ability to address the spiritual and material needs of great numbers of people who lived in chaotic times, its capacity to transcend tribal rivalries, and its offer of community and personal salvation. Its survival against great odds and bloody oppression in its first years gave it a militant cast. Its leaders believed in the idea of holy war (*jihad*), and through conquests and conversion Islam spread rapidly in all directions. In the West, by the year 732—a little more than one hundred years after Muhammad's first revelations—Muslim armies had penetrated deeply into France, where they were finally defeated at the Battle of Tours by Charles the Sledgehammer, Charlemagne's grandfather. The Arab-dominated Muslim army retreated behind the Pyrenees, where the Moors developed a splendid Islamic culture in Spain that contained beautiful cities, magnificent gardens with flowing water everywhere, great architectural monuments, and spacious centers of learning. There Muslim, Christian, and Jewish scholars worked side by side studying the manuscripts of the Greek philosophers, whose surviving copies were slowly being discovered and gathered in the great libraries of Seville, Granada, Cordoba, and Toledo. These libraries had no match in the Christian world. The products of the Muslim schools of translators slowly worked their way into Catholic-dominated Europe and caused a great stir, especially the translations of Aristotle and many commentaries on his works, most of which had been lost to the Christian world.

The Court of the Lions
The Alhambra—Granada

Averroës

One of the most influential of the Muslim philosophers in both the Islamic and Catholic worlds was Abul Walid Muhammad ibn Ahmad ibn Muhammad ibn Rushd, better known in the West as Averroës (1126–1198), who was born in Cordoba, Spain. His most impressive writings were his careful explications and analyses of Aristotle's philosophy. Aristotle's rediscovery had sent shock waves through the Muslim intellectual community. Averroës's commentaries were written in the context of a debate among Arab-speaking theologians as to whether the claims of Aristotle's philosophy were compatible with Muslim dogma. The Arab theologian Al-Ghazali (1058–1111) had written against Aristotle, and the Persian Avicenna (980–1037) had defended the Greek philosopher. Averroës rejected the arguments of both Al-Ghazali and Avicenna, claiming that they had both misread Aristotle. There still exists today a scholarly debate as to how Averroës himself should be read. According to one group of interpreters, Averroës wrote two types of commentary: one for more general consumption in which he asserted that all of Aristotle is compatible with Islam and that Aristotle's ideas can be used to explore and clarify Muslim belief, and another for a more sophisticated audience in which he defended Aristotle against Islam. According to a second group of scholars, Averroës's message is consistent throughout and is somewhere between the two extremes demarcated by the other two groups.[2] Averroës's commentaries came into the Christian world appearing to claim that there were two kinds of opposing truths, philosophical truth (i.e., Aristotelian) and religious truth, yet also claiming that the contexts of philosophical and theological discourse were so distinct that both truths could be accepted at the same time. Averroës's writings had a dizzying effect on the philosophers of the monasteries and newly established universities of the Catholic world. On the one hand, Averroës's work was indispensable for the understanding of Aristotle, but on the other, it was felt that his theory of the discrepancy between religion and philosophy would have to be refuted in the name of Christian dogma. Thomas Aquinas (whom we will study shortly) wrote a book called *On the Unity of the Intellect against the Averroists*, yet he so respected Averroës's explanations of Aristotle that he simply called him "the Commentator." Some Western theologians, led by Siger of Brabant (ca. 1240–ca. 1284), went against the grain (and got in trouble for it), defending what they took to be Averroës's **doctrine of double truth.** They were called the Latin Averroists.

Maimonides

What Averroës was to Muslim philosophy and Thomas Aquinas was to Catholic philosophy, Moises Maimonides (1135–1204) was to Jewish philosophy. Like his contemporary Averroës, Maimonides was born in Cordoba and also was most influential in the Catholic world for his insights into the philosophy of Aristotle. Thomas Aquinas revered Maimonides, and Thomas's demonstrations of God's existence were clearly influenced by those of Maimonides. In fact, Maimonides' first book, *A Treatise on Logic*, is a compendium of the categories of Aristotle's logic and an analysis of them. It was written in Arabic when Maimonides was sixteen years old.

Maimonides' most celebrated book is called *Guide of the Perplexed*. It purports to conduct educated but intellectually confused Jews through the labyrinth of philosophy and Judaic theology in their quest to resolve the conflicts between science and religion. The problem is, the *Guide* itself needs a guide, for it is a very difficult work, and it raises questions about its author's

Moses Maimonides

intentions similar to those raised about Averroës's. The most common way of understanding the book is to treat it as an attempt to reconcile Aristotelian philosophy with Jewish theology, showing that the Greek's theories provide tools for exploring and expanding on Judaism. Maimonides calls Aristotle "the chief of the philosophers" and calls Moses "the master of those who know."[3] But there have been very respectable scholars who see the book as subversive of religious values. Despite appearing to support religious values, the book in fact undermines them in a subtle and sophisticated way. For instance, Maimonides insists on what he claims to be the primary commandment of Judaism, to know God. Yet his theology is a negative theology, apparently showing that God cannot know us (an idea of Aristotle's, as you may recall) and that we can only know what God is not (a Neoplatonic idea that we have already seen in the work of John Scotus Eriugena). One Maimonidean scholar states the problem like this: Maimonides "records the duty to know God as the very first commandment. . . . Yet when we examine it in the total context and full development of his own analysis, we seemingly must conclude that this ideal is not only impossible, but empty of content and meaning."[4]

But if some scholars have seen Maimonides as a heretic destroying Jewish doctrine with Aristotelian logic, others have seen him as an anti-Aristotelian rabbi whose intention was to demonstrate the incoherence of so-called philosophical wisdom. Still others have seen him as holding a version of the doctrine of double truth attributed to Averroës, whose work he knew and admired. Whatever Maimonides' true intentions were, his astute clarification of Aristotelian categories and the use of Aristotelian arguments in his books left the impression in the world of Latin-speaking scholars that he was indeed a guide for those readers perplexed by Aristotle.

Despite the small minority of vociferous critics calling Maimonides a heretic, Jewish culture has for the greatest part been very proud of him from his day to ours. When Christian troops under Ferdinand and Isabella conquered the Moors in 1492 and expelled the Jews from Spain, there emerged this adage in Ladino, the Spanish spoken by the exiled Jews: "De Moisés a Moisés no ha habido nadie como Moisés" (From Moses to Moses there has been nobody like Moses).

The Problem of Faith and Reason

The problem being dealt with by Maimonides and Averroës, the problem of faith versus reason, was one that plagued the whole of medieval philosophy. In the Christian world it received its best medieval solution at the hands of Thomas Aquinas in the thirteenth century, as we shall soon see. The problem concerned the question of whether to emphasize the claims of divine revelation or the claims of philosophy in one's conception of reality, and among Christians there were extremists in both camps. We've seen that philosophers like John Scotus Eriugena had purely conceptual schemes in which there seemed to be no room for mere religious belief. Even St. Anselm's God seemed primarily philosophical and a far cry from the Stern Father and Vengeful Judge of the Old Testament. At the other end of the spectrum was the antiphilosopher Tertullian (169–220), whose

Credo Quia Absurdum

famous cry was *"Credo quia absurdum"* ("I believe that which is absurd"), with the implication that he believed it *because* it was absurd.

The debate between these two groups reached a high pitch and produced a number of startling claims, such as the view that we have seen attributed to the Latin Averroists, who produced the doctrine of double truth. Recall that according to this doctrine there are two mutually contradictory truths, one produced by faith and one by reason, but both valid from their respective points of view. So, for example, from the anatomical perspective, the human being is a compilation of organs that, when they cease to function, bring about the termination of the person; but from the theological perspective, the human being is a soul that is, through God's grace, immortal.

This theory, though logically unsatisfactory, did for a short time play the historically positive role of allowing science to develop without having to conceive of itself in theological terms.

The Problem of the Universals

The other vexing problem of the day, the problem of the universals, was the question concerning the referents of words. Augustine had inaugurated a concern about language that dominated philosophical thought throughout the Middle Ages. Remember that according to Augustine, God sees his creation as an eternal present—that is, past, present, and future all rolled up into one. If language represents reality, and if humans experience reality so differently from God, then the true "word of God" can be nothing like the language of humans, who perceive the world in terms of a temporal sequence in finite space. Human language, then, must be a kind of degradation of Godly language. (Notice that this situation is probably another one in which medieval thought is haunted by Plato's Simile of the Line, in which each level of the hierarchy of being is a poor copy of the one above it.) Yet human language can aspire to the truth, being God-given, so theological concerns necessarily overlapped linguistic ones. The specific version of the problem that would obsess Christian, Jewish, and Muslim philosophers for several centuries had been introduced by Boethius, who had been deeply influenced by Augustine and who had translated from the Greek an essay about Aristotle by the Neoplatonic author Porphyry (232–304). The latter had queried the ontological status of genera and species. We know that there exist individual things that we call "whales"; but does the genus *Balaenoptera*, or the species *Balaenoptera physalis* (fin whale), or the species *Balaenoptera musculus* (blue whale) exist in nature, or are these only artificial categories existing merely in the mind? (The same problem appears in sentences like "This dog is brown." Do the words "dog" and

"brown" only name the individual, or do they name the *classes* of canines and brown things, and are those classes real or artificial?)

The debate that ensued was, of course, similar to the debate between Plato and Aristotle over the status of the Forms, but the original works of the Greeks were lost to the philosophers of the early Middle Ages, and it took them 900 years to arrive at the point that Aristotle had gained in one generation. The issue reached such a state of confusion that John of Salisbury (ca. 1115– ca. 1180) claimed that in his day there were as many ideas on the subject as there were heads. The extremes in this debate were represented, on one side, by the strict Platonists (today called "exaggerated realists"). They held that classes were not only real but *more* real than individuals. Anselm himself was a representative of this view. The other extreme, represented by Roscelin (ca. 1050–1120) and William of Ockham (ca. 1280– ca. 1349), was the doctrine known as **nominalism,** from the Latin word for "name" (*nom*). According to this view, which was eventually found unacceptable by the Church, only particulars are real, and words denoting classes are merely names. According to the nominalists, the system of names creates differences and similarities that exist only in the mind of the speaker or in the system of language itself.

Currently, there exist as many theories on the topic as there are heads.

You and I may smile when we are told by anthropologists that an Amazonian tribe includes in the same class toads, palm leaves, and arm pits (namely, the class of entities that are warm and dry on top and damp and dark underneath), but the nominalist asks us if this classification is any more arbitrary than our claim that whales and moles are members of the same class (namely, the class of entities with mammary glands).

Saint Thomas Aquinas

As I mentioned earlier, it is Thomas Aquinas (1225–1274) who is generally credited with working out the best medieval solution both to the problem of faith versus reason and to the problem of the universals.

Thomas was an Italian nobleman who ran away from his family's castle to join the Dominican order (where, by the way, he was so well fed that a niche eventually had to be carved out of the dinner table

to accommodate his ample girth). Before I talk about his philosophy, let's look at the world he inhabited, thirteenth-century Europe.

More than 100 years had elapsed between Anselm's death and Thomas's birth. In that century, as we have seen, European scholars were becoming more and more acquainted with the "lost" works of the classical age, particularly the writings of Aristotle. Though the theories of Aristotle were found to be shocking by some, his philosophy was actually more compatible with the new this-worldly attitude of the thirteenth century than was the now somewhat stale other-worldliness of Platonic thought. The human race had survived the millennium. The year 1000 had passed without the world ending, as many people had expected.

The old apocalyptic prophecies faded further into the future, and as Europe emerged from the darkest moments of the Dark Ages, interest in the world of here and now was revived. Aristotle surfaced as the champion of these new interests. It fell to Thomas Aquinas to "Christianize" him—no easy task considering that Aristotle held such un-Christian views as

A. The earth is eternal. (There never was a creation.)
B. God, the Prime Mover, knowing only his own perfection, is indifferent to human affairs. (He doesn't even know we exist.)
C. The soul is not immortal.
D. The goal of life is happiness.
E. Pride is a virtue and humility a vice.

No surprise that Aristotle's works were banned by the University of Paris in 1210. (Indeed, Thomas's works themselves were condemned at Paris and at Oxford just after his death.)

Thomas Aquinas wrote more than forty volumes. His leading works are two encyclopedic projects, the *Summa theologica* and the *Summa contra gentiles*. These tremendously systematic works comprise a whole structure that has often been compared to the Gothic cathedrals, which were the new architectural style of his day. Like them, Thomas's work is not only a mirror held up to late medieval society but also a beacon unto it.

Thomas's main job was that of *reconciliation*, not only the reconciliation of Aristotle with Christendom but also that of reason with faith and of the warring sides in the debate over the status of universals. Concerning the latter, Thomas was able to take advantage of the Aristotelian solution: Universals are neither autonomous forms nor mere mental states. They are "embedded" in particular objects as their "whatness." The human mind has the power of *abstraction* based on its ability to recognize real similarities that exist in nature. These abstractions become *concepts*. This solution came to be known as **moderate realism.** It had been anticipated 120 years earlier by Peter Abelard (1079–1142), whose view is called **conceptualism.** The only difference between the two views seems to be one of emphasis. Both are grounded in Aristotle's insistence that essences do not exist apart from individual substances, even though as an intellectual act one can abstract the essence from the substances that exhibit essential similarities. For example, I can mentally and linguistically isolate the "dogness" that all dogs have in common, even though in fact that dogness exists only *in* real dogs. Abelard appears to concentrate more than Thomas does on the *conventionality* of the concepts in the human mind and therefore holds that there is a slight discrepancy between the concept in the mind and the essence (i.e., the real similarity existing among all dogs) that that concept is meant to represent. This view pushes Abelard a bit closer to nominalism than Thomas would be willing to go. The distinctions I am discussing here are subtle; nonetheless, precisely these kinds of fine points caused passionate intellectual battles in the Middle Ages.

Concerning the problem of reason versus faith, Thomas began by distinguishing between *philosophy* and **theology.** The philosopher uses human reason alone. The theologian accepts revelation as authority.

Philosophy

Theology

Then Thomas distinguished between revealed theology (accepted purely on faith) and natural theology (susceptible of the proof of reason). That is, he showed where philosophy and theology overlap.

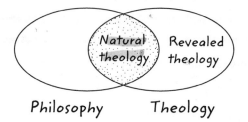

Thomas admitted that sometimes reason cannot establish the claims of faith, and he left those claims to the theologians (e.g., the claim that the universe has a beginning in time).

Most of Thomas's system is concerned with natural theology. Nevertheless, in order to establish that form of theology, he first developed a whole metaphysical system based on Aristotelian philosophy. Thomas agreed with Aristotle that there is nothing in the human mind that does not begin with observation and experience. Even though there are no innate ideas that explain how knowledge is possible (as in Plato's philosophy), according to Thomas, the soul does have the capacity for abstraction, contemplation, and reasoning. This ability allows humans to arrive at principles and causes that can explain the observable world even if those principles and causes are themselves unobservable. To arrive at these principles—which will also be the principles of his natural theology—Thomas first employed the Aristotelian conception of the world as a plurality of substances, which, you will recall, can be analyzed in terms of form and matter, or actuality and potentiality. Thomas stressed even more than did Aristotle the idea of actuality, which he called "act" (actus in Latin), and associated it strongly with the idea of "being" (esse in Latin). Esse is the actus whereby an essence or a form (what a thing is) has its being. "There is no essence without existence and no existence without essence."[5] In other words, chimeras and griffins do not have essences because they do not have being. They do not exist and never have existed. They are just fanciful constructions based on imaginative abstraction.

Aquinas placed this idea of "acts of being" in a context that is clearly more Platonic than Aristotelian, the context of a hierarchy of being. Reality is a system of "acts of being" in a hierarchical framework with God at the top and the lowliest "acts of being" taking place at the bottom. The word "being" (esse)

(After Sir John Tenniel)

here does not mean the same thing at each level of the hierarchy. The word has an analogical meaning rather than a single meaning. That is, esse at the bottom of the scale is something like esse at the top, but not identical to it. For example, according to Thomas, God is a pure act of being. He is, like Aristotle's Prime Mover, pure actuality with no potentiality to be anything other than what he is, whereas things further down the ladder have less actuality (they are lesser "acts of being") and have more potentiality to be something other than what they are at the moment. A tree can become lumber for a house, or it can rot, dry up, and turn into powder. It follows from this line of thinking that some substances have no physical matter, because matter has the most potentiality for change, according to Aristotle and Thomas. This lack of physical matter is true for God and humans, according to Aquinas. Here is where Thomas and Aristotle part company, because Aristotle called the human soul "the form of the body," implying thereby that the soul, along with the body, is mortal. But Thomas said that the soul is the form of the subject, the human individual, and therefore the soul is possibly immortal.

Saint Thomas Aquinas ◆ **131**

(Thomas could not logically *prove* that the soul is immortal, but as a theologian he accepted Christian revelation as establishing the truth of immortality.)

Thomas also believed that from this metaphysical scheme of reality as a hierarchy of substances one could deduce a priori that angels *must* exist to fill the gap between human souls—which are embodied—and God, who is pure, unembodied *esse*. Indeed, there have to be different levels of angels in the hierarchy, some more spiritual than others. The seraphim, for example, are higher than the cherubim. This deduction, for which Saint Thomas's followers gave him the title of the Angelic Doctor, shows not only how far the mind's capacity for abstraction can carry us beyond the confines of direct observation, but also provides a good example of a theological idea whose truth can be known both philosophically (natural theology) and by revelation (see Genesis 3:24 and Isaiah 6:2), according to Aquinas. Another, even more important, example of a truth that can be known both philosophically and through revelation is that of God's existence. In the *Summa theologica* Aquinas provided five philosophical arguments

**The Cherubim and the Flaming Sword Block
the Garden of Eden (Genesis 3:24)**

for God's existence. They are called **cosmological arguments**, as opposed to Anselm's ontological argument, because they all begin with observations derived from the natural world. (Remember, *kosmos* is the Greek word meaning "world.") Three of Thomas's "five ways" are very similar. I present here the second of the five as representative of Thomas's natural theology:

> In the world of sensible things we find there is an order of efficient causes. There is no case known (neither is it, indeed, possible) in which a thing is found to be the efficient cause of itself; for so it would be prior to itself, which is impossible. Now in efficient causes it is not possible to go on to infinity. . . . Now to take away the cause is to take away the effect. Therefore if there be no first cause among efficient causes, there will be no ultimate, nor any intermediate cause. . . . Therefore it is necessary to admit a first efficient cause, to which everyone gives the name of God.[6]

THE BUCK STOPS HERE

In the simplest reading of his demonstration, Thomas seems to be giving us a domino theory and merely saying that, if there is a series of causes and effects, such a series must be caused by a being who is itself uncaused; otherwise we will have an infinite regress, which Thomas found intellectually repugnant. This version of the argument was submitted to careful scrutiny (e.g., by David Hume in the eighteenth century). Thomas's alleged knowledge of an order of causes was challenged, as was his claim that an infinite series of causes is impossible. However, Thomistic scholars have demonstrated that Thomas's second way is more complicated than it appears to be, because it involves a horizontal system of causes (in which an infinite series cannot be disproved) and a hierarchical system of dependencies (which, according to Thomas, cannot admit of an infinite regress).

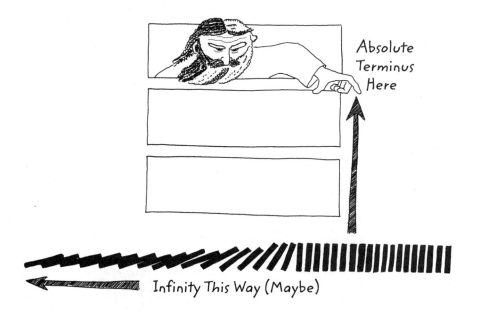

Absolute Terminus Here

Infinity This Way (Maybe)

Whatever their validity, the five Thomistic proofs have some historically notable features. Unlike the ontological proof of Anselm, they all begin with an **a posteriori** claim, that is, with an appeal to observation. This is one of the Aristotelian characteristics of the argument, and in its commitment to the reality of the observable world, it contrasts greatly with the Platonism of Anselm's a priori proof. Still, there are vestiges of Platonism in the five ways, including their appeal to a hierarchy of causes.

Like Aristotle's philosophy, all of Thomas's thought is teleological, especially his ethics. Human activity is viewed as a means-end structure. We choose desired goals and then choose among acts that lead to those goals. The acts are relative to the ends, but the ends (health, beauty, duty) are themselves relative to some absolute ends that give meaning to the relative ends; otherwise, every series of actions would lead to an infinite regress.

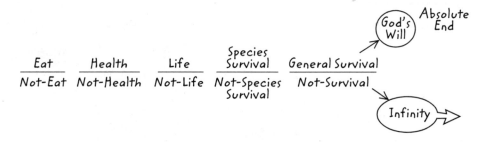

(Notice this argument is the same kind that led Thomas to posit God as an uncaused cause.) If we want to make correct choices, we must know what the ultimate goal is. Aristotle said it was happiness. Thomas agreed but thought he now knew what the Greeks did not—that happiness itself must be eternal to be an absolute. To be an absolute goal is to be a goal in and of itself, and not be merely a goal relative to some other goal (the way that taking aspirin is a goal relative to the goal of getting rid of a headache, which is a goal relative to the higher goal of maintaining health). Our happiness, hence our correct choices and acts, depends on knowledge of God—not just on philosophical knowledge of God but on the expectation of that full and final knowledge, the **Beatific Vision.** This possibility, when achieved, fulfills the Eternal Law of God, which is the law that sustains the universe—a divine ordering that governs nature. Just as this divine law that directs natural substances is obviously consistent with the essences of those substances and is reflected in their behavior, so is it reflected in human nature. "Natural law" is the term chosen by Thomas to designate the eternal law as it applies to humans. God also gave human beings freedom; therefore they are free to obey the natural law or not. (Notice that Aquinas's use of the phrase "natural law" is not related to modern science's application of it. In the scientific sense, humans are *not*

free to disobey natural law.) Obedience to natural law is "a rational participation in the eternal law of God."[7] Thomas argued that individuals have a sufficient knowledge of their own human nature to understand generally what is morally correct and to be able to regulate their own actions in the light of that understanding. They know, for instance, that they should seek to preserve themselves and that suicide is therefore wrong. They know that they should, as a species, reproduce. (I say "as a species" because individuals, such as nuns, monks, and priests, may choose to guard their virginity without going against the natural law.) Humans also know that they should care for their fellow

Multiply and be fruitful!

Six oranges times three is eighteen oranges

Three apples times eight is twenty-four apples

Two lemons times twelve is . . . uh . . . .

humans. But just in case self-knowledge is not strong enough in a weak-minded person to lead to these moral insights, revelation has also provided humans with the Ten Commandments. Thomas's moral philosophy, then, is yet another example of "natural theology," where both philosophy and biblical revelation lead to the same conclusion.

Thomas himself seems to have experienced some kind of ecstatic realization two years before his death (a prefiguring of the Beatific Vision?), which caused him to cease writing. He said that in the face of that experience, all his words were like mere straw.

The work of Saint Thomas Aquinas represents the apogee of scholastic philosophy. But at the very moment when **scholasticism** was being articulated by Thomas Aquinas and by other thirteenth-century philosophers such as John Duns Scotus (1265–1308) as the most excellent statement of the high medieval mind, there were already currents developing that would begin to undermine the scholastic synthesis, foreshadowing as they did the birth of a new, more secularly oriented world. These currents were the voices of men who, intentionally or unintentionally, separated the theological from the philosophical in ways that prepared the path for the "new science" of the Renaissance. Such was the thought of Roger Bacon (ca. 1212–ca. 1292), whose disdain for speculative metaphysics and whose curiosity about the natural world influenced other philosophers to move along the new path—philosophers such as John Buridan (ca. 1300–ca. 1358), Nicholas of Oresme (1320–1382), and Nicholas of Autrecourt (ca. 1300–?).

William of Ockham

The most influential of these antischolastic late medieval philosophers was William of Ockham (ca. 1280–ca. 1349), who has already been mentioned here for his nominalistic stance in the debate concerning the status of universals. William's name comes from his birthplace, the town of Ockham in Surrey, in the south of England. After entering the Franciscan order he studied theology at Oxford, where he proved himself to be a superb logician. His philosophy—if not his theology—is unabashedly empiricist. According to William, all knowledge other than revealed knowledge must be derived directly from sensorial observation of particular objects and events. Therefore, strictly speaking, there is no such thing as metaphysical knowledge (knowledge that goes beyond the physical). From the narrow epistemological foundation constructed by Ockham, Thomas Aquinas's metaphysical inferences are unwarranted. The search for knowledge must be governed by a methodological principle of simplicity according to which "plurality is not to be assumed without necessity." This principle, now known as Ockham's razor (or Occam's razor, after the Latinate spelling of William's name), would in later years come to be accepted as a guiding rule by all empiricists, and, indeed, it seems to have become a component of the scientific method itself. Its modern form has usually been worded as "Do not multiply entities beyond necessity," meaning that whenever a phenomenon can be equally well explained by a theory containing fewer elements rather than many, the simpler theory is to be chosen over the more complicated one. (Contrast these two theories: Your watch is powered by an electronic battery; or, your watch is powered by a workforce of invisible fairies.) William's principle of simplicity raised some ecclesiastical hackles. There were suspicions that his "razor" could be used to reduce the Holy Trinity to one, or even to

They're SWISS fairies!

shave God out of the picture. But William's goal was almost certainly not to attack religion. He was interested in ejecting universals and essences from metaphysical theories and, indeed, in shaving metaphysics itself from the realm of possible knowledge.

Ockham's razor also eliminates Aristotle's formal and final causes, concepts used extensively by the scholastic philosophers of the thirteenth century. In reducing causality to what Aristotle had called "efficient causes," William helped usher in the **mechanistic** conception of causality that would characterize modern science from the seventeenth through the nineteenth centuries. William's tight empiricist program also disallows the traditional proofs of God's existence, whether Anselmian or Thomist, depending as they do on the idea of a hierarchy of degrees of perfection or on the impossibility of an infinite series of efficient causes. According to Ockham, these ideas are illegitimate metaphysical notions that cannot be justified by empirical observation.

Ockham Wielding Razor

William's nominalism is such that only individuals are real, and universality is a feature of language, not of the world. That is, we can talk about "vegetables," for example, as a universal concept, but the universality inheres pragmatically in the linguistic category we use rather than in some universality actually existing in the various organic entities we call vegetables. William assumed that it is possible to create universal categories in language because of actual similarities between real individual objects in the world—individual carrots are not only similar to one another, but also to beets and to spinach—so his nominalism is not as radical as some later philosophers would carry it when they argued that even the concept of "similarity" is arbitrary, a conventional invention imposed on objects that are basically different from one another.

The genuine similarities and dissimilarities that exist among real objects and events permit a science of natural things, according to Ockham, including the cataloging of causal laws, but causality cannot be an absolute. There can be no *necessary connections* found among objects and events in the world. The reason for our failure to find necessity in the world is not the fault of our sensory apparata (as it will be in the radical empiricism of David Hume in the eighteenth century), but because of theological considerations. If God is omnipotent but inscrutable, as William thought Christians must believe, then all events in the natural world must be radically **contingent,** because divine omnipotence has the capacity to interrupt any series of events whatsoever, even those that we humans think are the most necessary. Indeed, there is historical and revelatory proof that such interruptions do happen, according to William, namely, the miracles recounted in the Bible.

In dealing with William of Ockham, we must constantly remind ourselves that in his own mind his radical philosophy did not undermine theology; rather, it strengthened it by preventing metaphysical ideas from claiming to impose constraints on God's ability. God's infinite freedom, inscrutable grace, and perfect omniscience are not limited by any human principles except the law of noncontradiction,

St. John the Divine Sees the End of the World

according to William. Indeed, these divine powers can even overturn the principles of empiricist philosophy, for *God* has the capacity to produce at will in the minds of his subjects appearances that are uncaused by any actual events in the world and yet that seem to be caused by such events. The proof of this claim is found in the visions that *God* allowed some of the biblical prophets to have of the future as if that future were contemporary with them. Also, revealed theology presents some paradoxes that cannot be resolved logically or philosophically, such as the compatibility of divine foreknowledge and human freedom. William rejected as sophistic the solutions to this problem of predestination that were offered by Saint Augustine, but he was unable to suggest a solution of his own.

Not surprisingly, a number of religious figures of his day found William's views to be heretical. His degree of Master of Theology from Oxford was held up by the chancellor of the university, who sent to the pope a complaint concerning the danger of allowing William's ideas to be circulated. Ockham was called to the papal palace in Avignon to be investigated. (This period in Catholic history—between 1309 and 1377—was later called by some theologians the "Babylonian captivity" of the papacy,[8] because the French cardinals had managed to outmaneuver the Italians and forced the papacy from the Vatican in Rome to Avignon in southern France.) William stayed in Avignon for four years without any judicial decision being reached.

At Avignon William got caught up in a controversy about the role of poverty among the clergy, because he supported the Franciscan doctrine of poverty against the stance of the pope. When he realized that the pope was about to issue a condemnation of his defense of apostolic poverty, William escaped to Bavaria and sought the protection of Emperor Ludwig, the antipapal regent there. Pope John excommunicated William in absentia. William probably died in Bavaria in 1349 of the Black Plague, which was ravaging Europe at that time. The epidemic deprived Europe of many of its most creative minds and contributed to a deterioration of culture that lasted well into the next century.

Renaissance Philosophers

The historical period that marks the transition between the Middle Ages and the modern world took place approximately between 1450 and 1600. It is called the Renaissance, meaning the "rebirth," which refers not only to the recovery of classical Greek and Roman art, ideas, styles, and forms, but also to a renewed enthusiasm for the more sensual aspects of the life as the ancient Greeks and Romans were imagined to have lived it. The exploration and exploitation of the "New World" by navigators and conquistadores such as Christopher Columbus, Ferdinand Magellan, and Hernan Cortés, along with the opening of trade routes to Asia, produced new economics, new classes of wealth, and demands for education outside the Church-dominated cathedral universities and cloisters. The culture that emerged put down its first and deepest roots in Italy, where the arts and literature were liberated from what the late-fifteenth-century citizens felt were the artificial strictures of the medieval world. Innovative and highly talented artists flourished, including painters (for example, Fra Angelico, Raphael, Michelangelo, and Leonardo da Vinci), sculptors (Donatello and Verrocchio), and architects (Giotto and Brunelleschi). In politics, the erosion of papal power opened channels for ambitious monarchs (for example, Charles I of Spain, Francis I of France, and Henry IV of England) and for influential religious reformers (such as Martin Luther, John Calvin, John Knox, and Jonathan Wycliffe). The works of the artists and writers of the period, as well as translations of the Bible into local languages, were made available for mass consumption for the first time because of the invention of the printing press and of engraving procedures.

Closer to the specific interests of this book, attention should be directed toward the end of the Renaissance, when some of the fields that we now recognize as the modern sciences began to establish independence from their philosophical and theological moorings, and a generation of scientific heroes emerged—men such as Nicolaus Copernicus (1473–1543), the Polish astronomer who articulated the modern version of the heliocentric (i.e., sun-centered) theory of the planets; Tycho Brahe (1546–1601) of Denmark, who gathered the astronomical data that would later be formulated into the laws of planetary motion by Johannes Kepler (1571–1630) in Germany; Galileo Galilei (1564–1642), the Italian physicist, mathematician, and astronomer who laid the foundations of contemporary science; and the English physician William Harvey (1578–1657), who discovered the circulation of blood.

Renaissance philosophers are in general not remembered today as well as the artists, scientists, politicians, and explorers who were their contemporaries. But there are in the Renaissance two related philosophical developments that should be reported: the emergence of humanism, and the battle between a newly articulated Neoplatonism and a revised Aristotelianism.

The word "humanist" was used in the Renaissance to designate those scholars whose interests were the studia humanitatis, the humanities. These philosophers were keenly interested in human affairs: politics, institutions, art, and mores as well as human freedom and dignity. In general, they were more concerned with moral philosophy than with metaphysics. They removed philosophy from the hands of ecclesiastical professionals and turned it into a fitting study for laypersons. To this end, they promoted translations of the Graeco-Roman masterpieces into modern European languages and experimented in writing their own works in those same vernacular languages—the language of the people. Although several important humanists were clergymen, they too participated in freeing philosophy from the institutional control of Christian authority. Their eventual power was such that even a number of popes were designated as humanists, most notably, Nicholas V (pope from 1447 to 1455).

The poet Petrarch (Francesco Petrarca, 1304–1374) is usually regarded as the founder of Italian humanism. Inspired as he was by the rhetorical skills and aesthetic qualities of the Roman poets and orators such as Cicero and Seneca, he objected not only to the content but also to the style of the works of the scholastic philosophers, which he found "barbaric, tediously pedantic, arid and incomprehensible." He had "nothing but contempt for what he regarded as their empty loquacity and their addiction to disputation for its own sake."[9] He attacked the scholastic addiction to Aristotle and touted Plato over Aristotle as the superior philosopher. These attacks did not mean that Petrarch had no respect for Aristotle. Despite not being able to read Greek well, he blamed the scholastic philosophers for mistranslating Aristotle, and despite never having read Averroës, he also blamed them for following the Arab philosopher's commentary on Aristotle. No Arab philosopher for Petrarch, only Latin and Greek!—and only those Latin and Greek philosophers whose works were compatible with Christianity. In all things, Petrarch's motivation came back to his religious beliefs. He summed up his project with this motto: Platonic wisdom, Christian dogma, Ciceronian eloquence.

Other important Renaissance humanists were Desiderius Erasmus (1466–1536) of Holland, whose *In Praise of Folly* cleverly satirized the overintellectualizing of the scholastics and called for a return to a simpler and happier Christianity; Thomas More (1478–1535) of England, whose *Utopia* combines Platonic, Epicurean, and Christian theories in a depiction of an ideal human life; the Italian Giovanni Pico della Mirandola (1463–1494), whose *Oration on the Dignity of Man* lauds human freedom and the human power of self-creation; and Michel de Montaigne (1533–1592) of France, whose influential *Essays* set forth in a witty manner his philosophy of skepticism. Even Niccolò Machiavelli (1469–1527) has been called a humanist, despite the fact that his book *The Prince* seems to be less "in praise of folly" than in praise of the manipulation of political power.

Despite the many differences between the medieval and the Renaissance philosophers, they had in common that their intellectual worlds were book centered and that their arguments were based on the appeal to the authority of ancient philosophers rather than to the arguments of reason or the data of experience, as would be the case with the modern philosophers who followed them. Not until the end of the Renaissance did thinkers begin to challenge all authorities—including the classics—and with that challenge the modern world began. The big philosophical debate in the early Renaissance was over the question of which ancient *auctor* (author), Plato or Aristotle, was the truer *auctoritates* (authority). To the Renaissance philosophers, was it Plato or Aristotle who had more genuinely anticipated the truths of Christianity? Which of the two had offered a better framework for a philosophical defense of Christian dogma?

So we see that despite the Renaissance reaction against medieval scholasticism, there was nevertheless a strong Aristotelian tradition throughout the period, but it was Aristotle in a new style as humanists tried to claim him for their own. If the scholastics had produced a perversion of the true Aristotle, then he must now be reclaimed for the new age. The Italian universities taught philosophy as a preparation for medicine, and in these teachings Aristotle's natural philosophy played a very different role from the role it had played at Oxford and Paris. Still, numerous empirically oriented philosophers continued to argue that Aristotle's philosophy—especially in its new, humanized guise—was better than Platonism for defending Christian dogma. However, as one Renaissance scholar noted, "even the most advanced Aristotelians did not progress from empiricism to experimentalism. They remained content to observe nature passively in order to confirm established doctrines rather than trying to devise methods of active intervention or validation."[10]

The Platonic philosophy that, during the Renaissance, tried to usurp the role that Aristotelian philosophy had played during the High Middle Ages was in fact an updated version of the Neoplatonism of the Low Middle Ages. Its tradition goes back to Plotinus, Proclus, Saint Augustine, the Pseudo-Dionysius, and John Scotus Eriugena. Renaissance Neoplatonism, especially that of the Florentine Academy, founded by Marsilio Ficino (1433–1499), was nevertheless not identical to its earlier incarnation. It was more humanized, yet it was also more entirely Christianized. The early Church fathers had speculated that Plato had learned of the Hebrew Bible during a visit to Egypt. This connection explained what the Platonized Christians took to be striking similarities between Plato's philosophy and Christianity, which to them was the fulfillment of biblical prophecy. Ficino translated all thirty-six

of Plato's dialogues, plus the *Enneads* of Plotinus, into Latin. Furthermore, he translated a manuscript attributed to Hermes Trismegistus, an Egyptian priest, that purported to show how Mosaic wisdom had been transmitted to Plato. This document was later discovered to be a forgery from the early Christian period, but in the Renaissance it added considerable stature to Plato's religious credentials.

The Neoplatonic Christians of the early medieval period had found it advantageous to interpret passages of the Bible not only literally but also allegorically and esoterically (finding layers of hidden meaning). The Platonism espoused in the Renaissance by Ficino and his teacher, Cardinal Bessarion (ca. 1403–1472), and by Nicholas of Cusa (1401–1464) in Germany, applied the same technique to the writings of Plato himself. This interpretation allowed them not only to find in Plato's writings cryptic allusions to biblical truth but also to explain away certain awkward features of Plato's philosophy, such as his apparent approval of homosexuality, his communism, and his doctrine of **metempsychosis** (according to which the soul exists in a heaven of souls before the body is born and enters the body at birth). Despite the mystical tendencies in Neoplatonism, in its Renaissance version it avoided Plato's apparent other-worldliness by seeing each individual object in the visible world as a microcosmic replica of the whole of reality. So, rather than viewing the physical world as disgusting, ugly, and sinful, humans could appreciate and even spiritualize the beauties of the material realm. The influence of humanism on Neoplatonism even permitted the glorification of pleasure and sensuality. This feature of Neoplatonism is perhaps best manifested in Renaissance art and allows that art to be paradoxically Platonic,

No, you may NOT look! This is NOT what Plato meant.

THE SYMPOSIUM

despite Plato's own suspicions about art and particularly about art's sensuous aspects.

Toward the end of the Renaissance, a revived interest in ancient Greek skepticism was employed to undermine *all* philosophical knowledge. Gianfrancesco Pico della Mirandola (1469–1533), nephew of the more famous Giovanni Pico della Mirandola, hoped to sweep away all philosophical learning and leave only the firm foundation of divine authority. He failed to foresee that that same skepticism would soon be used to chisel away at the bedrock of Christian dogma.

Giordano Bruno (b. 1548)—whom we could call the last man of the Renaissance—was burned at the stake by the Inquisition on February 17, 1600, for refusing to treat philosophical issues from the perspective that the religious authorities had deemed orthodox. At his trial he said that he pursued his ideas "according to the light of nature, without regard to any principles prescribed by faith."[11] Among his crimes was his espousal of the Copernican heliocentric theory of planetary motion.

Topics for Consideration

1. According to the information in this chapter, what is the relationship among the three major religions in the West: Judaism, Christianity, and Islam?

2. Write a short essay setting forth your own views about what is called in this chapter the problem of God's foreknowledge. If you agree with Augustine's solution, defend it. If you disagree with Augustine, criticize his solution.

3. Explain how the Christian philosopher John Scotus Eriugena could assert that God belongs in the category of "things that do not exist."

4. Explain why the opposite of a self-contradictory statement (i.e., the negation of such a statement) is necessarily true. Then explain why Saint Anselm asserted that the statement "God does not exist" is self-contradictory.

5. Describe the similarities that you find among the philosophies of Averroës, Maimonides, and Thomas Aquinas.

6. Explain what the problem of the universals is. Detail your explanation by analyzing the concept "dog" from the perspective of (a) the exaggerated realists, (b) the moderate realists, and (c) the nominalists. (Begin by looking up the words "dog" and "canine" in the dictionary.)

7. Compare and contrast Saint Anselm's ontological argument with Saint Thomas's cosmological argument.

8. Explain the ways in which the philosophy of William of Ockham, if true, would undermine the philosophy of Thomas Aquinas.

9. In your library find a book with reproductions of paintings from Renaissance Italy. Select a few and analyze each of them first from the point of view of Plato himself (see Chapter 2), then from the perspective of the Neoplatonic Renaissance philosophers.

Notes

1. Anselm of Canterbury, *Proslogium*, in *The Age of Belief*, ed. Anne Fremantle (New York: New American Library, 1954), 88–89.

2. This debate is discussed by Oliver Leaman, *Averroës and His Philosophy* (Richmond, England: Curzon Press, 1998). Leaman espouses the second of the two views.

3. Moses Maimonides, *The Guide of the Perplexed*, trans. Shlomo Pines (Chicago: University of Chicago Press, 1966), 29, 123.

4. Marvin Fox, *Interpreting Maimonides: Studies in Methodology, Metaphysics, and Moral Philosophy* (Chicago & London: University of Chicago Press, 1990), 21.

5. Frederick Copleston paraphrasing St. Thomas, in *A History of Philosophy*, vol. 2, *Medieval Philosophy*, part 2 (Garden City, N.Y.: Image Books/Doubleday & Co., 1962), 53.

6. Thomas Aquinas, *Summa theologica*, in *The Age of Belief*, 153.

7. Vernon J. Bourke paraphrasing Saint Thomas, in *The Encyclopedia of Philosophy*, vol. 8, ed. Paul Edwards (New York & London: Macmillan, 1972), 112.

8. The term "Babylonian captivity" refers by analogy to the enslavement of the Jews by the Babylonians between 579 and 338 B.C.E. Parts of the story of the complications of the Avignon papacy are nicely dramatized in Umberto Eco's best-selling novel *The Name of the Rose*, whose main character, William of Baskerville, is an amalgamation of William of Ockham and Sherlock Holmes.

9. Jill Fraye, "The Philosophy of the Italian Renaissance," in *The Routledge History of Philosophy*, vol. 4, *The Renaissance and Seventeenth-Century Rationalism*, ed. G. H. R. Parkinson (London & New York: Routledge, 1993), 17.

10. Ibid., 42.

11. Quoted by Fraye, 49.

5

Continental Rationalism and British Empiricism
The Seventeenth and Eighteenth Centuries

Descartes

Though there were a number of lesser philosophers during the Renaissance, the first truly magnificent philosophical system of the modern period was that of the Frenchman René Descartes (1596–1650). Descartes may not have been very good looking, but he was *smart!*

René Descartes

$$Z = X^2 + Y^2$$

Descartes first carved a niche for himself in the pantheon of intellectual giants by discovering analytical geometry, thereby fulfilling the old Pythagorean dream of demonstrating the relation between plane geometry and pure algebra.

Having made his contribution to math, in 1633 Descartes was about to publish his manuscript on physics, but when it dawned on

him that seventeen years earlier Galileo Galilei had been arrested by the Inquisition for teaching views about the physical world that were very close to Descartes's own views, Descartes ran, did not walk, to his publisher to withdraw his manuscript.

Galileo's crime had been to peer through his newly invented telescope and discover that the planet Jupiter had four moons.

Why should anybody care? Least of all, why should the Brothers of the Inquisition care?

Because the Renaissance mind had inherited from the medieval world the view that the Garden of Eden was the belly button of the

universe and that God had created the rest of the cosmos in con-
centric layers around the stage of the human drama.

Of course, there had been rumors floating around that the sun
and not the earth was the center of the planetary system, but the
scientific evidence against that view was the undisputed fact that
the moon orbits the earth. If the sun is the center of everything, then
why doesn't the moon orbit the sun instead of the earth?

So, if Galileo proved that Jupiter has four moons that orbit it, then he had pulled the last strut out from under the geocentric theory of the universe. As Freud was to say later, this discovery was the first of the three major blows against humans' conception of their own self-importance. (The other two were Darwin's revelation that we are only animals and Freud's discovery that we are *sick* animals.)

It was too much for the Brothers of the Inquisition, so off went Galileo to jail.

Descartes was a good but modern Catholic. He believed the Church had made a big mistake in the Galileo episode. He correctly saw that if religion tried to stem the tide of science, religion would be swept away. But Descartes did not want to have to go to jail to prove it.

So he decided to ease his ideas about

Stemming the Tide

physics onto an unsuspecting religious establishment by smuggling them into a book of philosophy called *Meditations*, which, in a groveling and self-effacing manner, he dedicated to "the Most Wise and Illustrious Doctors of the Sacred Faculty of Theology in Paris."

Meanwhile, to his friend he wrote, "the six Meditations contain all the fundamental ideas of my physics. But please keep this quiet."[1] Descartes hoped that the theologians would be convinced by his arguments before they realized that their own views had been refuted.

In his *Meditations on First Philosophy*, Descartes announced a massive intellectual project. He related his intention to tear down the edifice of knowledge and rebuild it from the foundations up.

To discover a firm foundation of absolute certainty upon which to build his objective system of knowledge, Descartes chose a method of "radical doubt," whose motto was *De omnibus dubitandum*—everything is to be doubted. So Descartes would doubt away anything that could possibly be doubted, no matter how weak the grounds were for doubting, until he could discover a proposition that

was logically indubitable. This proposition, if it existed, would be the absolutely certain foundation of all knowledge.

Descartes began his philosophical journal while sitting at his desk in front of the fire. He wrote, "Whatever I have so far accepted as supremely true I have learned either from the senses or through the senses."[2] But the senses are known deceivers, and it is not prudent ever to trust a known liar.

Descartes's point is clear. We all know about optical illusions (the "bent oar" in the pond, the "water" on the road, the tracks that "meet at the horizon"), as well as illusions associated with the other senses. So, in one fell swoop, radical doubt had deprived Descartes of all sensory information.

But Descartes immediately felt he had gone too far. Only a madman could stare at his hands and wonder if they really were his hands. It seemed that in one step, radical doubt had led not to philosophy but to lunacy.

But then Descartes recalled that on other occasions he had believed he was sitting before the fire, looking at his hands, only to awaken later to discover that it all was a dream. Much to his amazement, Descartes realized that there is no test to prove with absolute certainty that at any given moment one is not dreaming. (Any test you can *think*, you can *dream*, so it's no test at all.)

Therefore, consistent with radical doubt, Descartes assumed that it was always possible that he *was* dreaming. This assumption totally undermined the possibility that the senses could provide us with certain knowledge.

What about mathematics? Perhaps it can be a candidate for absolute certainty. Descartes said, "Whether we are awake or asleep, two plus three is always five, and the square never has more than four sides."[3] But radical doubt required Descartes to suspect even the simplest propositions of arithmetic if there was *any* reason for doing so. Well, what if the Creator of the universe was not the benevolent God of Catholicism, but an Evil Genius, a malevolent demon whose sole purpose was that of deception, so that even the simplest mathematical judgment would always be false? Could Descartes know for sure that such a demon did not exist?

No! There existed the logical possibility that Descartes's mind was being controlled externally by a malevolent force. So Descartes assumed that all the world was nothing but the diabolical fiction of the Evil Genius. Descartes asked, under these conditions could anything be certain?

Descartes concluded that there was one and only one thing that was absolutely certain—that he existed! His assertion "I think, therefore I am"[4] was true whether he was dreaming, whether the senses deceived, and whether there was an Evil Genius. It was, in fact, *necessarily* true. It could not be denied or even doubted without self-contradiction. (Try it! If you say, "I doubt that I exist," haven't you in fact proved that you do exist?)

Having discovered certainty in selfhood and having established that his self was his consciousness (for it is possible to doubt that you have a body, but it is impossible to doubt that you have a mind; therefore, your self and your mind must be identical), Descartes now had to find a way of escaping the confines of his own subjectivity and establishing the existence of an external world. To do so, he analyzed the contents of his mind and discovered it contained certain innate ideas (shades of Plato), including these: self, identity, substance, and God.

"SELF"
"IDENTITY"
"SUBSTANCE"
"GOD"

Of course, the innate idea of God, if veridical, would provide the first step in Descartes's advancement beyond his own subjectivity. But how did Descartes know that his apparently innate idea of God was not placed in his mind by the Evil Genius? Descartes had to prove God's existence and had to do so using only those data that

he could deduce
logically from the one certainty afforded him—the
immediate states of his own
consciousness. (Critics point
out that Descartes was over-
looking the fact that the process
of logical deduction is exactly the
kind of reasoning that the Demon could
distort. If it can distort math, it can distort logic. They are roughly
the same thing.) Nevertheless, Descartes did prove—to his own
satisfaction, at least—God's existence. He offered two arguments
to achieve this result. Here's the first:

> I can no more separate God's existence from his essence than a trian-
> gle' s angles equaling two right angles from the essence of a triangle,
> or the idea of a valley from the idea of a mountain. It's no less impos-

sible to think that God (the supremely perfect being) lacks existence (a perfection) than to think that a mountain lacks a valley.[5]

This argument is clearly a version of the ontological argument of Saint Anselm, whom Descartes failed to acknowledge as the author of this demonstration. (To be fair to Descartes we could say that it is precisely Descartes's appeal to reason rather than to authority that makes him a modern thinker.)

Here's a paraphrase of the second argument in four steps. (Such a condensation of his proof may be unfair to Descartes. The argument may be more convincing in all its detail. But Descartes takes four pages to develop it! Philosophy is long; life is short.)

    (A) The fact that I doubt proves that I am an imperfect being. (A perfect being would know everything, hence would have no doubts.)

    (B) I can only know that I am imperfect if I already understand the idea of perfection.

    (C) My idea of perfection could only be caused in me by something perfect. (Nothing can be more perfect than its cause, and nothing in my actual experience is perfect enough to cause the idea of perfection in my mind.)

    (D) Therefore, a perfect being (God) exists.

Descartes ended this argument with these words: "I am driven to this conclusion: The fact that I exist and have an idea in me of a perfect entity—that is, God—conclusively entails that God does in fact exist."[6]

Notice that doubting is a form of thinking—indeed, it has so far been Descartes's main form of thinking, given his method. Therefore the two main **Cartesian** philosophical arguments so far could be stated as

    1. I doubt, therefore I exist.
          and
    2. I doubt, therefore God exists.

Also notice that both proofs presuppose the Platonic hierarchy of being, where "most real" equals "most perfect," and vice versa.

If valid, Descartes's "proof" of God's existence disposes of the Evil Genius. (A perfect, omnipotent, omnibenevolent God would not allow such a Deceiver to exist.)

Therefore, Descartes recovered math into his system (the only objection to math had been the Evil Genius hypothesis). By applying math to his innate idea of corporeal substance, Descartes came up with what he took to be the correct account of reality—the world as known by mathematical physics. He thereby justified the "new science" inaugurated by Galileo precisely by proving God's existence. Descartes had pulled it off. He showed that you can have both God and Galileo!

NAIVE REALISM
"What you see is what you get."

However, Descartes did leave himself with a few problems. First, he had replaced the commonsense view of the relation between self and world (what philosophers call **"naive realism"**), but he replaced it with a most circuitous route, indeed. Second, he assigned all perceivable qualities ("red," "blue," "sweet," "warm," "melodious") to the mind and left only mathematically measurable quantities in the external world—a cold, colorless, odorless, soundless, tasteless world of matter in motion.

Furthermore, Descartes's picture of the world was hopelessly divided into substances that were defined in ways that mutually excluded each other. How could the mental world (a nonspatial, purely spiritual sphere) have any effect on the physical world of crass matter, and vice versa, in this radically dualistic scheme of

CARTESIAN REALISM
"What you see is <u>not</u> what you get."

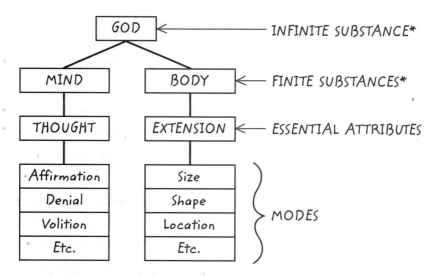

GOD ←——————— INFINITE SUBSTANCE*

MIND   BODY ←——— FINITE SUBSTANCES*

THOUGHT   EXTENSION ←——— ESSENTIAL ATTRIBUTES

Affirmation	Size
Denial	Shape
Volition	Location
Etc.	Etc.

} MODES

* Substance is defined as "that which can exist by itself, without the aid of any other substance."[7]

things? Descartes tried to solve the problem by claiming that mind meets body at the center of the brain, in the pineal gland.

It should have been obvious that this solution would not work. No matter *where* mind meets body, at that place it *becomes* body, because it then has *location*, which is a

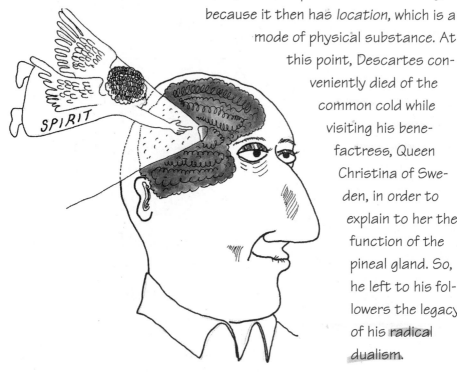

SPIRIT

mode of physical substance. At this point, Descartes conveniently died of the common cold while visiting his benefactress, Queen Christina of Sweden, in order to explain to her the function of the pineal gland. So, he left to his followers the legacy of his radical dualism.

Hobbes

Meanwhile, across the Channel, Thomas Hobbes (1588–1679) was dealing with problems similar to those addressed by his contemporary René Descartes. Hobbes was a contentious old codger who dabbled in everything. (His experiments in math led him to claim that he had squared the circle and cubed the sphere.) At one point or another he managed to antagonize every political party in Britain and had to flee to France.

Hobbes solved Descartes's dualistic dilemma simply by dismantling dualism. He loudly proclaimed a form of mechanistic materialism

Thomas Hobbes Squares the Circle

reminiscent of Democritus's atomism, thereby rejecting one side of Descartes's diagram; and Hobbes's thinly disguised atheism rejected Descartes's "infinite substance" as well. For Hobbes, the only things that existed in reality were bodies in motion. Despite his claim that "there exist everywhere only bodies," Hobbes did not actually deny the existence of thoughts. He simply held them to be "phantasms,"

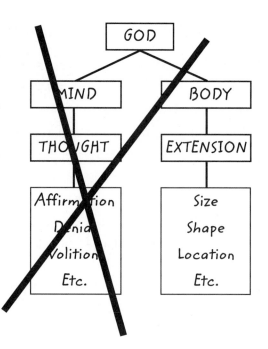

shadows of brain activity, mere epiphenomena that had no practical effect on the physical system. Similarly, though he was a determinist, he was, like the stoics and St. Augustine, a "soft determinist." (A soft determinist believes that freedom and determinism are compatible.) It was okay to talk about freedom as long as all one meant by it was "unimpeded movement." (Water flows down a channel both necessarily and freely.)

Hobbes's psychology is very pessimistic. Every living organism obeys laws of individual survival; therefore, all human acts are motivated by self-interest and the quest for power. Altruism is not just a bad idea; it is impossible. Far from being immoral, egoism is the only show in town: "Of the voluntary acts of every man, the object is some good to himself."[8]

What makes Hobbes's theory pessimistic, in my opinion, is that if it is true, then it is impossible for individuals to act except in ways that they take to be in their own interest. Anyone who makes a claim to the contrary is lying or is in a state of self-delusion, ignorance, or stupidity.

Hobbes is best known for his political philosophy, which is influenced by his egoistic theory of motivation. He recognized the state as an artificial monster (the "Leviathan") that restricts what little freedom there is in nature and flaunts its power over the individual, but Hobbes justified the existence of the political state by contrasting it to the notorious "state of nature," dominated by scarcity and fear, where "every man is enemy to every man" and where life is

"solitary, poor, nasty, brutish and short."[9] In the state of nature, there is no law, no morality, no property, and only one "natural right"—the right to protect oneself using any means at one's disposal, including violence and slaughter. If two people are on a desert island and there isn't an abundance of coconuts to eat, then neither dares turn a back nor sleep lest the other bash him or her with a rock in order to get all the coconuts. However, if both are rational, they will realize that the most likely way of surviving is to agree with each other to forswear violence and share the coconuts. The trouble is, given the selfish nature that Hobbes attributes to all of us, there is no reason at all for either party to keep the agreement if he

or she can figure a way to break
it with impunity. So there is
every reason for them to
distrust each other.
Despite their "agree-
ment," neither dares
yet to sleep a wink.
The solution requires
that a third party
be found. The first
two parties give to
the third party all
the rocks (and per-
haps an army), and

The Sovereign

they give up their right to violence. In exchange, she promises to use
her absolute power to guarantee that the first two parties honor
their agreement with each other. ("She" may be either a monarch or a
parliament—in either case she is the source of all authority.)

This is Hobbes's famous "social contract." He realized that there
is nothing to prevent the new sovereign from abusing her power (indeed, given *her* egoistic nature and innate lust for power, it is almost
inevitable that she would do so), but he believed that the state, even
with its necessary abuse of power, was better than the alternative—
the horrors of anarchy in "the state of nature."

(It should be mentioned that, typically, Hobbes's political theory
managed to please no one in Britain. The parliamentarians didn't like
it because of its absolutist implications, and the king didn't like it
because of its denial of the divine right of monarchs.)

Spinoza

Back on the Continent, the Dutch-born Jewish philosopher Baruch
Spinoza (1634–1677) was trying to resolve the dilemmas of Descartes's legacy while remaining within the rationalistic tradition that

Descartes exemplified. (Rationalists believe that the true source of knowledge is reason, not the senses, and that the correct philosophical model must be an a priori one, not one based on empirical generalizations.) Spinoza was, according to Bertrand Russell, "the noblest and most lovable of the great philosophers."[10] This is because he, more than any other philosopher, *lived* his philosophy, even though he realized that doing so would result in his

Baruch Spinoza

alienation from both the Jewish and the Christian communities. Spinoza accepted his excommunication from synagogue, church, and society without rancor, and he never sought fame or riches, or even a professorship, living out his life philosophizing and grinding lenses to earn a meager living. He accepted as his reward the state of tranquility afforded to him by his philosophy, and his motto could well have been his own epigram, "All excellent things are as difficult as they are rare."[11]

Spinoza tried to submit Cartesian metaphysics to a geometric method even more rigorous than that used by Descartes himself. Like Descartes's, Spinoza's philosophy is centered on a definition of substance, but Spinoza had detected a contradiction in Descartes's account. Descartes had said, "By substance, we can understand nothing else than a thing which so exists that it needs no other thing in order to exist." Then Descartes had gone on to say, "And in fact only one single substance can be understood which clearly needs nothing else, namely, God,"[12] which he called "infinite substance." Despite this admission that by definition there could exist only one kind of being that was absolutely independent, Descartes (in a contradictory manner, according to Spinoza) proceeded to distinguish between "infinite substance" and "finite substances"—the latter were called corporeal substance (body) and mental substance (mind). This radical dualism led Descartes to his notorious mind-body problem and his universally scorned pineal gland solution.

Spinoza avoided this embarrassment by accepting Descartes's definition of substance (as that which is absolutely independent) and taking deadly seriously the inference that there could be only one such substance. (If there were two, they would limit each other's independence.)

Furthermore, because finiteness would constitute a limitation on God's absolute independence, Spinoza defined God as having infinite attributes. So once again, one arrives at the conclusion that there can be but one substance because any substance other than God would have to possess attributes that have already been defined as belonging to God.

Let's look at a schematized comparison of the systems of Descartes and Spinoza:

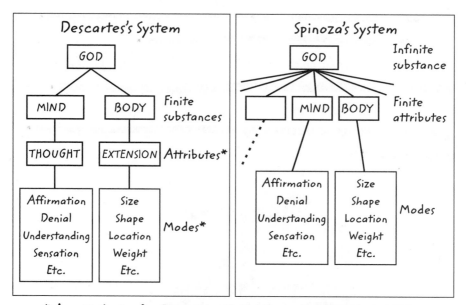

*An attribute, for Descartes, is a characteristic that is the essence of a substance (i.e., that which is essential to it). For Spinoza, an attribute is a characteristic that to the human intellect seems to be an essence. A mode is a specific modification of an attribute (i.e., a characteristic of a characteristic).

Like Descartes, Spinoza equated "infinite substance" with God, but he also equated it with nature. The equation "Nature equals God" makes him a pantheist. (It is also this equation that got him into trouble with both the Jewish and Christian theologians.) There are two human perspectives on reality (i.e., on God): one viewed through the attribute of mind (resulting in idealism, the claim that only mind exists) and one viewed through the attribute of body (resulting in materialism, the view that only matter exists). In theory, there are an indefinite number of other perspectives on reality, but only these two are open to the human intellect. A completely consistent idealistic or materialistic account of reality can be given, but no consistent dualism is possible. Dualism involves a confusion of perspectives. (So much for Descartes's pineal gland.)

Mais Monsieur Descartes, est-ce que vous avez mal à la glande pinéale?

I'm sure it's due to substance abuse.

The true philosopher attempts to transcend the purely human perspective and view reality *sub specie aeternitatis,* that is, from the perspective of reality itself. From this perspective, one comes to realize that the human has no privileged position in the cosmos, that the human has no more and no less dignity than anything else in nature. One must come to love everything, which is to say, to love God (because one must either love everything or nothing at all). The *love of God* is tantamount to the *knowledge of God,* which is to say, a philosophical knowledge of reality. This difficult intellectual love of God is a form of rationalism that, like Platonism, is tainted with mysticism. It also contains a stoic component, insofar as knowledge of reality leads one to realize that everything that happens, happens of necessity. There is no **randomness** and no freedom of the will. But the realization that there is no such thing as free will, neither for God nor for humans, can itself be a liberating realization because one is

The Unrequited Love of Nature

thereby freed from the demands of desire and passion, both of which were seen by Spinoza as murky emotions that manage to control us only because of our failure to grasp the rational structure of reality. With knowledge, these emotions can be transformed into clear and distinct ideas leading to a kind of blessedness and joy. Spinoza wrote, "There cannot be too much joy: it is always good: but melancholy is always bad."[13]

Leibniz

The third of the great Continental rationalists was the German Gottfried Leibniz (1646–1716). He was a universal genius who made significant advances in symbolic logic and who created a plan for the invasion of Egypt that may have been used by Napoleon 120 years later. Leibniz also invented a calculating machine that could add, subtract, and do square roots. Furthermore, he discovered infinitesimal calculus simultaneously with Sir Isaac Newton (and got into a squabble with him concerning who had stolen the idea from whom).

Gottfried Leibniz

Like Spinoza, Leibniz wished to correct the errors of Cartesian metaphysics without rejecting its main structure, but Leibniz was not

"Leibniz was one of the supreme intellects of all time, but as a human being he was not admirable."[14]

Bertrand Russell

satisfied with Spinoza's pantheistic monism nor with his naturalism (i.e., his view that all is nature and that the human being has no spe-

cial status in reality). Leibniz wanted a return to a Cartesian
with real individuals and a transcendent God. Leibniz's syst/
set forth in his *Monadology* and *Essays in Theodicy*, can be ~~
rized in terms of three principles: the **principle of identity,** the principle of sufficient reason, and the principle of internal harmony.

In his principle of identity, Leibniz divided all **propositions** into
two types, which later philosophers would call **analytic propositions**
and **synthetic propositions.** Take a look at the following table:

ANALYTIC	SYNTHETIC
A. True by definition (They are true merely by virtue of the meanings of the words in the sentences.)	A. Not true by definition (Their truth or falsity depends not on <u>meanings</u> but on facts in the world.)
B. Necessary (Their opposites are self-contradictions. They <u>cannot</u> be false.)	B. Not necessary; rather, contingent (They <u>could</u> be false if facts were different.)
C. A priori (Their truth is known independently of observation.)	C. A posteriori (Their truth or falsity is known by observation.)

Following are some examples of analytic sentences:

A. All bachelors are men.
B. 2 + 3 = 5
C. Either A or not–A

This category includes definitions and parts of definitions
(example A) and arithmetic and the principles of logic (examples B
and C). Analytic propositions were said by Leibniz to be based on the
principle of identity in the sense that this principle is the positive
counterpart of the **principle of noncontradiction** (which says that it
cannot be the case that A and not–A at the same time) in that the
negation of every analytic sentence is a self-contradiction (e.g., "Not
all bachelors are men" implies the contradictory assertion "Some

men are not men" because the definition of "bachelor" is "unmarried man").

Following are some examples of synthetic sentences:

A. The cat is on the mat.
B. Caesar crossed the Rubicon in 49 B.C.E.

Now, having drawn what many philosophers believe to be a very important distinction, Leibniz made the surprising move of claiming that all synthetic sentences are really analytic. *Sub specie aeternitatis;* that is to say, from God's point of view, it is the case that all true sentences are necessarily true, even though it doesn't seem to be the case to us humans. For Leibniz, Tuffy the cat's characteristic of "being on the mat at time T" is a characteristic necessary to that specific cat in the same way that "being a feline" is necessary to it.

This line of reasoning brings us to the principle of sufficient reason. According to Leibniz, for anything that exists, there is some reason why it exists and why it exists exactly as it does exist. Leibniz claimed that this second principle is the main principle of rationality and that anyone who rejects this principle is irrational. If the cat is on the mat, then there must be some reason why the cat exists at all, and why it is on the mat and not, for example, in the dishwasher.

You see, I couldn't <u>not</u> be on the mat!

Both these reasons should be open to human scientific inquiry, though perhaps only God can know why the cat exists necessarily and is necessarily on the mat.

What is true of the cat is true of the whole cosmos, said Leibniz. There must be a reason why the universe exists at all, and this reason ought to be open to rational human inquiry. The deepest question, according to Leibniz, is "why there exists something rather than nothing."[15] Like Saint Thomas, he concluded that the only possible answer would be in terms of an uncaused cause, an all-perfect God whose being was itself necessary. So if Leibniz was right, we can derive the proof of the existence of God from the bare notion of rationality, plus the self-evident proposition that something rather than nothing exists.

This conclusion leads us to the principle of internal harmony. If there is a God, God must be both rational and good. Such a divinity, Leibniz told us, must desire and be capable of creating the maximum amount of existence possible ("metaphysical perfection") and the maximum amount of activity possible ("moral perfection"). Therefore, at the moment of creation, God entertained all possibilities. He actualized only those possibilities that would guarantee the maximum amount of metaphysical and moral perfection. For example, God did not just consider the individual "Caesar" in all of Caesar's ramifications (would write *The Gallic Wars*, would cross the Rubicon in 49 B.C.E., would die on the Ides of March) before actualizing him. Perhaps God considered actualizing (i.e., creating) in Caesar's place "Gaesar" and "Creasar," who, as potential actualizations, were identical to Caesar in all respects except that Gaesar would cross *not* the Rubicon but the Delaware River in 49 B.C.E., and Creasar would cross the Love Canal. God saw that only Caesar was compatible with the rest of the possibilities that he would activate, and therefore he actualized him and not the others. A similar thought experiment could be performed with God's creation of Brutus (as opposed, perhaps, to "Brautus" and "Brutos"). So the relation between Caesar and Brutus is not a causal one but one of *internal harmony*. And the same holds true of the relations among all substances. God activates only substances that will necessarily harmonize with each other to the greatest extent possible. This principle now explains why all true sentences are analytic. If Tuffy is on the mat at 8 P.M., that is because *this cat* *must* be on the mat at 8 P.M. (otherwise it is not Tuffy, but another cat). It also explains Leibniz's notorious claim that *this is the best of all possible worlds*. His actual words are "Hence the world is not only the most admirable machine, but in so far as it consists of minds, it is also the best Republic, that in which the minds are granted the greatest possible happiness and joy."[16] The world may appear very imperfect to you, but if you knew what the alternative was, you would be very grateful indeed to God. (It is this feature of Leibniz's philosophy that was to be lampooned by Voltaire in *Candide*.)

This is the best of all possible worlds, . . . this is the best of all possible worlds . . .

Candide Inspects the Ruins of Lisbon after the Earthquake of 1755

Every philosopher in the 250-year period after the publication of Descartes's *Meditations* conceived of reality in terms of substances. Leibniz called these substances *monads*, which he defined as units of psychic force. They are "substances" in that they are the simplest and realest "things" that can exist independently of one another. They are not *material* substances, however, as were both the "atoms" of Democritus and the "corporeal existence" of Descartes, because materiality is not an irreducible substratum but a quality that is a product of the relation between certain monads—

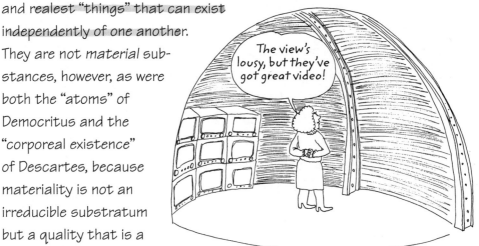

The Monads Have No Windows

the way that liquidity is a product of relationships between certain molecules of hydrogen and oxygen, even though neither hydrogen nor oxygen is itself liquid. Monads are simple (i.e., they have no parts), and each is "pregnant"[17] with all its future states. Each monad is a mirror of the entire universe (God actualized only those monads that *would* mirror the rest of the universe), but they perceive the rest of reality only as features of their own inner states. "The monads have no windows."[18] All monads have a psychic life, but some have a higher

After a Philosophy Lecture,
Three Students Actually Find
a Monad behind a Pile of Old Socks

degree of psychic life than others. These monads (or communities of monads clustered around a "dominant monad") are conscious. Some conscious clusters of monads are also free, and these are human beings. (Of course, in Leibniz's theory, as in the theory of Saint Augustine, God already knows how these human beings will spend their freedom.)

Perhaps it can be said that Leibniz's philosophy solves the problems of Descartes's dualism, but it does so at the expense of common sense and seems to be fraught with as many problems as Descartes's theory. It should come as no surprise that a philosopher would soon rise to the defense of common sense and of observation, reacting against the speculative flights of fancy of a Spinoza or a Leibniz. Such a philosopher was John Locke.

Locke

John Locke (1632–1704) was the first of the classical British empiricists. (Empiricists believed that all knowledge derives from experience. These philosophers were hostile to rationalistic metaphysics, particularly to its unbridled use of speculation, its grandiose claims, and its epistemology grounded in innate ideas.) In his *Essay Concerning Human Understanding*, Locke began his attack on Descartes's "innate ideas" by threatening them with Ockham's razor. (Recall that Ockham's razor is a principle of simplification derived from William of Ockham. It cautions,

John Locke

"Do not multiply entities beyond necessity." Given two theories, each of which adequately accounts for all the observable data, the simpler theory is the correct theory.) If Locke could account for all human knowledge without making reference to innate ideas, then his theory would be simpler, hence better, than that of Descartes. He wrote, "Let us then suppose the mind to be, as we say,

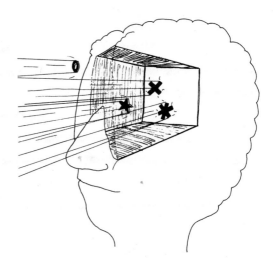

The Tabula Rasa Being Marked by Experience

white paper, void of all characters, without any ideas: How comes it to be furnished? . . . To this I answer, in one word, from *experience*."[19] So the mind at birth is a *tabula rasa*, a blank slate, and is informed only by "experience," that is, by sense experience and acts of reflection. Locke built from this theory an epistemology beginning with a pair of distinctions: one between simple and complex ideas and another between primary and secondary qualities.

Simple ideas originate in any one sense (though some of them, like "motion," can derive from either the sense of sight or the sense of touch). These ideas are simple in the sense that they cannot be further broken down into yet simpler entities. (If a person does not understand the idea of "yellow," you can't explain it. All you can do is point to a sample and say, "yellow.") These simple ideas are Locke's primary data, his psychological atoms. All knowledge is in one way or another built up out of them.

Complex ideas are, for example, combinations of simple ideas. These result in our knowledge of particular things (e.g., "apple"—derived from the simple ideas "red," "spherical," "sweet"), comparisons ("darker than"), relations ("north of"), and abstractions ("gratitude"). Even abstractions, or general ideas, are nevertheless *particular ideas* that stand for collections. (This doctrine places Locke close to the theory known in the medieval world as "nominalism." All the empiricists share with the nominalists the anti-Platonic thesis that only particulars exist.)

Locke's distinction between primary and secondary qualities is one that he borrowed from Descartes and Galileo, who had in turn borrowed it from Democritus. Primary qualities are characteristics of external objects. These qualities really do inhere in those objects. (Extension, size, shape, and location are examples of primary qualities.) Secondary qualities are characteristics that we often attribute to external objects, but that in fact exist only in the mind yet are *caused* by real features of external objects. (Examples of secondary qualities are colors, sounds, and tastes.) This view of the mind has come to be known as *representative realism*. According to it, the mind represents the external world but it does not duplicate it. (Naive realism, the view that the mind literally duplicates external

The Problem: To Construct Knowledge from Simple Ideas

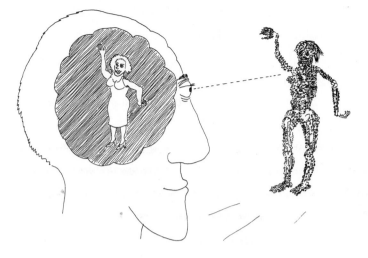

What Appears to Be Out There   **What Is Out There**

reality, was discussed earlier in this chapter.) The mind is something like a photograph in that there are features of a photo that very accurately represent the world (e.g., a good picture of three people correctly depicts the fact that there are three people and that each of them has two eyes, one nose, and one mouth) and there are features of the photograph that belong exclusively to the photo (its glossiness, its two-dimensionality, the white border around its content). So in Locke's system, as in Descartes's system, there is a real world out there and it has certain real qualities—the primary qualities. Now, these qualities—what are they qualities of? In answering this question, Locke never abandoned the basic Cartesian metaphysics of substance.

A real quality must be a quality of a real *thing*, and real things are substances. (Once again, everything in the world is either a substance or a characteristic of a substance.) Well then, what is the status of this pivotal idea of "substance" in Locke's theory? Recall that Descartes had claimed that one cannot derive the idea of substance from observation precisely because perception can only generate qualities. For this very reason, it was necessary to posit the idea of substance as an *innate idea*. But Locke was committed to the rejection of innate ideas and to the claim that all knowledge comes in through the senses. So what did he say about the idea of substance? Rather amazingly, he said the following:

> So that if anyone will examine himself concerning his notion of pure substance in general, he will find he has no other idea of it at all, but only a supposition of he knows not what *support* of such qualities which are capable of producing simple ideas in us.[20]

So, having claimed that he could account for all knowledge purely in terms of experience and having arrived at the concept that had dominated philosophy for the last several generations, Locke proclaimed it a mystery and even joked about it. (He compared the philosopher trying to explain substance to the Indian who explained that the world was supported by a great elephant, which in turn was supported by a tortoise, which in turn was supported by—"something, he knew not what.") Locke's conclusion is a bit embarrassing, and it is either a rather inauspicious beginning for empiricism or the beginning of the end of the metaphysics of substance. (We will soon see that it is the latter.)

John Locke concerned himself not only with epistemology but with politics as well. In his theory, developed in *Two Treatises on Government,* Locke, like Hobbes, drew a distinction between the "state of nature" and the "political state." However, what he meant by "state

of nature" was very different indeed from what Hobbes meant by it. Far from being a condition in which there is no justice nor injustice, no right nor wrong, "no mine and thine distinct,"[21] Locke's "state of nature" is a moral state—the state into which we are all born as humans, where we are all bestowed with certain God-given natural rights, the right to "life, health, liberty and possessions."[22] Recall that for Hobbes, there was only one natural

The State of Nature according to Hobbes

right, the right to try to preserve one's life. Hobbes seems to have believed that a kind of instinct for survival authorized that right. Locke's theory contains several natural rights, all of which are moral rather than instinctual, and they derive their authority from God. Hobbes purposely left God

The State of Nature according to Locke

y because he was trying to escape medievalism, where
resupposed God's existence. Hobbes was particularly
here was no such thing as a "natural right to prop-
nature there is no property, only possession ("only
man's, that he can get; and for so long as he can
keep it").²³ Locke, on the contrary, claimed we have a natural right to
whatever part of nature we have "mixed our labor with."²⁴ So if I till
the soil, or cut down a tree and make a house from it, then this garden and that house are *mine* (and will be my children's when they
inherit them from me). Locke did put qualifications on this natural
right to property. One can accumulate as much "natural property"
as one can use, as long as:

A. It does not spoil in its accumulation.
B. Enough has been left for others.
C. Its accumulation is not harmful to others.

What are you complaining about? You have plenty for your meager needs.

Locke's wealthy friends
were probably glad to hear
that "gold and silver may be
hoarded up without injury to
anyone."²⁵

(It is noteworthy
that Locke's theory pre-
supposes a state of
abundance in nature,
whereas Hobbes's pre-
supposes a state of
scarcity. It may be
true that human
nature would express
itself very differently
in these vastly dis-
similar "states of
nature.")

According to Locke, individual political states are to be evaluated in terms of how well they protect the natural rights of the individuals living in those states. A good state is one that guarantees and maximizes those rights; a bad state is one that does not guarantee them; and an evil state is one that itself assaults the natural rights. Locke's version of the "social contract" is that all citizens consent to be ruled by a government elected by a majority for just as long as that government protects the natural rights. But a tyrannical government is illegitimate and ought to be revolted against. Note that, unlike Hobbes, Locke is able to distinguish between a legitimate and an illegitimate government and provides a theory of justifiable revolution. It is clear that the Founding Fathers used Locke's theory to justify the American Revolution, and they incorporated his ideas into our Declaration of Independence and Constitution. Perhaps what is best in the American system derives from what is best in Locke's theory, and some social critics claim that what is worst in the American system is derived from what is worst in Locke's theory. America can be seen as a great Lockean experiment.

Berkeley

The second of the British empiricists was the Irishman George Berkeley (1685–1753), a teacher at Trinity College in Dublin who eventually became the Anglican Bishop of Cloyne. As a philosopher, he was very impressed by Locke's work and wanted to correct what he took to be its errors and inconsistencies while remaining true to the basic platform of empiricism ("blank slate" theory, **psychological atomism,** nominalism, commitment to Ockham's razor). In fact, he applied Ockham's razor to the idea of material substance so scrupulously that he shaved it clean away and was left with a type of subjective idealism—the view that only minds and ideas exist.

Early in his *Principles of Human Knowledge,* Berkeley attacked Locke's distinction between primary and secondary qualities. Recall that the former were said to inhere in material substance that existed independently of the mind, whereas the latter existed only in

George Berkeley

the mind (or, as Berkeley put it, their *esse is percipi*—their "being" is "to be perceived"). Berkeley pointed out that our only access to so-called primary qualities is through secondary qualities. The only way we can know the size, shape, location, or dimensionality of an object is by feeling it or seeing it (i.e., through the secondary qualities of tactile or visual sensation). Berkeley's conclusion was that descriptions of primary qualities are really only interpretations of secondary qualities—different ways of talking about colors, sounds, tastes, odors, and tactile sensations. Therefore, primary qualities too exist only in the mind. Their *esse* is also *percipi*.

To explain how this translation of secondary qualities into primary qualities is possible, Berkeley drew a distinction between *direct perception* and *indirect perception*. Direct (or immediate) perception is the passive reception of basic **sense data** (Locke's secondary qualities and simple ideas). Indirect (or mediate) perception is the *interpretation* of those sense data. Consider the process of learning to read. The small child confronts a written page and sees only black "squigglies" on a white background. (This is direct perception.)

Through a process of acculturation, the child eventually learns to see these markings as words loaded with meanings. (This is indirect perception.) It is an interesting fact that once we've learned to read, it is very difficult to recover the child's "innocent eye" and see the words again as mere squigglies. This distinction explained to Berkeley why we adults perceive the world as groupings of things rather than as sense data. Nevertheless, claimed Berkeley, the things we see in the so-called external world are really only collections of ideas, philosophically analyzable into their component sense data. Said Berkeley,

> As several of these [sense data] are observed to accompany each other, they come to be marked by one name, and so to be reputed as one thing. Thus, for example, a certain color, taste, smell, figure and consistence having been observed to go together, are accounted one distinct thing, signified by the name "apple"; other collections of ideas constitute a stone, a tree, a book, and the like sensible things.[26]

What's true of the component parts of a stone is true of the whole stone. Its esse is also percipi.

Notice that the notion of material substance (Locke's "something, I know not what") has simply disappeared in Berkeley's system. And the role played by the rationalists' innate idea of substance in explaining how we come to know the world as a concatenation of individual physical objects has been taken over by language. We teach our children words, which organize the ideas in their minds into "things." Berkeley's subjective idealism holds that each of us lives in his or her own subjective world composed of the sense data of the five senses. This is the same world we entered into as infants. But we were taught a language, which is to say, taught to "read" our sense data. Language is also the cement of intersubjectivity. I am able to bridge the gap between my private world and yours through the shared use of conventional symbols. Without language I would be stuck **solipsistically** in the echo chamber of my own mind.

Berkeley believed that with these two categories (sense data and language) he could account for all possible human knowledge—

all except the knowledge of God. (Berkeley was a bishop, after a[l]
don't be surprised to find God playing a key role in Berkeley's p[hiloso]
phy, even if it was a bit embarrassing to him that *God's esse is no[t]
percipi*.) God's existence can be deduced from the regularity and pre-
dictability of sense data. If the so-called physical world's "being" is to

When I said that ESSE IS PERCIPI, of course I didn't mean that YOURS was!

"be perceived" and hence is dependent on the mind, then why is it
that when I return to an empty room that I had vacated earlier,
everything is just as I left it? Why didn't the room disappear when I
stopped perceiving it? Because God was perceiving it while I was out.

Why Doesn't the Room Disappear When We Leave It?

God is the guarantor of the laws of nature. When the Bible says that God created the world, it means that he created sense data and minds (spirits, selves) to perceive them. God did *not* cause there to be some unperceivable, mysterious stuff—"material substance"—which in turn causes ideas. Believing in the existence of such a "stuff" was the error of Locke's representative realism. Locke failed to see that the representation *is* the reality. Berkeley has merely eliminated the "middle man." His theory explains everything that Locke's does but is more economical; hence, according to Ockham's razor, it is *better* than Locke's. So Berkeley believed.

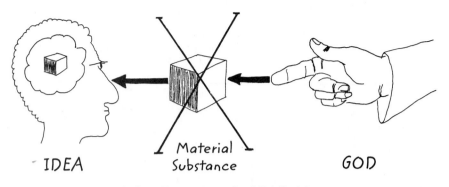

IDEA   Material Substance   GOD

Berkeley Eliminates the Middle Man

Hume

The third of the "Holy Trinity" of British empiricism is the Scot David Hume (1711–1776). He published his first book, *A Treatise of Human Nature,* when he was twenty-seven and he hoped to achieve fame and fortune from it, but, by his own reckoning, it "fell dead-born from the press." Ten years later he rewrote it and published it as *An Inquiry Concerning the Human Understanding.* This book was considerably more successful than its predecessor, possibly because it was a bit more moderate. Today Hume is recognized as the most acute, if the most perplexing, of the British empiricists.

Hume's philosophy began with a revival of Leibniz's analytic-synthetic distinction, or, in Hume's words, a distinction between "relations of ideas" and "matters of fact." It will be recalled that analytic propositions are expressed by sentences

A. whose negation leads to a self-contradiction,
B. that are a priori,
C. that are true by definition, and, therefore,
D. are necessarily true.

Synthetic propositions are expressed by sentences that are the opposite of sentences expressing analytic propositions; that is, they are sentences

A. whose negation does *not* lead to a self-contradiction,
B. that are a posteriori,

David Hume

C. that are *not* true by definition, and
D. when they are true, they are *not necessarily* true (they *can* be false).

Now, in accepting this distinction, Hume was admitting that there are such things as *a priori necessary truths*. It would seem that any empiricist who accepted such truths was jeopardizing the program of empiricism by recognizing the legitimacy of the rationalists' dream, but Hume defused this situation by adding one more characteristic to the list of features of "relations of ideas." He said that they are all *tautological*; that is, they are all redundant, repetitive, merely verbal truths that provide no new information about the world, only information about the meaning of words. Thus, given the conventions of the English language, it is certainly true that "all sisters are siblings," but this statement tells us nothing about any particular sister that wasn't already known by calling her a sister in the first place. Similarly, anybody who really understands the concept "five" and the concepts "three," "two," and "plus" already knows that 3 + 2 = 5. So the rationalistic dream of a complete description of reality that is a priori and necessarily true is a will-o'-the-wisp because a priori truths aren't descriptions of *anything*, according to Hume. Only synthetic claims—"matters of fact"—can correctly describe reality, and these claims are necessarily a posteriori. Therefore, all true knowledge about the world must be based on observation. This is, of course, the central thesis of all empiricism.

Mommy! Today I learned that all brothers are siblings. It is not the case that it is raining and not raining at the same time. All red things are members of the class of red things.

Yes but *is* the cat on the mat?

What Hume was claiming was that there are basically only three categories of analysis. Any proposition whatsoever is either analytic, synthetic, or nonsense. Hume said:

> When we run over libraries, persuaded of these principles, what havoc must we make? If we take in our hand any volume—of divinity or school metaphysics, for instance—let us ask, *Does it contain any abstract reasoning concerning quantity or number* [i.e., analytical truths]? No. *Does it contain any experimental reasoning concerning matter of fact and existence* [i.e., synthetic truths]? No. Commit it then to the flames, for it can contain nothing but sophistry and illusion.[27]

(No wonder Hume lost his job as a librarian.)

David Hume—Librarian

There is, then, very clearly a "Humean method" of philosophizing. One takes any claim that one would like to test and asks a series of questions about that claim:

1. *Is it analytic?*

    (This is determined by negating the sentence in which the claim is expressed. If the resultant negative sentence is a self-contradiction, then the original sentence is analytic.)

    ☐ YES (If the answer is YES, the claim is *true* but philosophically trivial.)

    ☐ NO (If the answer is NO, go to the next question.)

2. *Is it synthetic?*

    This question is posed by Hume in the following way: "When we entertain . . . any suspicion that a philosophical term is employed without any meaning or idea (as is but too frequent), we need but inquire, *from what impression is that supposed idea derived?* And if it be impossible to assign any, this will serve to confirm our suspicion."[28]

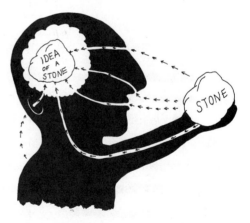

In other words, question 2 can be answered affirmatively only if it is possible to trace its ideas back to sense data ("impressions"). For example, all the ideas in the sentence "This stone is heavy" can be traced back to sense data; hence, it passes the empirical criterion of meaning.

☑ YES

But what if, in a particular case, the answer to question 2 is negative?

☑ NO

That is, what if a particular idea cannot be traced to a sense impression? In that case, according to Hume, we must be dealing with vacuous ideas, that is to say, with *nonsense.*

Now, with Hume's method in hand, if we turn to some of the traditional philosophical topics, such as God, world, and self, we arrive at some pretty startling conclusions. Let's start with the sentence "God exists."

1. Is this proposition analytic?

That is to ask, is its negation ("God does not exist") a self-contradiction? Most people would answer no. Of course, there are some who would answer yes—namely, all those defenders of the "ontological proof of God's existence" (e.g., Anselm, Descartes, Spinoza), but Hume would respond to them by saying that if the sentence "God exists" is analytic, then it is tautological and tells us nothing about reality. The true sentence "A being whose existence is necessary would be one that necessarily exists" still doesn't tell us whether there is a necessary being.

✔ NO

So if we assume that "God exists" is not analytic, the next question is,

2. Is this proposition synthetic?

Hume believed it was impossible to trace the idea of God back to sense data. He said, "Our ideas reach no farther than our experience: We have no experience of divine attributes and operations; I need not conclude my syllogism. You can draw the inference yourself."[29] So, although Hume didn't actually say so, his method seems to imply that the idea of God is vacuous and that statements about God are literally nonsense.

So much for God in Hume's system. What about the world? Berkeley, using Ockham's razor, had already eliminated "material substance" from empiricism. Material substance was one of the key concepts philosophers had used to explain the world. Hume now turned to another, one that was employed not only by philosophers but also by scientists and by ordinary people of common sense—that of **causality.**

Let's take the sentence "X causes Y," where X and Y are both events. (We'll use Hume's example: X is the event of billiard ball A striking billiard ball B, and Y is the event of ball B moving after being struck.)

1. Is the sentence "X causes Y" analytic?
   (That is to say, is the sentence "X does not cause Y" a self-contradiction? Obviously not, because it is perfectly possible to conceive of A striking B and B *not* moving.)
   ☑ NO

2. Is the sentence "X causes Y" synthetic?

Now, it seems that the answer will be affirmative because there should be no difficulty in tracing back the idea of "cause" to sense data. But Hume *found* a difficulty. When he analyzed the concept, he broke it down into three components: (a) priority, (b) contiguity, and (c) necessary connection. Priority (the fact that X precedes Y) can be traced to sense data. So can contiguity (the fact that X touches Y). But no matter how many times Hume observed ball A strike ball B, he could not find any *necessary connection* (the fact that if X happens, Y *must* happen), yet this was exactly what needed to be found if the concept of causality was to be sensible.

Hume Observing Causality

So the concept of "causality" proved to have the same status as "material substance" and "God." This embarrassment has far-reaching consequences. It means that whenever we say that event A causes event B, we are really only reporting our own *expectation* that A will be followed by B in the future. This statement expresses a psychological fact about us and not a fact about the world. But if we try to show the rational grounding of our expectation, we cannot do so. Even if A was followed by B innumerable times in the past, that does not justify our claim to know that it will do so again in the future. Hume did not, however, conclude that no causality exists in the world. He never doubted that objects and events stand in causal relations to each other, but he did doubt that an adequate philosophical account of causality was available.

Hume's discovery has come to be known as the problem of **induction**. What makes us so certain that the future will behave like the past? If we answer "because it has always done so in the past," we are begging the question, because the real question is, *Must it do*

so in the future just be-
cause it has always done
so in the past? Nor can
we appeal to the "laws of
nature," because then the
question is, What guaran-
tees that the laws of
nature will hold tomorrow?
There is no analytic or
synthetic guarantee of
the laws of nature. The
concept of causality is
one of the key ideas that
are needed to understand
the world. Hume concluded
that neither reason nor
experience could justify
the idea of "necessary
connections," which is the
main component of the notion of causality.

**Hume Discovers the Self—
Such As It Is**

"Hume's fork" (the analytic-synthetic distinction) has equally
disastrous results for the concept of self. There is no sense datum
to which the concept can be traced. Far from finding the self to be
the simple, indubitable, absolutely certain, eternal soul that Descartes had claimed it to be, Hume found, according to his method,
that "there is no such idea" as "self." The so-called self proves to be
"a bundle or collection of different perceptions [. . . heat or cold, light
or shade, love or hatred, pain or pleasure . . .] which succeed each
other with an inconceivable rapidity, and are in a perpetual flux and
movement."[30]

David Hume had consistently and vigorously followed the program of empiricism to its logical conclusion. The results were disastrous for the philosophical enterprise. The sphere of rationality was
found to be very small indeed, reduced as it was to verbal truths and

descriptions of sense data; yet nearly everything that interested people as philosophers or nonphilosophers fell beyond those limits. Hume believed he had shown that human life was incompatible with rationality and that human endeavors always extend beyond philosophical justification. (Rationally, I can never know that the loaf of bread that nourished me yesterday will nourish me today; hence, I can never be rationally motivated to eat.) But Hume knew perfectly well that the human being could not be sustained by the meager fruits of philosophy. Even while writing his philosophical manuscript he knew that, once he put down his pen, he too would revert to the normal, unfounded beliefs of humanity—namely, beliefs in self, world, and causality (if not in God). He even suggested, maybe with tongue in cheek, that perhaps we should abandon philosophy and take to tending sheep instead.

David Hume—Shepherd

Kant

It would be fair to say that the history of philosophy would have ended with Hume if his views had prevailed. To survive Hume's attack, philosophy needed a powerful, subtle, and original mind to come to its defense. It found such a protector in the German Immanuel Kant (1724–1804). Kant spent the whole of his life in the old Hanseatic city of Königsberg in the northeastern corner of Prussia (today, Kaliningrad, Russia), where, at least until his fiftieth year, he passed his days complacently in the bourgeois life of a respected professor of the university. This old bachelor, whose personal life was so methodical that his neighbors used to set their clocks by his afternoon walks, had been trained in the rationalistic metaphysics of Christian von Wolff, an undistinguished disciple of Leibniz, and Kant had found no reason to doubt any of its tenets—that

Herr Professor Immanuel Kant on His Daily Walk

is, not until one fine day in his late middle age when a copy of Hume's *Inquiry* crossed his desk. Kant's reading of it "awakened him from his dogmatic slumber," as he later reported. He realized that Hume's powerful argument undermined everything Kant had believed and that no honest progress in philosophy could be made until Hume's skeptical arguments had been refuted.

Kant's response to Hume, and his attempt to synthesize what he took to be the best of Hume's philosophy with the best of what was left of rationalism after Hume's full-scale frontal assault on it, is found in *The Critique of Pure Reason*. There Kant accepted Hume's analytic-synthetic distinction as the key philosophical tool of analysis. Kant agreed with Hume that all analytic propositions are a priori

l a posteriori propositions are synthetic, but he disagreed
s claim that all synthetic propositions are a posteriori and
riori propositions are analytic (hence tautological). That is
cording to Kant, there is such a thing as a synthetic a priori truth, a meaningful statement about reality whose truth is known
independently of observation.

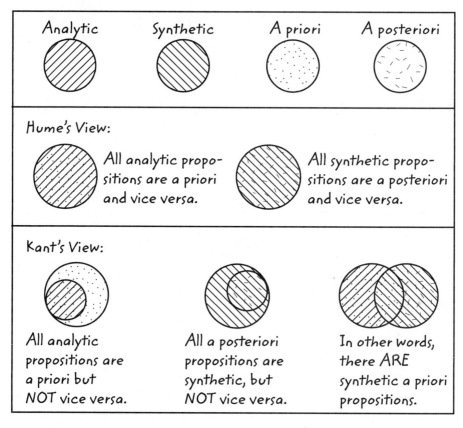

| Analytic | Synthetic | A priori | A posteriori |

Hume's View:

All analytic propositions are a priori and vice versa.

All synthetic propositions are a posteriori and vice versa.

Kant's View:

All analytic propositions are a priori but NOT vice versa.

All a posteriori propositions are synthetic, but NOT vice versa.

In other words, there ARE synthetic a priori propositions.

Kant believed that only by demonstrating the existence of such
truths could Hume be refuted and philosophy, science, and common
sense (and perhaps religion) be made respectable again. This demonstration would be done by showing that the knowledge that Hume
denied was, in fact, grounded in synthetic a priori truth, as were the
very arguments that Hume had mustered against such claims of
knowledge. Kant began by dividing the mind into three "faculties"—
intuition (i.e., perception), understanding, and reason—and then performing what he called a "transcendental" analysis of each faculty.

Kant first dealt with the faculty of intuition. Here the primary question that concerned Kant was not "What is perception" nor "Is perception possible?" Rather, it was "*How* is perception possible?" That is, he began with the commonsense view that we *do* perceive the world and asked what conditions must hold for that to be possible. For example, he wanted to know how it was possible that we are able to utter true sentences about the height of the Matterhorn if the empiricists were right to say we never perceive space, only sense data. And he wanted to know how

it was possible that we are able to utter true sentences about the amount of time it takes to get to Berlin if the empiricists were correct to say we never perceive *time*, only sense data. Kant's solution was to demonstrate that space and time are the synthetic a priori foundations of the faculty of perception. An a posteriori sentence like "The cat is on the mat" *presupposes* the truth of the sentence "Objects exist in space and time." According to Kant, we sometimes know the first sentence to be true, yet *it* cannot be true unless the second is also true. The latter is not analytic, and it is not a posteriori (there is no sense datum of space or time—Hume was right about that), so it must be a synthetic a priori truth.

Kant called this method of analysis a "transcendental **deduction**" because it transcends direct observation or, better, gets behind and underneath it to discover its necessary conditions. This analysis led Kant to conclude that space and time were not features of external reality. Rather, they were features of the *structure of the mind*. The human mind analyzes the data it receives in terms of space and time. Space and time are the "irremovable goggles" through which we perceive the world. They are not like pieces on a chess board (things in

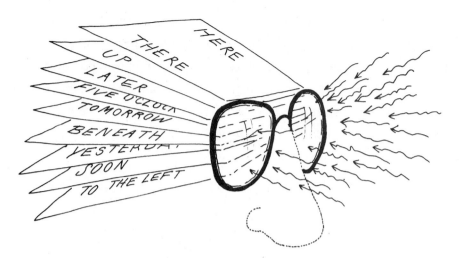

The Irremovable Goggles

the world); rather, they are like the rules according to which we play chess and in whose absence chess would not exist.

Having discovered the synthetic a priori foundations of the faculty of intuition, Kant then turned to the faculty of understanding. This faculty enables us to understand facts about the world (that Mt. Whitney is higher than Death Valley, that the cat is on the mat). Once again, Kant began not by asking "Can there be knowledge of the world?" Instead, he began with the commonsense assumption that we *do* have such knowledge and asked how such knowledge was possible. He found that it was grounded in the synthetic a priori foundations of the faculty of the understanding, which he called "the categories of the understanding." These categories included those of unity/plurality/totality, causality, and substantiality. These concepts are not deduced by the mind from reality; on the contrary, the mind brings them to reality. This is why Hume had been unable to find them "out there" when he looked for them. A sentence such as "Every event is caused" (which to Hume was neither empirical nor true by definition) is, according to Kant, a synthetic a priori truth.

Kant also claimed that mathematics belonged in the category of the synthetic a priori. First, math has an a priori status because our knowledge of it is independent of observation. (Your first grade teacher, Miss Green [you remember her!] was wrong when she pointed to two piles of chalk and said, "Two pieces of chalk plus three pieces of chalk is five pieces of chalk. *Therefore, 2 + 3 = 5.*" No, 2 plus 3 would equal 5 even if chalk had never been created.) But math also has a synthetic status. It tells us something about the world. A mathematical proposition is not merely an empty tautology in the way that definitions are.

Obviously, Kant's theory of the synthetic a priori is reminiscent of the Platonic-Cartesian doctrine of innate ideas, but there is a major difference. Kant did not claim that we are born with a group of *ideas* but that the mind is structured in such a way that it analyzes its data in terms of a particular set of synthetic *a priori rules,* which are like a permanent program in a computer and which produce ideas when fed information by the senses. If you are a human being, then you make sense of the world in terms of such concepts as time/space/substantiality/causality. The mind *must* order the world in terms of "thingness," though there is nothing "out there" corresponding to our idea of substance. The mind *must* understand the world in terms of causal series even though there is nothing out there that could correspond to our idea of *the* cause of any event.

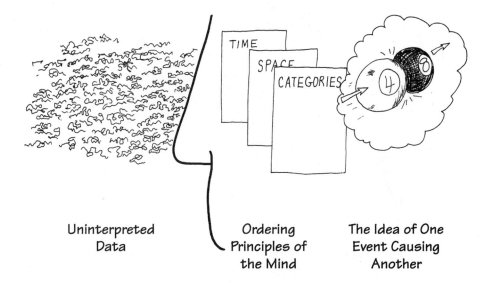

Uninterpreted
Data

Ordering
Principles of
the Mind

The Idea of One
Event Causing
Another

Kant's position was meant to represent a compromise between the warring rationalists and empiricists. His famous assertion "thoughts without content are empty, intuitions without concepts are blind"[31] was meant to grant to the rationalists that sense data alone could not provide knowledge and to grant to the empiricists that there could be no knowledge in the absence of sensorial contribution. Kant's solution seemed to many to be successful; however, it had the consequence of putting him in the disconcerting position of admitting that there does exist some kind of ultimate reality (what he called the **noumenal world,** or the "thing-in-itself" [*das Ding-an-sich*]) but that the human mind is incapable of knowing it. The noumenal world (from a Greek word meaning "the *thing* that appears," as contrasted with "phenomenon," from a Greek word meaning "the *appearance* of a thing") is the reality behind appearances, and we can

Kant Peers beyond the Curtain of the Phenomenal World and Sees Nothing

know that such a reality does exist because appearances must be appearances *of* something. But we humans of necessity have no access to this noumenal world; rather, we are limited to knowledge of what Kant called the "phenomenal world"—the world as perceived, conceived, imagined, interpreted, analyzed, and theorized about by the human mind. That is, we can only know a world that has passed through the human mind, through the gridwork of space and time and the categories of the understanding. Contrary to Hume's conclusion, Kant's conclusion was that common sense and science are valid but only insofar as their claims are about the phenomenal world. But nothing positive can be said about ultimate reality, other than that it exists. The concept of a noumenal world is what Kant calls a *limiting* concept. We can say *that* a noumenal reality exists, but not *what* that existence comprises. This limiting concept meant that traditional metaphysics of the type attempted by philosophers from Plato through Leibniz was impossible. Kant deduced this conclusion from his transcendental analysis of the faculty of reason.

The faculty of reason was supposed by Kant to be the faculty that produced the "pure" concepts (i.e., concepts uncontaminated by the senses) such as "God" and "soul." Were there any synthetic a priori foundations for this faculty? (Which is another way of asking, can we hope to know any "higher truths" about ultimate reality?) Kant's notorious answer—which was so scandalous to the metaphysicians and theologians—was *no!* Traditional metaphysics was impossible because it was always the result of illegitimately applying notions of space, time, and causality to the noumenal world when in fact these concepts can be applied only to the observable world. Therefore, all proofs of God's existence must fail, along with all attempts to describe ultimate reality in terms of that mysterious category "substance." We humans must therefore despair of ever knowing of God, justice, immortality, or freedom, because all these ideas overreach the human capability for knowledge.

If Kant had concluded *The Critique of Pure Reason* at this point, he would have satisfied the Humean critics of metaphysics and

**The House of Metaphysics
before and after *The Critique of Pure Reason***

theology while pleasing the defenders of common sense and science, but he would not have satisfied those impulses in the human heart toward higher sentiments. To these stirrings, Kant addressed the rest of his *Critique*. There he claimed the following: There is no logical necessity to conceive of the world in terms of God, immortality, justice, and freedom (in the way that there *is* a logical necessity of conceiving of the world in terms of time, space, and causality); nevertheless, without such inspirational concepts, many humans would lose their enthusiasm for life. If one could not believe, for example, that

No God, no immortality, no justice. I can't stand it! Barkeep, bring me another.

the human soul is free and that ultimately justice will triumph, then one might well lose the motivation required for the engagement in the day-to-day world. Therefore, according to Kant, one has the right to *believe* (but not to claim to know) that God, soul, immortality, justice, and freedom exist, not as *metaphysical necessities*, but as *practical* (i.e., moral) necessities. We have the right to treat these topics as if they were synthetic a priori truths if doing so will make us better, more successful human beings.

Kant's attempt to distinguish knowledge from belief, yet ground belief in moral necessity, was acceptable to many who were tired of the extravagant claims made by metaphysicians and theologians but who were also looking for a legitimate role for *belief* in the modern world. Kant's critics, however, accused him of merely "kicking God out the front door in order to let him in through the back door."

After *The Critique of Pure Reason*, Kant wrote a number of other important philosophical works, including *The Critique of Practical Reason* and *The Foundations of the Metaphysics of Morals*, both of which addressed specifically the problem of ethics. In its emphasis on intention and duty, Kant's theory demonstrated Christianity's influence on him, and in its attempts to ground duty in reason, Kant's theory showed him to be a thinker of the Enlightenment. By positing freedom as if it were grounded in a synthetic a priori truth (for without freedom there can be no moral acts), one can derive an ethical code from its foundations in reason. Being a rule-guided activity, reasoning itself is based on a respect for rules and laws. From such respect, Kant deduced a moral command, which he called the *categorical imperative:* "Act only according to that maxim by which you can at the same time will that it should become a universal law."[32] All moral acts are modeled on principles that may be universalized without contradiction. Kant thought that, as creatures of reason, we are duty-bound to obey such principles, or "maxims," as he calls them, meaning subjective rules of conduct—subjective in that we must choose to submit ourselves to them. Here, I am going to oversimplify this idea a bit to see what Kant was talking about.

Let's suppose that you owe a friend five dollars, and, to your annoyance, he pressures you to repay. So you say to yourself, "If I kill him, I won't have to repay the debt." But as a true Kantian, you first check to see if you could universalize the maxim governing the proposed action. You ask yourself, What if everyone accomplished his or her goals by killing someone? Could there exist a universal law that

states, "Everyone ought to kill someone"? This law would be an impossible law because if everyone complied with it, there would be no one left to comply with it. Therefore, we are duty-bound not to kill as a way of solving problems. Okay, then, what if you lie to your friend, telling him that you already repaid the debt? Can the principle behind this proposal be universalized? Could there be a general law

that states, "Everyone ought always to lie"? Obviously not, because it would be impossible even to state the law without breaking it. Furthermore, if everyone always lied, then there would be no such thing as a lie, or, lies would be the truth. (For the same reason, if all money were counterfeit, then there would be no such thing as counterfeit money. Counterfeit money would be real money.) This law would be self-contradictory. Therefore, we are duty-bound not to lie. Well, what if you repay the five dollars and then steal them back? Can the principle behind this act be universalized? Imagine a general law that states, "Everyone ought always to steal."

Where Theft Is the Law of the Land

But this too is an impossible law because the concept of stealing is parasitical upon the concept of property. But if everyone always steals, there can be no property; there can be only temporary possession, that is, stuff passing from person to person. So we are also duty-bound to refrain from stealing. (If you are a true Kantian, it's beginning to look as though you will have to pay your debt!)[33]

Kant formulated the categorical imperative in a number of ways, not just in terms of the principle of universalizability. One such formulation was this: "Act so that you treat humanity, whether in your own person, or in that of another, always as an end and never as a means only."[34] By saying we should treat people as ends and not merely as means, Kant was, of course, admonishing us against *using* other people as a means to our own ends. He thought that morality entailed the recognition of the *dignity* of each person as a person. If there were no *persons* in the world, only *things*, there would be no *values*. Nothing would be worth anything more or less than anything else. But there are persons in the world—that is, individual entities having not only desires (because animals, too, have desires) but also rationality and freedom. Therefore, as the source of values, humans have *dignity*, which Kant defines as something so valuable that nothing could transcend it in worth. To claim our status as humans—that is, to claim our dignity—we must value above all else that which bestows dignity and humanity, namely, rationality, freedom, and autonomy. We must value these qualities in ourselves, but also in other individuals as well. Or, in Kant's words, we must treat other individuals as *ends* and not as *means*. The principle of universalizability behind the categorical imperative makes this our duty as rational beings. This side of Kant's ethics has widespread practical implications for such issues as sexual relationships, discrimination, informed consent, and death with dignity.

If we dwelt solely on the first formulation of the categorical imperative (the one based on universalizability), Kant's ethics might seem quite bloodless; but this second formulation adds some warmth to his moral doctrine. Nevertheless, there is a *bit of coldness* at the heart of his view. He was so intent on making morality a question of *duty* that he refused to grant any worth to *inclination*. According to him, if a person who was motivated by feelings of empathy toward humanity rendered assistance to a helpless, needy person, this act would be of less moral value than would be the same act performed by someone who actually loathed humanity but who was motivated purely by a sense of duty.

Kant's ethical conclusions, like his metaphysical conclusions, were essentially conservative in nature. His theory rationalized all the virtues that his Lutheran upbringing had extolled. (Lutherans had always known that a human's relation to God was one of belief, not of knowledge; and they had always known that they were duty-bound not to murder, lie, or steal.) Nevertheless, it is striking that Kant derived his principles from reason and not from divine commandment. Here he was more of an Enlightenment figure than a Lutheran. And many believe that Kant, in saying that certain kinds of metaphysical speculation are a waste of time, revealed something essential about the limits of human reasoning, and in saying that morality requires acts to be viewed from a perspective other than that of self-interest, he revealed something essential about ethics.

Topics for Consideration

1. Discuss the role that God plays in Descartes's philosophy. Based on the evidence provided in this chapter, defend one of these views:

   A. Descartes was an atheist who used the idea of God to disguise the true nature of his enterprise from religious authorities who were hostile to the new mechanistic sciences.

   B. Descartes gave God so much power in his system that without God the system would collapse, which proves that Descartes was a religious philosopher as well as a supporter of science.

2. Discuss Descartes's method of radical doubt, which he used to establish an absolutely certain foundation for his philosophy. Are you convinced that Descartes's method achieved that goal? If so, say why. If not, explain what you think goes wrong.

3. Explain why Descartes's philosophy leaves us with what has been called the "mind-body problem," and briefly show how Hobbes, Spinoza, and Leibniz, respectively, dealt with that problem.

4. State the thesis of Hobbes's **psychological egoism,** and then either defend it or criticize it.

5. Explain how Hobbes justified the legitimacy of governments and the absolute power of sovereigns within governments.

6. Replace the word "God" as used in Spinoza's philosophy with the word "nature," and report what differences, if any, such a change makes in his philosophy.

7. Central to the theories of both Leibniz and Hume is the distinction between analytic and synthetic propositions. What differences exist in

their respective treatment of these categories that can explain why their general philosophies are so much in opposition to each other?

8. Explain the different views that Descartes, Spinoza, and Leibniz had of the idea of "substance," and show the consequences that these differences produced in their respective philosophies.

9. Show the further development of the idea of "substance" in the philosophies of Locke and Berkeley.

10. Contrast the idea of the "self" in the theories of Descartes and Hume.

11. It was suggested on page 190 that in conditions of abundance, Locke's optimistic view of human nature may be correct, and in conditions of scarcity, Hobbes's pessimistic view may be correct. If this suggestion is valid, what are the implications for the idea of "human nature"?

12. Critically discuss Berkeley's claim that descriptions of so-called primary qualities (size, shape, location, etc.) are really only interpretations of secondary qualities (colors, sounds, tastes, etc.).

13. Explain the idea of "necessary connection" in Hume's discussion of causality. Why do you think Hume held that necessary connections are required in true causal relations, and why did he hold that propositions attempting to describe necessary conditions are neither analytic nor synthetic?

14. Using examples from the text, explain why Descartes, Spinoza, and Leibniz are all called rationalists, and why Locke, Berkeley and Hume are called empiricists.

15. What, in your opinion, does Kant's theory of knowledge have in common with rationalism? What does it have in common with empiricism?

16. Try to construct an argument showing that the following maxim is ultimately self-contradictory and that willing it as a universal law would therefore be impossible: "Everyone desiring to escape an onerous obligation should kill the person to whom he or she is obligated." (See note 33.)

Notes

1. René Descartes, *Essential Works of Descartes,* trans. Lowell Blair (New York: Bantam Books, 1966), x.

2. René Descartes, *Meditations on First Philosophy,* in *A Guided Tour of Descartes' "Meditations on First Philosophy,"* 2d ed., ed. Christopher Biffle, trans. Ronald Rubin (Mountain View, Calif.: Mayfield Publishing, 1996), 22.

3. Ibid., 23.

4. Descartes's version of this idea as expressed in the *Meditations* is simply, "I am, I exist" (*Meditations*, 35). I have used "I think, therefore I am," the version from the *Discourse on Method*, because it is better known than the other. Indeed, it may be the most famous line from the history of Western philosophy. See René Descartes, *Discourse on Method*, in *The Essential Descartes*, ed. Margaret D. Wilson, trans. E. S. Haldane and G. T. R. Ross (New York: New American Library, 1969), 127.

5. Descartes, *Meditations*, 87.

6. Ibid., 63.

7. René Descartes, *Objections and Replies*, in *The Essential Descartes*, 274.

8. Thomas Hobbes, *Leviathan: On the Matter, Forme and Power of a Commonwealth Ecclesiasticall and Civil* (New York: Collier Books, 1962), 105.

9. Ibid., 100.

10. Bertrand Russell, *A History of Western Philosophy* (New York & London: Simon & Schuster, 1972), 569.

11. Baruch Spinoza, *Ethics* and *On the Correction of the Understanding*, trans. Andrew Boyle (New York: Dutton/Everyman's Library, 1977), 224.

12. René Descartes, *The Principles of Philosophy*, in *The Essential Descartes*, 323.

13. Spinoza, 171. I have tampered a bit with Boyle's translation of the Latin word *hilaritus*, which Boyle renders as "merriment" and I have changed to "joy." The word "mirth," chosen by R. H. M. Elwes, is, to my ears, even less Spinozistic than "merriment."

14. Russell, 581.

15. Gottfried Wilhelm von Leibniz, *Monadology and Other Philosophical Essays*, trans. Paul Schrecker and Anne Martin Schrecker (New York: Bobbs-Merrill, 1965), 87.

16. Ibid., 90–91.

17. Ibid., 151.

18. Ibid., 148.

19. John Locke, *An Essay Concerning Human Understanding* (Cleveland & New York: Meridian Books, 1964), 89.

20. Ibid., 185.

21. Hobbes, 102.

22. John Locke, *The Second Treatise of Civil Government*, in *Two Treatises of Government* (New York: Hafner, 1964), 124.

23. Hobbes, 102.

24. Locke, *The Second Treatise*, 134.

25. Ibid., 144.

26. George Berkeley, *A Treatise Concerning the Principles of Human Knowledge*, in *Principles, Dialogues, and Philosophical Correspondence*, ed. Colin Murray Turbane (Indianapolis & New York: Bobbs-Merrill, 1965), 22.

27. David Hume, *An Inquiry Concerning Human Understanding* (Indianapolis: Hackett, 1993), 114.

28. Ibid., 13.

29. David Hume, *Dialogues Concerning Natural Religion*, in Focus on "Dialogues Concerning Natural Religion," ed. Stanley Tweyman (London & New York: Routledge, 1991), 108.

30. David Hume, *A Treatise of Human Nature* (Oxford: Clarendon Press, 1941), 252–53.

31. Immanuel Kant, *Critique of Pure Reason*, trans. Norman Kemp Smith (New York: Humanities Press, 1950), 93.

32. Immanuel Kant, *Foundations of the Metaphysics of Morals*, trans. Lewis Beck White (Indianapolis: Bobbs-Merrill, 1976), 39.

33. When I said in the text that I had oversimplified the presentation of Kant's theory of universalizability, what I meant is that I was going to ignore for the moment some of the problems related to interpreting this theory. For example, there is a debate concerning the generality or specificity of the maxim to be universalized. Some Kantian scholars believe that the correct rendition of the categorical imperative requires adding the phrase "similarly circumstanced," for example, to each of the laws I mentioned in my examples. For instance, when you think about killing your friend to avoid repaying your debt, rather than testing the morality of your action by suggesting a law that states, "Everyone ought to kill someone," you should propose the maxim "Everyone desiring to escape an onerous obligation should kill the person to whom he or she is obligated." (There would be similarly circumstanced maxims in the case of lying to the lender or stealing from him.) These formulations stressing circumstance would make it harder for Kant to demonstrate the self-contradictoriness of these maxims, but they would perhaps save Kant from the charge of inconsistency sometimes leveled against him for his support of capital punishment and of the killing of enemies during "just" wars.

34. Kant, *Metaphysics of Morals*, 47.

6
Post-Kantian British and Continental Philosophy
The Nineteenth Century

If Kant believed that his "critical philosophy" would spell the end of speculative metaphysics, he was sorely mistaken. Even during his lifetime, there was emerging a generation of metaphysicians, some of whom, ironically, were using Kantian principles to advance their speculations well beyond the limits that Kant lay down in his *Critique*. Kant was especially embarrassed by the use of his ideas and terminology by philosophers who were calling themselves Kantians while creating a kind of highly metaphysical idealism of the type Kant had repudiated. But it must be said that he himself was somewhat responsible for this turn of events. After all, he had defined nonhuman reality as a noumenal thing-in-itself and then announced that it was inaccessible to human thought, with the consequence that human thought had access only to itself. As that earlier idealist George Berkeley would have pointed out, an inaccessible noumenal world is hardly better than no noumenal world at all. Indeed, this new generation of German philosophers derived their idealism from their dissatisfaction with Kant's claim that there existed a nonmental world that was unknowable.

Hegel

Primary among the ranks of the German idealists were Johann Gottlieb Fichte (1762–1814), Friedrich Wilhelm Joseph von Schelling (1775–1854), and Georg Wilhelm Friedrich Hegel (1770–1831).

G. W. F. Hegel

Of these, it was Hegel who achieved the greatest prominence, and it will be he who will represent German idealism for us.

Kant had argued that the appearances of ultimate reality are processed by the human mind, which thereby creates a world for us humans to inhabit. Hegel went further and claimed that the mind did not merely *structure* and *regulate* reality but actually *generated* it and *constituted* it. That is to say, reality is simply mind or spirit (*Geist* in German). This claim left Hegel with a philosophy that he himself called "absolute idealism." It is *absolute* idealism not only in the sense that absolutely nothing but ideas exists, but also because ultimately Hegel equated "mind" with "divine mind," or "absolute mind." This meant that if mind = reality, then reality = God. This view, in some ways similar to Spinoza's, made Hegel a pantheist. Furthermore, besides equating *Geist* with reality and God, Hegel also equated it with history. Kant had seen the mind as structurally identical from individual to individual, culture to culture, and historical period to historical period. Hegel criticized Kant's view as static and ahistorical. According to Hegel, even though the mind does have a universal, abstract structure, its content changes evolutionarily from period to period. There exists a mode of philosophical introspection that reveals the general structure of Mind and

The Evolution of the Mind

even allows us to reconstruct history in an a priori manner. In our attempt as philosophers to investigate the nature of the mind, we can reconstruct the *logical* (not chronological) beginnings of creation. They go something like this:

In the beginning, God, pure Mind, and hence Pure Being, attempted to *think himself*. But the thought of pure Being is an impossible thought; therefore, when God attempted to think Being, he thought *nothing*. That is, he thought the opposite of Being.

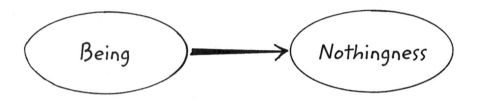

But remember, in the unusual system being suggested here, *God is God's thought*; therefore, in his failure to think pure Being, God has distanced himself from his own essence. This is what Hegel calls God's *self-alienation*. The "truth" of Hegel's insight can be seen in biblical symbolism in the relation between God and Satan. Satan is a fallen angel. He has "fallen away" from divinity. He is, in Hegel's way

Satan Falls Away from God—Divine Self-Alienation

of thinking, divinity self-alienated. Another biblical indication of Hegel's "truth" can be seen in God's answer to Moses when God spoke to him through the burning bush. When the shrub burst into flame, Moses asked it, "Who art thou?" and God answered, "I am that which is" (or, in ungrammatical Hebrew, "I am that what am"). Here we see that God cannot say himself without dividing his essence into a sub-ject– object relationship. ("I am . . ." [= subject]  "that which is" [= object]. If the subject is the object, then it is not itself as subject.) Hegel's God, then, is in a kind of identity crisis. But if God ex-periences an identity crisis, so does the human because the human mind is nothing but a manifestation of the Divine Mind. The history of an indi-vidual's mind, like history itself, is the process of self-awareness and self-recovery.

Returning to the di-chotomy Being ⟷ Noth-ingness—can there be any reconciliation between the two? Well, these two impos-sible thoughts (neither Pure Being nor Pure Nothingness

God's Identity Crisis

can truly be thought) represent the absolute limitation of all thinking and all reality. That is, all thought and all reality must fall somewhere between these two extremes. Hegel's term for anything occurring between these polar opposites is "Becoming." So we can call Being a *thesis* (positive, +), Nothingness an *antithesis* (negative, −), and Becoming a *synthesis* (combination of positive and negative +/ −). Hegel calls this universal structure of all thought and reality the dialectic.

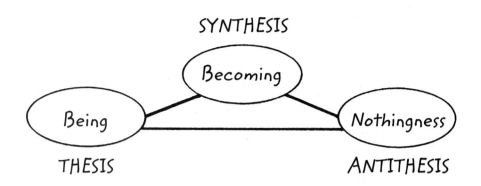

SYNTHESIS

Becoming

Being   Nothingness

THESIS   ANTITHESIS

Therefore, anything in the world—a table, for instance—is in fact a *process* synthesizing a positivity and a negativity. It *is* the table by *not* being the chair or the floor. This process is the nature of thought, language, and reality, which are systems of positivities created by negativities, and vice versa. Every thought, word, and thing exists only as a part of a system of exclusions. Again, a thing is what it is by *not* being its other, yet that "otherness" is what defines it as a being. This fact now explains why the thoughts of Pure Being and Pure Nothingness are impossible. Thought and language only function in a system of contrasts, yet Pure Being encompasses all; hence, there is nothing to contrast with it, *except* Nothingness, which is nothing. (Are you following this dizzying "logic"?) Furthermore, it can be deduced from this system that every synthesis must become a new thesis, and, defined as it is by its opposite, this new thesis must spawn its own antithesis. So history is an

BECOMING

HISTORY

BEING

NOTHINGNESS

eternal process of the dialectic, with each historical moment being a concatenation of contradictions—the tension between the positive and the negative. These forces are opposed to each other, yet mutually dependent on each other. Eventually, the tension between the thesis and the antithesis destroys the historical moment, but out of its ashes a new historical moment is born, one that *brings forward the best of the old moment.* Here is Hegel's optimism: progress is built into history. And if we individuals think we see regression and backsliding at specific times in history, this is because we are blind to "the cunning of Reason," which uses *apparent* retrograde movements to make hidden progress. Such is the nature of Reason's (i.e., God's) process of self-recovery. Consider, for example, the period of Graeco-Roman democracy. On the one hand, there existed among the Greek and Roman democrats the commitment to self-determination, freedom, and human dignity (as seen, e.g., in Pericles' "funeral speech"). On the other hand, during their democratic periods, both Greece and Rome were imperialistic, slave-holding states. These two essential features of the society in question were contradictory but, ironically, were mutually dependent on each another. The slaves existed for the pleasure of the new democratic class, but without slavery and the booty from plundering there never would have been a class of men liberated from toil who could dedicate their time, skills, and intellect to the creation of a democratic state. Yet eventually the *conceptual* contradiction between freedom and unfreedom, the two pillars of Graeco-Roman democracy, tore the society apart and prepared the way for a new kind of society, medieval feudalism.

Now, feudalism might not seem to you and me like a progression over earlier democratic societies, and, in fact, it might seem like a retrogression. But from Hegel's point of view, medieval society represents an advance in freedom over Greece and Rome because in feudalism there were no slaves. Even the most humble serf had legal rights.

What happened in history also happens individually. Each of us passes through various stages in our conceptions of our self and our

freedom. There is the stage at which we believe we can be free only by escaping the domination of others and by dominating them. Then we come to realize that in dominating them we ourselves are dominated because we become dependent on those we dominate, both materially and in terms of self-identity. (Who am I? I am the lord. But only as long as I am recognized as such by the bondsman. Without his recognition, I am nobody. Hence, in effect, *he* is the lord, and *I* am the bondsman.) Only by acknowledging that neither we nor others around us are free can we

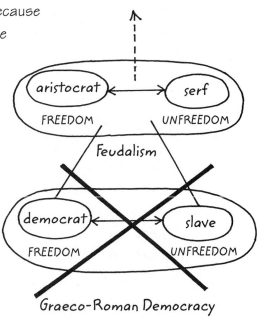

transcend the unfreedom of relationships of domination and discover higher forms of freedom—which is to say, discover the path of Reason and Divinity.

This sample of Hegelian thinking gives us an inkling of the psychological, sociological, historical, and theological dimensions of Hegel's thought. What we miss in this sampling is the absolute systematization of his philosophy. An outline of one of his several proposals for such a system follows:

The System

I. The idea-in-itself (= logic)
    A. Being
    B. Nothingness   This we've just
    C. Becoming   discussed.

II. The idea-outside-itself (= nature, i.e., the material world qua *material* that is the opposite of spirit but must be *potentially* spirit. The *goal* of inanimate matter is spirit.)

III. The idea for itself (= spirit; the idea recovered from its loss into its opposite.)
    A. Subjective spirit (Mind as self-conscious and introverted.)
    B. Objective spirit (Mind projecting its own laws outward, creating a human world.)
        1. Law (Exterior—comes to the individual from without.)
        2. Morality (Interior—comes from within the individual.)
        3. Ethics (Synthesis of the law exteriorized and interiorized.)
        a. Family
        b. Society
        c. State
    C. Absolute spirit
        1. Art
        2. Religion
        3. Philosophy

Notice that this whole system is structured in terms of interrelating triads of theses—antitheses—syntheses (even though Hegel

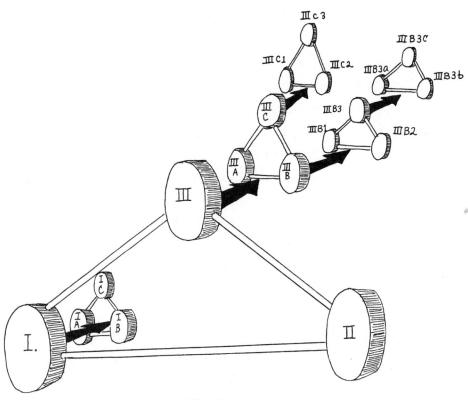

The System

rarely used those terms) and that the state is the highest form of objective spirit. Many of Hegel's critics point this out when they call attention to his eventual worship of the authoritarian, repressive Prussian state. Some even claim his whole system was contrived to be in the political service of the newly restored Prussian monarch, Hegel's paymaster.[1]

A more positive interpretation of Hegel's objective spirit concentrates on his designation of Napoleon as a sign of the end of history.[2] On this account, *history* is the history of the opposition between masters and slaves, or lords and bondsmen. The labor of the bondsmen had created a world of culture that transcended nature. Before the French Revolution the fruit of their labor was enjoyed only by the lords, who had finally proven themselves to be useless. The rise of Napoleon marked the end of the reign of the lords and the advent of a new universal and homogeneous state where lords no longer looked down contemptuously on bondsmen; rather, this new state was one in which "one consciousness recognizes itself in another, and in which each knows that reciprocal recognition";[3] that is, each person will recognize all other people's individuality in their universality and their universality in their individuality. Napoleon's cannons at the Battle of Jena, which Hegel could hear as he hurried through the last pages of his *Phenomenology of Mind,* were finishing off the old world of masters and slaves. Napoleon himself was the harbinger of the posthistorical world. Yet to Hegel it was no surprise that people caught up in the turbulent events of the moment did not grasp their significance at the time. The end of history cannot be understood by those *in* history. This is the meaning of Hegel's aphorism "The owl of Minerva spreads its wings only with the falling of dusk."[4] But perhaps in Hegel's mind his own philosophy represented the posthistorical world even more than did Napoleon. It also must be noted that it is not objective spirit that is the apogee of Hegel's system; rather, it is absolute spirit, and the highest pinnacle of absolute spirit is not the state but *philosophy* (and, one assumes, particularly *Hegel's* philosophy).

The Owl of Minerva

Schopenhauer

Arthur Schopenhauer (1788–1860) was one of Hegel's sharpest critics. He was a younger contemporary who refused to be intimidated by Hegel's immense fame. As a beginning philosophy teacher at the University of Berlin, Schopenhauer had scheduled classes at the same time as Hegel's, knowing full well that thereby he was guaranteeing for himself few, if any, students. This arrogant young philosopher's opinion of Hegel was one of undisguised contempt, as can be seen in the following unflattering portrait he drew.

> Hegel, installed from above by the powers that be as the certified Great Philosopher, was a flat-headed, insipid, nauseating, illiterate charlatan, who reached the pinnacle of audacity in scribbling together and dishing up the craziest mystifying nonsense.[5]

Arthur Schopenhauer

Schopenhauer, in fact, showed deep respect for only two Western philosophers: Plato and Kant. He also admired the philosophical traditions of India. To Schopenhauer, the rest of the philosophers throughout history had been merely "windbags." Schopenhauer began his work demanding a return to Kant, and, indeed, the first part of Schopenhauer's main work, *The World as Will and Idea*, was fundamentally a repetition of Kantian ideas. He agreed with Kant that the human mind is incapable of knowing ultimate reality, that the only reality we are capable of grasping intellectually is that which has passed through the grid work of space and time and through the categories of the understanding. Schopenhauer wrote:

> "The world is my idea":—this is a truth which holds good for everything that lives and knows, though man alone can bring it into reflective and abstract consciousness. If he really does this, he has

The History of Philosophy as the History of Windbags

attained to philosophical wisdom. It then becomes clear and certain
to him that what he knows is not a sun and an earth, but only an eye
that sees a sun, a hand that feels an earth; that the world which sur-
rounds him is there only as idea.[6]

Now, when Kant turned to the noumenal world, he claimed that
we could not know it, though we had the right to hold various beliefs
about it based on certain of our practical needs. Recall that for
Kant, these beliefs were extremely optimistic ones: faith in God,
freedom, immortality, and eternal justice. Furthermore, Kant had
pointed out certain human experiences, certain positive intuitions
of ours, that he hoped might be extrarational hints about the nature
of that unknowable noumenal world. For example, there were those
feelings of the sublime that we experience when we look deeply into
the sky on a clear summer night, and equally inspiring to Kant were
the feelings of moral duty that we experience in certain moments
of crisis. As Kant put it, "Two things fill the mind with ever new and
increasing admiration and awe . . . the starry heavens above and the
moral law within."[7]

Well, Schopenhauer too believed that there were certain intuitive
experiences that should be heeded because they might well give us an
extrarational insight into ultimate reality. But Schopenhauer's examples of such insights were very different indeed from those of Kant.

For example, Schopenhauer wondered why it is that when some-one is told of the death of an acquaintance, the first impulse that person experiences is the urge to grin—an urge that, of course, must be suppressed. And Schopenhauer wondered why it is that a respectable businessman or government official, who may have worked tirelessly for years to achieve the success and power that he has finally obtained, is willing to risk all of it for a moment's sexual

It's Not Nice to Giggle at Funerals

pleasure with a forbidden partner. These and similar human experi-ences left Schopenhauer with a much more pessimistic hunch about the nature of ultimate reality than that held by Kant. Schopen-hauer's dark suspicions quickly became "truths" in his system. (The curious status of these nonepistemological truths has not escaped the eyes of Schopenhauer's critics.) Said Schopenhauer: "This truth, which must be very serious and impressive if not awful to everyone, is that a man can also say and must say, 'The world is my will.'"[8]

**Schopenhauer Peers beyond the Curtain
of the Phenomenal World**

Schopenhauer's awful truth amounts to this: Behind appearances, behind the phenomenal veil, there does lie a noumenal reality; but, far from being the benign sphere where Kant hoped to find God, immortality, and justice, Schopenhauer found there a wild, seething, inexorable, meaningless force that he called "will." This force creates all and destroys all in its insatiable demand for "More!" (More of *what* it does not know—it only knows that it wants more.)

The best phenomenal images for understanding Schopenhauer's will are images of sex and violence. Not only in nature but even in the human sphere, every event is an act of procreation or destruction. Our actions, whether intentional or unintentional, motivated consciously or unconsciously, are, in fact, actions that in one way or another are in the service of procreation and destruction. (If you are familiar with Freud's theories, you know now where he got his idea of the id. Even the name "id" [Latin for "it"] indicates the same noumenal indeter- minacy as Schopen- hauer's will. Freud himself said in 1920, "We have unwittingly steered our course into the harbour of Schopenhauer's philosophy.")[9]

More! More! More!

According to Scho- penhauer, everything in the phenomenal world is merely the manifestation of this perverse will, or, as he called it, an "objectification of the will" (that is to say, the will passed through the categories and the grid work of space and time).

Even though Schopenhauer's images of the will are ones of dumb brutality, he also conceived of the will as immensely cunning. The will is capable of disguising its heartless purposes from any of its own "experiments" that might be capable of taking offense or even taking reprisals against the will. In other words, the human mind is con- structed in such a way as to be self-deceiving, even concerning its view on the world. The will is denatured as it passes through the grid work and the categories. Nevertheless, if we could strip away our natural optimism, itself a product of the cunning of the will, we could look into nature and see that it cares not a whit for the happiness or well-being of any of its creatures beyond the bare needs of repro- duction. Schopenhauer illustrated his point with descriptions of the giant turtles of the South Pacific that were known to have been smashed to death by the hundreds against the rocky coast in storms during mating season as they tried to get to shore to lay their eggs in the sand. Schopenhauer also called attention to that strange species of moth that emerges from its cocoon with full reproductive and digestive systems; yet nature forgot to give it one little detail—a mouth! So the moth reproduces and then finds food but quickly starves to death. Yet nature does not care; the moth has laid its little eggs. And, according to Schopenhauer, what's true of the turtle and the moth is true of the human being. If you are over eighteen years of age, your body is deteriorating. Your body, which is just the scaffolding for the reproductive system, begins to die once it has held its eggs in place and given them a chance to duplicate themselves.

Waiter, there seems to be a problem here.

This news is terrible indeed. Why do people not realize that we are all in a state of bondage to the irrational, meaningless will? Precisely because of the cunning of the will. Human culture itself is nothing but one more experiment of the will, and human optimism and hope are simply the will's gift to us to guarantee that we continue to deceive ourselves about the true state of affairs. The whole of human culture is nothing more than a grand deception. Art, religion, law, morality, science, and even philosophy are only **sublimations** of the will, sublimations that are still acting in its service. Hegel's glorification of higher culture is simply proof of the absolute triumph of the will.

All our hopes and aspirations will be dashed. Happiness is an impossible dream. It is absurd that anyone can remain an optimist after even a glance at the newspaper on any given day. A mudslide swallows up whole villages. A mad assassin's bullet strikes down the hope of a people. A single parent, mother of three, is killed by a painful disease. The drums of war never cease beating, and an inglorious

The Human Being in the Grip of the Will

What Seems to Be the Case

What Is the Case

death awaits all. Verily, only a fool can remain optimistic in the face of the truth.

Surely philosophy was never so disheartened and disheartening as in the case of Schopenhauer. But, according to him, his pessimism was a *rational* pessimism, and he sought a *rational* solution to it. There had, of course, been others who understood the truth and sought rational responses to it. Both Jesus and the Buddha had been pessimists, according to Schopenhauer, but their solutions were chimerical and still in the service of the will (besides, their doctrines were perverted by the cunning of the will manifested in the optimism of their disciples who presented their masters' pessimistic messages as "good news"). Plato too had offered a *nearly* successful solution, but his eternal Forms were still part of the world of idea, hence of the will.

It might seem that suicide should be the only recommendation that Schopenhauer's philosophy could make. But, in fact, Schopenhauer recommended against suicide on the grounds that self-murder

Plato's Solution

would be a last, desperate act of will, hence still a manifestation of the will (that is to say, no act requires as much concentration of will as does suicide; hence, suicide cannot possibly be the negation of the will).

Do not despair! There is a Schopenhauerian solution. Even though all culture is nothing but a sublimation of sex and violence, hence an experiment of the will, there is a point at which the cultural world can achieve such a degree of subtlety that it can break off from its own unconscious origins and set up an independent sphere that

Elvis's Solution

is, in fact, counternature and therefore antiwill. This autonomy from the will occurs in a specific corner of the art world—that of music. But not just *any* music. Certainly, popular music won't do, evoking as it does the imagery and emotions of the phenomenal world. Nor will most classical music serve. For example, in Beethoven's works, the imagery is still too strong; hence its link to the will is too obvious. (When listening to the "Pastoral," we see the cows in the meadow, the bright green grass and the wildflowers, and the puffy little white clouds in the blue sky.) No, an escape from the will can be achieved only in the contemplation of purely *formal* music, a music without words and without imagery. There is a kind of baroque music that fits the bill—a music of pure mathematical formalism: point, counterpoint, point. It is possible to dedicate one's life to the disinterested contemplation of such music, and Schopenhauer recommended precisely this contemplation as his version of Nirvana—an escape from the world into pure

Schopenhauer's Solution

form and hence a triumph over the will. It was this goal toward which Plato and the Buddha were clumsily struggling.

Schopenhauer's philosophy was deeply influential among intellectuals in the German-speaking world. The work of Friedrich Nietzsche, Sigmund Freud, and Thomas Mann is hardly conceivable without Schopenhauer. Yet nobody seems to have taken Schopenhauer's solution very seriously. It was perhaps too obvious, as Nietzsche was to point out, that baroque music is the most sensual of all music and that the desire to immerse oneself in it is after all a *desire*, hence still the work of the will.

Kierkegaard

Schopenhauer's method of dealing with Hegel was first to call him names and then to ignore him. But the generation of Continental

Søren Kierkegaard

philosophers who followed Schopenhauer had to deal more directly with Hegel, whose influence by the 1830s had become immense. One of the most curious members of this generation was the Dane Søren Kierkegaard (1813–1855). Kierkegaard, who is generally recognized today as the father of **existentialism,** thought of himself primarily as a religious author and an antiphilosopher. In truth, he was not opposed to philosophy as such but to *Hegel's* philosophy. Nevertheless, like the rest of his generation, Kierkegaard fell more under Hegel's spell than he would have liked to admit.

Kierkegaard blamed Hegel for much of what he took to be the dehumanization of the intellectual life of a whole generation. This dehumanization was the result of a "correction" that Hegel made to Aristotelian logic. Aristotle had laid down the three basic principles of logic as

1. The principle of identity (A = A)
2. The principle of noncontradiction [not (A and not–A)]
3. The **principle of the excluded middle** [either (A) or (not–A)]

Hegel believed these principles to be erroneous. His new dialectical logic overturned them. In the dialectic, everything is in some sense its opposite; therefore, it is not the case that A = A because A = not–A. (Greek democracy was in some sense equivalent to Greek slavery; hence, it was its own opposite.) If the principle of identity falls, then the principles of noncontradiction and of the excluded middle collapse too. Kierkegaard took offense at the pompousness of Hegel's suggestion. He mocked it with vignettes like the following:

> If you marry, you will regret it; if you do not marry, you will also regret it; . . . whether you marry or do not marry, you will regret both. Laugh at the world's follies, you will regret it; weep over them, you will regret that; laugh at the world's follies or weep over them, you will regret both. . . . Believe a woman, you will regret it, believe her not, you will also regret that; believe a woman or believe her not, you will regret both. . . . Hang yourself, you will regret it, do not hang yourself, and you will also regret that; hang yourself or do not hang yourself, you will regret both. . . . This, gentlemen, is the sum and substance of all philosophy.[10]

This is not really the sum and substance of all philosophy. It is the sum and substance of *Hegel's* philosophy, a philosophy in which all oppositions are swallowed up, creating absolute apathy and demoralization, and which, by abrogating the principle of the excluded middle, thereby annuls the "either/or" of decision making—and therewith denies freedom, which, for Kierkegaard and his existentialist followers, is the essence of human existence. Therefore, Kierkegaard published the foregoing "ecstatic lecture" in a book that he called *Either/Or*, whose very title was an attack on Hegel.

Not only had Hegel collapsed the distinction between the "either" and the "or," but he had also abolished the difference between epistemology and ontology by asserting "the Rational is the Real and the Real is the Rational,"[11] which is another way of saying that existence and thought are identical. Kierkegaard inverted Hegel's assertion, claiming that existence is the one thing that cannot be thought. This claim is a double entendre, meaning (1) Thought and existence are *not identical*, and (2) it is impossible to think "existence."

Recall that Hegel's god had found himself incapable of thinking pure existence (Pure Being). Kierkegaard pushed this limitation to the fore, claiming not just that *pure* existence is impossible to think but that *any* existence is unthinkable, because, in Kierkegaard's Platonic theory of meaning, thought is always a form of abstraction. Words are signifiers that denote concepts, and concepts are general categories. Every word in the sentence "The brown dog obeys its master" denotes for Kierkegaard an abstraction. Language abstracts from experience and suppresses differences in order to allow the possibility of thought and communication; hence, thought (which is language-bound) distances us from real existence, which is never abstract but always *concrete*.

Language Alienates One from Lived Experience

Kierkegaard's philoso-
phy, as opposed to the
abstractions of Hegelian
philosophy, would
return us to the
concreteness of
existence. But he
was not so much
interested in the
concreteness of
existence of things
in the world as he was
in the concreteness of
individual human exis-
tence. René Descartes
had been right to begin
philosophy with the self

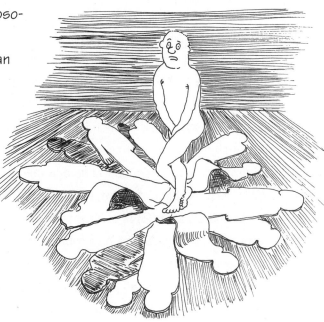

**When All the Roles Have Been Stripped
Away, What's Left Is My Existence**

("I think, therefore I am"), but he had been wrong, as was Hegel after
him, to equate the self with thought. "To think is one thing, to exist is
another," said Kierkegaard. I can think and say many things about
myself—"I am a teacher, I am a man, I am an American, I am in love,
I prefer chocolate to vanilla." Yet, when I am done talking and thinking
about myself, there is one thing remaining that cannot be thought—
my existence, which is a "surd" (an irrational residue). I cannot *think*
it; rather, I must *live* it.

My lived existence, according to Kierkegaard, is equated with
passion, decision, and action. None of these categories can be
exhausted by thought. But Kierkegaard is not saying that there is no
connection between existence and thought. In fact, existence must
be interpenetrated with thought. What kind of thought? An "existential probing" that "dedicates itself more and more profoundly to the
task of existing, and with the consciousness of what existence is,
penetrates all illusions, becoming more and more concrete through
reconstructing existence in action."[12]

To explain this notion I must clarify a distinction that Kierkegaard drew in his *Concluding Unscientific Postscript to the Philosophical Fragments* between "objective thought" and "subjective thought." The first category is a kind of thinking for which there exist objective criteria of truth, such as in the case of math, science, and history. If you wonder whether "3 + 2 = 5," "f = ma," or "Caesar crossed the Rubicon in 49 B.C.E.," recognized standards can be used to determine the truth of these assertions.

Objective truths exist, then, but they are existentially indifferent. That is, they have no essential relationship to my existence. If I found out that one of them was false, I might be surprised, but I would not thereby become a different person. Therefore, Kierkegaard's philosophy is uninterested in objective truths.

Subjective thought, however, is thought for which there exist no objective criteria of truth. Subjective thought exists, for example, in the case of values, for instance, ethical and religious claims. If I tell you that it is immoral to cause unnecessary misery to others and if you challenge my assertion, ultimately there are no objective standards for me to appeal to and I cannot prove my claim. (Kantianism won't work, according to Kierkegaard, because it presupposes a valuing of notions of consistency and noncontradictoriness. But what if you refuse to accept that value?) Similarly, if I claim that "God is love" and you challenge me, I cannot appeal to any objective criterion of truth to justify my assertion.

Nevertheless, these subjective truths are essential to my existence in the way that objective truths are indifferent. We pretty much *are* what we do, and what we do—the actions we perform—is the result of *decisions*, which are embodiments of *values* chosen. Yet those values cannot be grounded in certainty but are always accepted on faith—a faith in the uncertain.

This need for values and decisiveness in the face of the uncertainty of all things provokes, according to Kierkegaard, a kind of dizziness and loss of footing that reveals the true human condition as one of anguish and despair. Hegel was wrong. The real is not the rational. Rather, the lived experience of true human reality lies underneath rationality as a kind of despairing nothingness longing to be a something. (Yet, had Hegel not said this too?)

There are other subjective truths besides those of moral and religious valuation. But these truths can

Vertigo in the Face of the Uncertainty of Reality

only be communicated indirectly, Kierkegaard told us. They can be hinted at, alluded to, overstated, understated, misstated, joked about, poeticized, or ignored. But they cannot be *said*—or at least, if they are said, they can't be directly understood. Such a truth would be the truth of "my death." Now, I know that all humans die and that, being a human, someday I *too* will die. I know much about death from the studies I have made in my history and biology classes. But that knowledge does not mean that I have grasped my death as a subjective truth. In the *Postscript*, Kierkegaard relates the story of a man who meets a friend on a street corner of Copenhagen and is invited to dinner by him. The invitee enthusiastically promises to attend, but at that very moment the prospective guest is struck and killed by a tile that happens to fall from the roof. Kierkegaard mocks the dead man, saying that one could laugh oneself to death over this case. Here is a person who makes an absolute commitment into the future, yet whose existence is whisked away by a gust of wind. After chuckling for a while over the irony of this story, Kierkegaard then asks himself if he is not being too harsh on the chap. Surely we don't expect the guest to respond to his invitation saying, "You can count

on me, I shall certainly come; but I must make an exception for the contingency that a tile happens to blow down from a roof, and kills me; for in that case I cannot come."[13] Yet the reader of the *Postscript* comes to the realization that that is exactly what Kierkegaard wanted. When we reach the understanding that after every utterance we make about the future, we can correctly add the rider: "However, I may be dead in the next moment, in which case I shall not attend," then we will have grasped the subjective truth of *our* death.

The point of Kierkegaard's story is not to provoke a sense of morbidity. According to him, the discovery of one's death as a subjective truth becomes the pretext for another discovery—that of "one's existence" as a subjective truth. Only against a backdrop of the yawning abyss of eternity can the immediacy and fragility of

The Individual before the Yawning Abyss of Eternity

existence be understood. Most people are oblivious to the proximity of nothingness, and they spend their lives engaged in petty thoughts and pointless projects. ("Do my socks have holes? What will people think of me if I wear a soiled tie?") But the discovery of our subjective truths concretizes and intensifies our existence. It helps us to order our priorities and clarify our values and to recover the self from its alienation into social roles, material possessions, and linguistic abstractions. It reveals (and at the same time creates) the self that had been invisible to the self.

For Kierkegaard, the self is essentially subjectivity, and subjectivity is constituted by the individual's commitment to his or her subjective truths. The authentic self, for Kierkegaard, is one that "chooses itself" by a form of self-reflective activity that both clarifies and creates values while assuming total responsibility for those values. It was this process that Hegel had left out of his system, according to Kierkegaard; or, more correctly, it was this process that any system would necessarily swallow up. Therefore, Kierkegaard was antisystematic and titled one of his books *Philosophical Fragments*, yet another slap in Hegel's face.

Kierkegaard saw as his task not the development of a new epistemology nor the creation of a new system of metaphysics, but the creation of a whole new kind of human being—people who could grasp their own freedom and create their own destiny. (In this task he was joined by two other wayward nineteenth-century thinkers at whom we have yet to look: Karl Marx and Friedrich Nietzsche.) Kierkegaard called his version of the new human being "a Knight of Faith." This person, for Kierkegaard, has an almost superhuman kind of strength and greatness. Kierkegaard wrote of the archetypal Knight of Faith,

> Not one shall be forgotten who was great in the world. But each was great in his own way . . . each became great in proportion to his expectation. One became great by expecting the possible, another by expecting the eternal, but he who expected the impossible became greater than all. Everyone shall be remembered but each was great in proportion to the greatness of that with which he strove. For he who

strove with the world became great by overcoming the world, and he who strove with himself became great by overcoming himself, but he who strove with God became greater than all.[14]

These knights have grasped the absurdity and contingency of all existence. David Hume had meditated on the disconnectedness of all things. But Hume had *only* meditated on it, whereas the Knights of Faith feel it in their bones. Yet they find the strength within themselves to unify their world, to hold it together with an act of will, which Kierkegaard called "faith." These knights are individuals who have looked profoundly into the world of humans and seen that at the deepest level we are alone. We are in "absolute isolation"—an aloneness that constitutes a kind of madness, or "divine madness,"

That Other "Knight of Faith"

for Kierkegaard's heroes are alone with their god. In fact, Kierkegaard's Knights of Faith, his "new humans," are not new at all. Rather, they are based on Kierkegaard's tortured interpretation of the biblical patriarch Abraham, who heard a voice in the night telling him to sacrifice his son. Abraham took full responsibility for the meaning of the message—it was *his* meaning, his subjective truth—and for his

actions, thereby becoming a Kierkegaardian hero. Kierkegaard wrote of him, "Abraham was greater than all, great by reason of his power whose strength is impotence, great by reason of his wisdom whose secret is foolishness, great by reason of his hope whose form is madness."[15] Hegel had transformed human existence into pure thought. Kierkegaard counteracted Hegel's rationalization by introducing into philosophy a new category, "the category of the absurd," and putting it in the heart of his ideal human being.

Marx

Of course, Søren Kierkegaard was not the only philosopher of his generation to be deeply influenced by Hegel. When Karl Marx (1818–1883) arrived as a young philosophy student at the University of Berlin in the mid-1830s, Hegel had been dead of cholera for five years, but his spirit still reigned supreme. To do philosophy in the Germany of the 1830s was to do Hegelian philosophy. Nevertheless, the Hegelians were by no means in agreement as to what "doing philosophy" truly consisted of. In fact, they had broken into two warring camps, the

Hegel's Spirit Reigns Supreme

The Manifest Content

The Latent Content

"Hegelian Left" and the "Hegelian Right." The Right gave the more orthodox reading of Hegel and was composed mostly of older, more conservative members of their generation. They were primarily interested in what Hegel had to say about religion and morality. The Left was composed of younger, more radical philosophers. They sometimes called themselves the "Young Hegelians." They were mostly interested in developing what they took to be still inchoate Hegelian notions about social and political issues. They believed that Hegel's ideas as he himself understood them were false but that there was a hidden truth in them that needed revealing. Their attitude toward Hegel's writing was very much like Freud's attitude toward dreams. There is a "manifest content" (the dream images) and a "latent content" (the true meaning of the dream, which can be discovered only by interpreting the manifest content). Sometimes the analysis of the imagery, like Freud's dream analysis, demonstrates that the meaning is the opposite of what it appears to be.

Needless to say, Marx fell under the influence of the Hegelian Left, not the Right. The foremost practitioner of the art of Hegelian Leftism was Ludwig Feuerbach (1804–1872), whose *Essence of Christianity* became holy scripture to a whole generation of progressive German youth.

Feuerbach's book, which was meant to be a kind of anthropological analysis of religion, contained an inversion of a key Hegelian idea. Hegel had asserted, "Man is God self-alienated." Feuerbach reversed this proposition, saying, "God is man self-alienated." That is, the idea of God is the perversion of the idea of man. Feuerbach believed that there were certain (Platonic) universal values to which all humans aspired. Every culture throughout history has longed for truth, beauty, justice, strength, and purity. It is part of the human essence to have these longings. But as historical peoples were frustrated in their attempts to achieve these ideals, the ideals themselves became alienated from the human and were projected onto an Ideal Being, a God who demanded that all be sacrificed to his glory. Feuerbach believed that as long as we humans continued to alienate our ideals into some nonhuman extraneous being, we would never be able to achieve the fullness of our own being. Hegel had caught only a glimpse of the truth.

Man *is* God, but we can only become the god that we are by an act of self-recovery that can be brought about exclusively by annulling our traditional concept of religion. For example, consider the Feuerbachian concept of the Holy Family.

According to Feuerbach, only by abolishing the image of the heavenly family can we bring peace, happiness, and love into the earthly family, because as long as we hold the image of the former before us, we will consider the earth merely a place of trial and punishment. Workers will attend church on Sunday, confess their sins, become resigned to misery as the human lot, and on the next payday return to the tavern to drink away their meager salaries.

This is the heavenly family. It is the idealization of the earthly family. Here peace, happiness, and love reign.

This is the earthly family. The frustrated father comes home drunk from the tavern where he has spent much of the pittance that is his weekly wage. He expends his rage terrorizing his wife and children.

Marx fell directly under Feuerbach's influence. As a young philosophy student, Marx wrote, "One cannot do philosophy without passing through the fiery brook." (In German, *Feuerbach* means "fiery brook.") But Marx soon became disenchanted with Feuerbach, and his own philosophy began with a critique of his old mentor. Feuerbach had prided himself on having escaped from Hegel's idealism, proclaiming himself a materialist. But Marx criticized Feuerbach as a crypto-idealist, that is, an idealist who believed himself to be a materialist. Marx pointed out the idealistic implications of Feuerbach's account of the heavenly family. According to it, we could bring about changes in the *material* configurations of the earthly family by changing the *idea* of the heavenly family. Marx, to the contrary, argued that all change must begin at the level of material configurations. In his "Theses on Feuerbach" he wrote, "Once the earthly family is discovered to be the secret of the holy family, the former must then itself be theoretically criticized and radically changed in practice."[16] Consistent with this attitude, Marx ended his tract against Feuerbach with the following famous line: "The philosophers have only *interpreted* the world in various ways: the point however is to *change* it."[17] Marx believed that once the family was revolutionized (i.e., once its hierarchy of power was restructured, along with the hierarchy of power in the society of which the family was the mirror image), then the idea of the holy family would simply disappear. Religion would not need to be abolished; it would simply dissolve. This disappearance would occur because, contrary to what Feuerbach believed, religion is not the *cause* of alienation; it is, rather, a *symptom* of alienation and sometimes even a remonstration against it. Marx's statement that religion is the opiate of the masses is often taken out of context and misunderstood. What he actually said is this: "*Religious distress is at the same time the expression of real distress and the protest against real distress.*

The Disappearance of the Heavenly Family

Religion is the sigh of the oppressed creature, the heart of a heartless world, just as it is the spirit of an unspiritual situation. It is the opium of the people."[18] Here the word "opium" refers to the drug's power to dull pain.

Like Feuerbach and Hegel before him, Marx was interested in analyzing **alienation** (the process of the subject being split from its natural object). Although Marx discussed alienation in a number of its manifestations (alienation from nature, social alienation, and self-alienation), he was most philosophically original perhaps in his account of "the alienation of labor." Marx believed that it was the nature of human beings to be producers. We create of necessity, Marx thought. He preferred the designation *homo faber* (man the maker) to *homo sapiens* (man the knower) because our *knowing* is dependent on our *doing*. According to Marx, to a great extent we are what we make. We create our products and our products re-create us. Our minds begin to take on the features of the objects we create. If we create in piecemeal, fragmented ways, we become piecemeal

You Are What You Make

and fragmented ourselves. If we create useless objects, we ourselves become useless human beings.[19] Unfortunately, the processes of production are influenced by historical forces that are not always in our control. When these forces, usually socio-politico-economic ones, drive a wedge between individual humans and their products, the result is "alienated labor." This alienation happens if the work a person performs is not the expression of a natural creative need but is motivated by the necessity of fulfilling other needs, such as economic or avaricious ones. Further alienation occurs if the product that a worker creates is for the profit of another person and if the product enters into an economic system meant to fulfill desires of greed rather than true human needs. And above all, alienated labor comes about if the worker's product returns to the worker as a disabling alien force. (Extreme case: The worker produces cigarettes, which give that worker lung cancer.) It will come as no surprise to you to hear that, according to Marx, of all the historical socioeconomic systems, with the exception of slavery, capitalism is the one that promotes the most intense

The Worker Confronts Himself as an Alien

forms of alienated labor. Alienated labor, in turn, produces self-alienation—workers confront themselves as strangers and as strangers to the human race. (This is Marx's version of Hegel's divine identity crisis.) The goal of the young Karl Marx's communism was to create a society in which all alienation would be overcome and in which humans would recover their lost essence as *homo faber*.

In converting Hegel's idealism into a form of materialism (thereby "standing Hegel on his head"), Marx created a philosophy unique in history. We have run across materialists before, of course; Democritus and Hobbes were such. But each of them, in claiming that ultimately everything resolves into matter, chose to define the key category in terms of physics. Their material reality was simply mass in motion. But Marx chose his key category not from physics but from economics. He did not try to explain the whole of reality but only human reality. Marx used an analytic model involving a foundation and a super-structure. According to him, the foundations of the social world are material ones: natural resources, means of production, and means of distribution, as well as the human work relations involved at this level. Built on this foundation is a

Marx Stands Hegel on His Head

level composed of certain other social relations, such as legal and political arrangements, and above this is yet another level, comprising

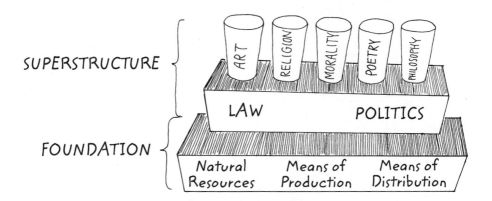

"higher culture," such social features as art, religion, morality, poetry, and philosophy. According to Marx,

> In the social production of their life, men enter into definite relations that are indispensable and independent of their will, relations of production which correspond to a definite stage of development of their material productive forces. The sum total of these relations of production constitutes the economic structure of society, the real foundation, on which rises a legal and political superstructure and to which correspond definite forms of social consciousness. The mode of production of material life conditions the social, political,

and intellectual life process in general. It is not the consciousness of men that determines their social being, but, on the contrary, their social being that determines their consciousness.[20]

In this and similar passages, Marx made the relationship between the foundation and the superstructure seem simple. Higher culture, or what he called the "ideological" sphere, was merely a "reflex" or a "sublimate" of the socioeconomic foundation. Later he modified this, admitting that the ideational superstructure and the material foundation mutually influenced each other, though ultimately the foundation dominated. The ideational features of society never ceased to be **ideology,** that is, a system of unconscious propaganda for the foundational economic structure in which the contradictions

Portrait of Louis XIV
(after Hyacinthe Rigaud)

Laws Establishing
Aristocratic Privilege
(e.g., antipoaching laws)

Property Ownership
by the Nobility

Art as Ideology

in that structure are disguised or denied. Therefore, to find out the true status of the symbols in a society, you simply ask, "Who owns the foundation?" Find out who controls the natural resources, the means of production, and the means of distribution (the raw materials, the factories, the trucking lines, and the distribution outlets), and you will discover the secret behind the laws, the politics, the science, the art, the morality, and the religion of any society. As the old saw has it, "He who pays the piper calls the tune." Marx's version is, "The ruling ideas of each age have ever been the ideas of its ruling class."[21]

Add to Marx's materialistic model of foundation and superstructure his dialectical interpretation of the foundation. The possession of a society's material wealth by a specific group of people automatically creates a class system—basically, the owning class (the "haves") and the class controlled by the owning class (the "have nots"). Since the interests of these two classes are always in opposition, these classes must be in perpetual conflict. In the first line of *The Communist Manifesto*, Marx announced, "The history of all

ARTISTIC, MORAL, RELIGIOUS AND PHILOSOPHICAL FORCES PROPAGANDIZING FOR BOURGEOIS PRIVILEGE

ARTISTIC, MORAL, RELIGIOUS AND PHILOSOPHICAL FORCES UNDERMINING BOURGEOIS PRIVILEGE

CULTURE

LEGAL AND POLITICAL FORCES ATTEMPTING TO SOLIDIFY BOURGEOIS DOMINATION

LEGAL AND POLITICAL FORCES OPPOSING BOURGEOIS DOMINATION

LAW   POLITICS

CAPITAL FORCE ATTEMPTING TO DEFEND BOURGEOIS OWNERSHIP SYSTEM

WORKING FORCE ATTEMPTING TO OVERTURN BOURGEOIS OWNERSHIP SYSTEM

NATURAL RESOURCES   MEANS OF PRODUCTION   MEANS OF DISTRIBUTION hitherto existing society is the history of class struggle."[22] This conflict, which began in prehistoric times with the creation of tools, had, in Marx's time, reached what he took to be its most clearly delineated stage, and, indeed, according to him, it had reached its final stage, a struggle between the owning class of capitalism (the bourgeoisie) and the working class that capitalism exploited (the proletariat). Marx spent the bulk of his mature years describing the structure of capitalism in all its internal contradictions (memories of the Hegelian dialectic!). Here are some examples: capitalism's emphasis on competition leads to its own opposite, monopoly—and the consequent expulsion of some former members of the economic elite into the ranks of the paupers; capitalism's constant need for new

As per Karl Marx's Prediction, Capitalism Collapses in the Middle Because of Its Own Excesses

sources of raw materials, cheap labor, and dumping grounds for its products leads to imperialistic wars among capitalist states; capitalism's need to solve the problem of unemployment, achieved by pumping more money into the system, thereby creates inflation, and its need to solve the problem of inflation is achieved by increasing unemployment. Marx thought that these internal contradictions of capitalism, along with the massive unrest that would be caused by the ever-growing misery of its dispossessed, would necessarily bring on a simultaneous internal collapse of capitalism and a revolt of the working class that would produce Marx's notorious "dictatorship of the proletariat," whose function it would be to ensure that the victorious proletariat did not reconstitute the institutions of classism. (After all, these conquering street fighters themselves grew up in conditions of alienation and hence in "**false consciousness.**")[23] According to Marx, once this dictatorship has performed its essential service, it will simply step down from power—"wither," as Marx worded it. Marx's critics are quick to point out that he did not deal with the question of the abuse of power in his socialistic utopia. Perhaps this neglect was due to the philosophical optimism he inherited from Hegel. (Unfortunately, as the Stalinist period in the Soviet Union proved, Lord Acton's pessimism was more realistic than Marx's optimism. It was Acton who said, "Power corrupts, and absolute power corrupts absolutely.") This relinquishing of control by the dictatorship, predicted Marx, will usher in a classless society, which will end the dialectic of conflict and therefore end history as we know it. (Marx defined history, after all, as "the history of class conflict.") Humans will live under optimum conditions for the first time since aboriginal times. Private ownership will be abolished, as well as the division of labor (i.e., the type of spe-

cialization where a person is defined throughout life by the practice of one speciality). We will all be artists and philosophers, and we will "hunt in the morning, fish in the afternoon, rear cattle in the evening, criticize [poetry] after dinner, just as [we] have in mind, without ever becoming hunter, fisherman, shepherd or critic."[24] Elsewhere Marx's picture of the ideal world includes socializing in the pub, going to dances, going to the theater, buying books, loving, theorizing, painting, singing, and even fencing. (Fencing?) Sometimes Marx's true communist society seems more like a bourgeois pastoral than a working-class paradise; and sometimes, as was the case with Kierkegaard's "new human being," Marx's "new human being" seems to be a very "old human being," though one not from the historical past but from the mythical Golden Age.

The New Golden Age?

Nietzsche

Friedrich Nietzsche (1844—1900) was the third post-Kantian who responded to the crisis of his time not by demanding a new "critique of reason" but by calling for a new kind of human existence. (The other two, as we have seen, were Kierkegaard and Marx.) Nietzsche was a solitary thinker who liked Alpine trails more than the halls of academia (which he abandoned in his mid-thirties). He spent most of his life using his authorship in an attempt to triumph over the powerful influences on his childhood: Lutheranism, German nationalism, and the domination of his forceful mother, granny, aunts, and sister. (His attempts were more successful in some of these endeavors than in others.) The material result of his efforts was an unprecedented stream of the most eccentric books ever to have been introduced into the history of philosophy, including such titles as *The Birth of Tragedy, Beyond Good and Evil, The Genealogy of Morals, Thus Spake*

Friedrich Nietzsche

Zarathustra, and his outrageous intellectual autobiography, pretentiously titled *Ecce Homo* ("behold the man"—the phrase with which Pilate introduced Jesus to the masses), with such chapter headings as "Why I Am So Wise," "Why I Am So Clever," and "Why I Write Such Good Books." Nietzsche's short, prolific authorship ended in 1888 with the onset of syphilis-induced insanity.

Nietzsche's epistemological theory constituted a radical return to the sophistic period. His theory is usually called perspectivism, and it derived from Nietzsche's early training in **philology.** Philologists, those students of ancient languages, knew that what were called the Bible, the Vedas, the Upanishads, and the *Iliad* were not direct translations of single existing documents; rather, they were compilations of fragments of conflicting evidence derived from a dizzying number of sources. The dream of the philologists was to find *the* original texts of each of the great scriptures in history. Nietzsche's conclusion as a philologist was that *there is no original text*. Each of these books is simply the result of a *decision* to let a particular interpretation represent an end product, even though, in fact, that "end product" is merely an emblem of a relationship that exists among a number of fragmentary documents, reports, historical studies, and items of gossip.

There is no original text.

Nietzsche translated his philological insight into an ontological and epistemological doctrine. Just as in philology there is no original text, so in reality and knowledge there is no "pure being" nor "original datum." There are no gods, no

Platonic Forms, no substances, no "things-in-themselves," or even any "things." There exist only flux and chaos, upon which we must impose our will. Therefore, said Nietzsche, there can be no such thing as *knowing* in the Platonic sense. All "knowing" is inventing, and all inventing is lying. But then, there are lies, and there are *lies*. Inauthentic lying is *self-deception*. According to Nietzsche, self-deceivers are people who "lie traditionally," that is, who lie in terms of established traditions.

Nietzsche's recommendation in the face of what appears to be a condemnation to a life of lying is to "lie creatively," which is to say to invent, or "know," creatively. To lie creatively is to express what Nietzsche, borrowing and subverting a Schopenhauerian idea, calls "will to power." To express will to power is to force reality to submit to one's own creative might. Nietzsche also calls will to power "the urge to freedom." All our biological instincts expend themselves as manifestations of this desire for freedom, even though in most cases these instincts have been constrained by the forces of normalization (themselves other manifestations of will to power, or manifestations of the will to power of others).

Not only our biology but also our thought and language are manifestations of will to power. But at the same time, language and thought are the main vehicles of self-

Forcing Reality to Bend to One's Will

deception. According to Nietzsche's radical *nominalism* (reminiscent of William of Ockham's nominalism), language functions precisely by lying, that is, by denying real dissimilarities and inventing fictitious similarities. For example, the only way we can classify as "leaves" all the forms of foliage that sprout from trees and shrubs is by ignoring and, indeed, suppressing the fact that no two of these entities are alike and by asserting an identity among them that does not, in fact, exist. So language can be and usually is a medium of **reification** and petrification of being. It produces errors that "tyrannize over us as a

condition of life."[25] But the fact that language *must* lie is also the source of the creative possibilities inherent in language. Nietzsche rejected the traditional view of language, namely, that its poetic

function is peripheral to its literal function. He felt that the so-called literal function was merely a subclass of its poetic nature. Language, according to Nietzsche, is "a mobile army of metaphors, metonyms and anthropomorphisms."[26] (Reminder: A metaphor is a form of speech in which one image replaces another, importing the new meaning into the old context, such as "Achilles is a lion in battle." A metonym is a form of speech in which meaning is displaced from one image onto an adjacent image that now bears the weight of both images, such as "He likes the bottle too much." **Anthropomorphisms**—the projections of human traits onto the nonhuman

Language: A Mobile Army of Metaphors,
Metonyms, and Anthropomorphisms

world, such as "The rose is striving to reach the light"—are themselves usually unconscious metaphors or metonyms.) Whole chains of metaphors and metonyms can create a poetic rendition of reality. Nietzsche recognized these chains of reasoning as felicitous expressions of will to power.

In fact, as Nietzsche understood full well, his own term "will to power" was the product of such a metaphorical/ metonymical chain of reasoning, as were his other key terms, such as "the overman," "eternal recurrence," and "the death of God." It follows, then, that a claim of Nietzsche's—such as "life simply *is* will to power"[27]—constitutes not a philosophical insight into the ultimate nature of life but simply another poetic interpretation of life. (When confronted with this charge, Nietzsche responded, "Well, so much the better!")[28]

If it is true that there are only interpretations, are all interpretations equally valid? Despite his relativism, Nietzsche did not think so. Only those lies that affirm life are truly *noble* lies for him. All other lies are nihilistic and on the side of death. This belief is why Nietzsche says will to power must be full of laughter, dancing, and affirmation and why we must condemn Platonism ("that fear of time") and Christianity ("Platonism for the people"),[29] which in longing for another world deny reality as it is (i.e., they refuse to recognize reality as chaos and flux that must be molded in the image of each will), and thereby long not for being but for nothingness and death. (One detects Hegel in all this, somehow.) Nietzsche embodied his doctrine in a *goal* that he called "the overman" (*der Übermensch*). The overman represents the triumph of the will to power. Besides teaching laughter and dance, the overman teaches the death of God and eternal recurrence. Of course, there can be no single correct answer to the question, What did Nietzsche mean by "the death of God"? (any more than there can be to the question concerning what Prufrock meant when he said, "I should have been a pair of ragged claws scuttling across the floors of silent seas"), but surely Nietzsche at least meant to announce the end of traditional

Der Übermensch?

forms of authority: historical, political, religious, moral, and textual. (For an interesting reading of Nietzsche's phrase "God is dead," try replacing the term "God" with the term "Santa Claus." Why is the claim "Santa Claus does not exist" less tragic than the claim "Santa Claus is dead"?)

What is true of the death of God is true of eternal recurrence. There has been a great river of literature trying to interpret this enigmatic doctrine. But whatever else it means, it was certainly meant to

The Death of Santa Claus

assert Nietzsche's allegiance to reality as it is. Nietzsche advocated what he took to be the opposite of the Schopenhauerian ideal of pessimism, namely,

> the ideal of the most high-spirited, alive and world-affirming human being who has not only come to terms and learned to get along with whatever was and is, but who wants to have *what was and is* repeated into all eternity.[30]

> Let us think this thought in its most terrible form: existence as it is, without meaning or aim, yet recurring inevitably without any finale of nothingness: *the eternal recurrence.*[31]

It is easy enough to criticize Nietzsche for his inconsistency and faulty logic. (How can we will life as it really is if there is no such thing as life or will—only interpretations of interpretations? If everything is a lie, then isn't the claim that everything is a lie also a lie?) But this criticism misses Nietzsche's point. He meant to teach neither

The Thought in Its Most Terrible Form:
The Eternal Recurrence

consistency nor logic but a radically new kind of subversive subjectivity that would undermine all previous forms of thought and being. However, there is a price to pay for such subversiveness. One will have disciples that one might not have hoped for. And, indeed, many diverse groups have claimed the Nietzschean heritage, including Nazis, psychoanalysts, existentialists, and, currently, a group called "deconstructionists," whom some people see as the new liberators and others as the new nihilists.

Utilitarianism

Let us leave the extravagant frenzy of Nietzsche's (ultimately) deranged mind and turn to the orderly and complacent minds of his contemporaries in the British Isles (whom Nietzsche dismissed as "blockheads"). Despite Hume's facetious suggestion that philosophy be abandoned altogether, a philosophical empiricism was alive and thriving in mid-nineteenth-century Britain. It derived from a side of Hume's thought that was not explored in this book and that is difficult to square with his radical skepticism.

Despite his denial of the possibility of true knowledge concerning causality, self, and the external world, Hume held that what is commonly taken as "knowledge" in these areas is really a set of reasonable beliefs that are well founded because they are based on experience. The tradition deriving from this more practical side of Hume was inherited by a group of philosophers known as the utilitarians,

Nietzsche's View of a Meeting of the Utilitarian Society

headed by Jeremy Bentham (1748–1832) and his wayward follower John Stuart Mill (1808–1873), who were interested in applying the principles of empiricism to moral and social issues.

Bentham

The eccentric Jeremy Bentham (whose fully dressed, mummified body still presides over the trustees' meetings at University College in London because his fortune was left to them with the provision that he be able to attend all their meetings) concluded that all theory, including moral and political theory, must be grounded in empirical fact. He claimed that in the case of the human sciences this fact would have to be the primacy of the pleasure principle. That is to say, all analyses of human behavior and all recommendations for change in behavior would have to begin with the fact that humans are motivated by the desire for pleasure and by the aversion to pain. In this way of thinking, of course, he was not unlike Hobbes, though Bentham's conclusions were much more liberal.

**John Stuart Mill with the
Mummified Head of Jeremy Bentham**

The doctrine that only pleasure can (or should) have value is known as hedonism, and we have seen this philosophy before, not just with Hobbes but also with Epicurus and Callicles. Bentham's innovation was the claim that hedonism doesn't have to be egoistic; it can be social. That is, one can (and should) be motivated to act in the name of the pleasure of others as well as for one's own pleasure. His social hedonism is reflected in his most famous maxim, "It is the greatest happiness of the greatest number that is the measure of right and wrong"[32] (where "happiness" is defined in terms of pleasure). This principle, in association with the "one person, one vote" principle (i.e., each person gets to define his or her version of happiness), gave Bentham's utilitarianism a distinctly democratic cast. Furthermore, it meant that the moral worth of an act depended exclusively on the amount of happiness or unhappiness that the act promoted. This view is sometimes called consequentialism (because it is the consequence of the act that determines the act's value), and it is the opposite extreme from Kant's moral perspective, according to which the moral worth of an action depended on the *intention* of the agent, on whether the act was motivated by a desire to do one's duty, and on whether the act was consistent with the laws of rationality.

Kant and Bentham between them have provided us with the two key moral models used in Western ethics. Unfortunately, the conclusions drawn from these two models sometimes contradict each other, and, when applied to specific cases, sometimes the utilitarian view seems much more reasonable than the Kantian one; yet in other cases, the Kantian view seems better than the utilitarian one. For instance, the Kantian ethic tells us we are duty-bound never to lie. But what if an armed man, frothing at the mouth, asks us where Bill Jones is? Do we have a duty to tell the truth, knowing full well that doing so may lead to Jones's death? Here Bentham's principle seems better: The act of lying is not immoral if by lying we can prevent grievous harm. But consider another famous example: What if you pay a visit to a friend in the hospital, and a utilitarian physician decides to sacrifice you and distribute your vital organs to five patients who will die if they do not receive immediate organ implants? The doctor is acting on the "greatest amount of happiness for the greatest number of people" principle and maybe even on the "one person, one vote" principle. But most of us probably feel that Kant would be right to call this sacrifice immoral.

As we saw, Bentham believed that happiness could be defined in terms of pleasure, and he held that the study of pleasure could be refined to a science. Pleasures could be experienced in terms of seven categories. These categories could be articulated in terms of a set of seven questions:

1. Intensity (How intense is the pleasure?)
2. Duration (How long does the pleasure last?)
3. Certainty (How sure is the pleasure?)
4. Proximity (How soon will the pleasure be experienced?)
5. Fecundity (How many more pleasures will follow in the train of this pleasure?)
6. Purity (How free from pain is the pleasure?)
7. Extent (How many people will experience the pleasure? [It is this category that makes Bentham's hedonism a social one.])

On a scale of one to ten, this is about a ten in all categories.

When considering any act whatsoever, one should analyze it in terms of the pleasure it will produce in these seven categories, which Bentham called "the calculus of felicity."

He thought that after some practice one could learn to apply this calculus rather intuitively, but until that point, one should actually work out the figures as often as possible. (Indeed, the story goes that Bentham himself used the calculus of felicity in choosing between remaining a bachelor or marrying. [He married!]) Try out the calculus on a decision such as that between studying for a chemistry midterm exam and going to the beach with some friends. Obviously, the beach party will be strong in some categories (1, 3, 4, 6), and weaker in others (2, 5). Studying will be weak in most categories but strong in a few (2 and 5, and 7 also, if other persons have an

Beach Guilt

interest in your succeeding in college). Are the assets of studying strong enough to overcome its deficits, in the face of the fun enticing you to the beach? (Of course, the guilt you would experience at the beach has to be taken into consideration too.) According to the "one person, one vote" principle, each person must decide for himself or herself.

Mill

John Stuart Mill, who was raised in strict adherence to Benthamite tenets, developed certain qualms about those views after suffering a nervous breakdown at twenty-one years of age. Among other concerns, he was worried about the beach/chemistry–type decision, or perhaps more about the six-pack of beer/ Shakespearean sonnet–type decision. If the average person were given the choice between reading a Renaissance poem and guzzling beer while watching the 49ers on the tube . . . well, you can't force people to read poetry or watch football if they don't think it's fun. But in a democracy, under the "one person, one vote" principle, what if you gave people a choice of making public expenditures for the teaching of Shakespeare in universities or receiving a tax rebate? Mill feared the worst

and thought it bode ill for the advancement of civilization. If we let ourselves be guided by the calculus of felicity, perhaps the pig would prove to be right; wallowing in the mud might rank higher than studying philosophy.

Mill solved the problem by saying that only those who are competent judges of *both* of two competing experiences can "vote" for one or the other of them. (You get a vote only if you know beer *and* Shakespeare or have wallowed *and* read Plato.) Mill's conclusion was that "some kinds of pleasure are more desirable and more valuable than others."[33] We assume that he had in mind the reading of Shakespeare and Plato.

Mill claimed that in abandoning the calculus of felicity, he was simply defining pleasure in qualitative and not merely quantitative terms. His critics charge, however, that in asserting that some pleasures are better than others, Mill had abandoned the "principle of utility" (i.e., the pleasure principle) altogether. They have also charged him with elitism and with undermining the democratic foundation that Bentham had given utilitarianism. For what it's worth, Mill's doctrine did leave us some questions to ponder: In a democracy, must the "one person, one vote" principle apply at all levels of decision making? And if so, are democracy and higher culture compatible?

In his most famous book, *On Liberty*, Mill outlined his doctrine of *laissez-faire* (hands off!). There are certain spheres where the government has no business interfering in the lives of its citizens. Mill's principle of liberty states, "the only purpose for which power can be rightfully exercised over any member of a civilized community, against his will, is to prevent harm to others."[34] In other words, Mill was against state paternalism, the condition in which the state tells a citizen what to do for his or her own good. For Mill, there could be no such thing as a victimless crime. If a man decides to ride his Harley without a helmet, get bombed on cheap wine or drugs in the privacy of his own house, visit a prostitute, or even *become* a prostitute, that's his own business and not the state's.

For moral reasons, we should perhaps try to persuade this man of the error of his ways, but we have no business passing laws to protect him from himself as long as he is doing no harm to others. (Contemporary commentators point out that it was probably easier

**A Drunken Male Prostitute without a Helmet
Riding His Motorcycle in the Privacy of His Own Home**

to draw this distinction in Mill's day than in our own. In today's world, very few acts are purely private. If you go to a hospital because of a motorcycle injury, my tax dollars may well have to nurse you back to health.)

Mill also believed in the hands-off doctrine in the marketplace. He said, "*Laissez-faire . . . should be the general practice: every departure from it, unless required by some great good, is a certain evil.*"[35] He thought that under most conditions, the government should not interfere in the exchange of commodities, that the law of supply and demand should determine the nature and quality of production.

Even though Mill was considered a liberal in his own day, in many ways his views sound to us more like those that today we associate with political conservatism. But the proof that he was not a pure supply-side theorist can be seen in the restrictions he placed on the laissez-faire doctrine. He excluded from the application of his hands-off policy any products that the buyer is not competent to

"The Uncultivated Cannot Be
Competent Judges of Cultivation"

judge and any product "in the quality of which society has much at stake." Mill said,

> There are . . . things of the worth of which the demand of the market is by no means a test, things . . . the want of which is least felt where the need is greatest. This is peculiarly true of those things which are chiefly useful as tending to raise the character of human beings. The uncultivated cannot be competent judges of cultivation.[36]

Frege

The city of Jena in central Germany had been the site of Napoleon's decisive defeat of the Prussian forces in 1806. It was then and there that G. W. F. Hegel hastily finished his metaphysical masterpiece, The Phenomenology of Mind, as Napoleon's cannon fire blasted the city walls. We began our overview of nineteenth-century philosophy in Jena, and we now return there, seventy years later, to complete it. In Jena we encounter Hegel's countryman Gottlob Frege (1848–1925), but Frege's work is in every way the opposite of Hegel's—and, indeed, is radically different from that of everyone presented in this chapter, which treats a period that has been called "the wild years of philosophy."[37] Frege toiled in relative obscurity at his office in the mathematics department of the University of Jena attempting to solve problems concerning the foundations of arithmetic that seemed at the time to have very little to do with philosophy. But his efforts to support his mathematical hypotheses led him to develop a general theory of meaning that would eventually have a major impact on the history of philosophy. He died without realizing that his accomplishments would come to be seen as the initial steps in what is now called **analytic philosophy** and that he would be looked back on as a pioneer. Frege directed philosophy toward new themes and new techniques that would come to dominate British and American philosophy throughout the twentieth century and that would have a large impact on the Continent as well.

I am the sole member of the set of all authors of the Begriffschrift. The set also includes Gottlob Frege and my mother's eldest son. How is that possible?

"Analytic philosophy" may appear to be the name of a kind of philosophy, but in fact many of its practitioners have argued that it is the only kind of legitimate philosophy left to pursue. Analytic philosophy began as a disgusted response to the speculative philosophy that had dominated the nineteenth century. The outrageous metaphysical schemes that had proliferated on the Continent were seen to be like a dense jungle whose covering was so thick that it allowed no light to penetrate into the damp and steamy atmosphere that it generated. To cut through this kind of metaphysical speculation, these philosophers developed and honed certain tools of logical, linguistic, and conceptual analysis that would allow them to reveal the massive abuses of language that these metaphysicians employed to camouflage the confusion that they passed off as theories. The founders of analytic philosophy, including Frege, were interested in defending against the idealism of the metaphysicians a kind of **realism**—the view that there is a real physical world "out there" and that this world is correctly grasped either by common sense and ordinary language or by scientific investigation. Many analytic philosophers eventually abandoned the task of generating philosophical theories at all and came to think that philosophy's job was quite simply the analysis of meaning. Some analytic philosophers have held that the key task is the conceptual analysis of philosophically puzzling features of natural languages, that is, the analysis of the meaning of concepts employed in everyday discourse—concepts like "mind," "body," "perception," "ought," "art," and "justice." Others have seen the main task as the analysis of an artificial logical language that can be detected as a hidden structure behind natural languages, that is, the analysis of categories like "number," "equivalence," "inference," "disjunction," "necessity," and "contingency." A group of philosophers related to the previous one sees the philosopher's job as the logical analysis of the key concepts of science, ideas like "causality," "probability," and "natural law." Despite their differences, all analytic philosophers owe a debt to Frege, partly because two of the most famous analytic philosophers—Bertrand Russell and Ludwig Wittgenstein—read his work with great interest, discussed his ideas with him, and were influenced by his theories.

For Frege, questions about meaning were ultimately related to questions about *logic*. Our best philosophical arguments about any topic whatsoever are only as good as the logic that structures them. We can say that modern logic began in 1879 with the publication of Frege's *Begriffschrift*.[38] This book lays out the first extensive discussion of the ideas of existence and generality in logic—the relation between propositions asserting, "There exists at least one X where X is Y," and those stating, "All X is Y." This apparently simple notion had been completely missing from Aristotle's logic, which had dominated philosophy from his time until the eighteenth century, when Leibniz had made significant contributions. (In fact, Leibniz had stuck most of his papers on logic in a desk drawer, and they saw the light of day only in the twentieth century. Much of the actual notation in contemporary symbolic logic derives from Leibniz's scribblings, but much of it also comes from Frege.)

Frege's next book, *The Foundations of Arithmetic* (1884), addresses the need for a theory proving that arithmetic is internally self-consistent (a "consistency proof"). Frege tries to show that an extension of the basic principles of logic generates all the fundamental notions of arithmetic and that therefore the consistency of arithmetic can be proved from purely logical considerations. A successful definition of "number," for example, could be derived from the principle of identity, that is, $A = A$. This finding means, in fact, that arithmetic can be reduced to logic (yet another step in the history of reductionism that commenced with the pre-Socratics). If arithmetic derives from logic, then it has a purely analytic a priori status. This thesis, if true, eliminates Plato's and Descartes's claim that mathematics is grounded in innate ideas, and it gets rid of Kant's mathematical synthetic a priori category. (You may want to review all these terms in the Glossary.) But it also replaces the unconvincing thesis of empiricists like Mill, who asserted that mathematical truths are empirical generalizations. ("Well, whenever in the past we have put two things together with three things, we've ended up with a total of five things, so we will hazard that "$2 + 3 = 5$" is true, or at least

"I don't get it! Every time I count them, I come up with a different number"

John Stuart Mill Inspects His Rabbit Collection

highly probable. Still, it's not certain. Nobody knows for sure that we won't get six things next time!")

As good as Frege's discovery appears, in 1903 the young Bertrand Russell (whom we will study in the next chapter) found a contradiction in the **set theory** around which Frege had constructed his proof. Russell's letter to Frege announcing the contradiction arrived just as the second volume of Frege's *Foundations* was about to be published. A horrified Frege hastily added some new material as damage control, but he was never satisfied with his inability to dispose of the contradiction completely. Much of the last twenty years of his life were unproductive, and he apparently suffered long bouts of depression during this period. He eventually came to the conclusion that the whole project of trying to derive arithmetic from logic was erroneous, and his last ideas on the subject drifted back toward Kant's synthetic a priori grounding of mathematics. Most of the logicians who were influenced by Frege's work chose not to follow him in that direction. They believed that his first theory was on the right track and that, despite his failure to resolve all the problems in the theory, his accomplishment was brilliant enough to establish him as the first true philosopher of mathematics.

Furthermore, philosophers were impressed with the general theory of meaning that Frege had developed to support his mathematical theories. A main feature of the *Foundations* was its attack on "psychologism" in theories of meaning. According to that prevalent form of theorizing, the meaning of a word must be closely related to the images that the word provokes in the minds of the speaker and the audience. According to Frege, the mental events aroused by words have nothing to do with a word's meaning. The meaning of a word is determined by the role the word plays in establishing the *truth conditions* of sentences in which the word appears. For example, consider these sentences:

> A quadrilateral figure with equal sides and at least one right angle is a square.
> The walls of Fort Apache were built in the form of a square.
> Circles are square.
> The base of the Mayan pyramids was a square.
> The earth is square.
> In Kansas, basketball is played with a square ball.

Frege does not care what images these sentences conjure up in your mind. He is interested in the conditions that would have to exist to establish the truth or falsity of any of these sentences. These conditions are what determine the meaning of the word "square."

Versions of this thesis are accepted today by most philosophers who dedicate themselves to the problem of meaning. They

Oh no! Not again!

THUNK

look back at Frege's formulation as the first pronouncement of an analytic device that must be present in any successful theory explaining how mere noises (words) can take on meaning.

A related feature of Frege's theory that is repeated in one version or another in many contemporary discussions of the topic of meaning is a distinction he drew between *Sinn* and *Bedeutung*, usually translated as "sense" and "reference." These terms are meant to be applied to the analysis of **proper names.** (If you are unfamiliar with this phrase, check it out in the Glossary.) The older view about these terms was that their meaning was exhausted in the function of naming, or referring to, or pointing at, the object that they named. For example, the meaning of the name "George Washington" would be the actual person named. The words simply stand for him and have no meaning other than the function of designation. But Frege points out a major difficulty with this commonsense account. Take three proper names: (A) the morning star; (B) the evening star; and (C) Venus. (A) refers to a heavenly body appearing in the east immediately before sunrise, used for centuries by sailors to navigate the morning seas. (B) refers to a heavenly body appearing in the west immediately after sunset, used for centuries by sailors to navigate the evening seas. (C) refers to the most brilliant planet in the solar system, second in order to the sun. Now, it was an empirical discovery that (A) = (B) = (C), that is, that the so-called morning star and the so-called evening star are in fact the same body and, furthermore, that that body is the planet Venus. Now, suppose that the meaning of a proper name is simply the object named; call that object "X." In that case, the sentence "The morning star is the evening star, which in fact is the planet Venus" means "X = X, which in fact = X." In other words, the sentence is a tautology that conveys no information at all. Yet, clearly the sentence in question *does* convey information. Anyone who knows it to be true knows *more* than did the ancient mariners. Therefore, concluded Frege, there must be a third element to meaning in these cases in addition to the *name* and

**The Rime of the Ancient Mariner
(A Collaborative Work of Art by Praxiteles,
Coleridge, Palmer, and an Anonymous
Author of Annoying Kiddie-Jingles)**

the *object named*, and he called that third element *Sinn* (pronounced
"zinn" in German), or sense. The sense in each case "sheds a different light" on the object referred to. It is a "mode of presentation" of
the object—a way of representing it.

Frege's theory has not satisfied all the analytic philosophers
that descended from Frege, but it pointed out an important problem
with which any serious theory of meaning must deal. Furthermore, it
set the tone for the whole school of analytic philosophy that now
reveres Frege as a founding father.

Topics for Consideration

1. Hegel's philosophy is teleological. History is revealed as progressive, directed toward a goal. Explain how progress takes place in his system, and why, according to Hegel, that advancement may appear to us to be backsliding.

2. Use Hegel's master/slave dynamics to explain relations in traditional society between husband and wife, parent and child, teacher and student, and employer and employee.

3. Discuss those features of Schopenhauer's philosophy that are in agreement with Kant, and those that are in disagreement.

4. Discuss Kierkegaard's notion of subjective truths, and say why they can be communicated only indirectly.

5. Compare and contrast Hegel, Feuerbach, and Marx on the idea of alienation.

6. Pick an example of a work of art that you think would support Marx's claim that most art is ideological.

7. Explain what you think Nietzsche means when he recommends that we lie creatively.

8. It has been said that Kierkegaard, Marx, and Nietzsche did not demand a new critique of reason; rather, they demanded a whole new kind of human. Explain what it means to say this.

9. After reviewing Kant's discussion of the categorical imperative (pp. 215–18), contrast Kant's moral idea with Bentham's greatest happiness principle; What, would you say, is the strongest and weakest point of each moral system?

10. Do you think Mill contradicts himself when he says both that pleasure is the ultimate criterion of value and that some pleasures are more valuable than others? Defend or attack his view.

11. Using examples other than those in the text, explain why Frege believes that the meaning of proper names must involve more than simple denotation (that is, more than reference to the object named).

Notes

1. See, for example, Karl Popper, *The Open Society and Its Enemies*, vol. 2, *Hegel and Marx* (Princeton, N.J.: Princeton University Press, 1966).

2. See, for example, Alexandre Kojève, *Introduction to the Reading of Hegel: Lectures on the "Phenomenology of Spirit,"* trans. James H. Nichols Jr. (Ithaca, N.Y., and London: Cornell University Press, 1993).

3. G. W. F. Hegel, *The Phenomenology of Mind*, trans. J. B. Baillie (New York and Evanston, Ill.: Harper Torchbooks, 1967), 457. The newer translation is *Phenomenology of Spirit*, trans. A. V. Miller (Oxford and New York: Oxford University Press, 1977). But I "grew up" on Baillie's translation and prefer it.

4. G. W. F. Hegel, *The Philosophy of Right*, in *Hegel: The Essential Writings*, ed. Frederick G. Weiss (New York: Harper Torchbooks, 1974), 256. In Roman mythology Minerva is the goddess of wisdom, and the owl symbolizes her.

5. Quoted by Popper, 32–33.

6. Arthur Schopenhauer, *The World as Will and Idea*, vol. 1, trans. R. B. Haldane and J. Kemp (London: Routledge and Kegan Paul, 1964), 3.

7. Immanuel Kant, *Critique of Practical Reason*, trans. Lewis White Beck (Chicago: University of Chicago Press, 1949), 258.

8. Schopenhauer, 4–5.

9. Sigmund Freud, *Beyond the Pleasure Principle*, trans. James Stachey (New York: Bantam Books, 1963), 88.

10. Søren Kierkegaard, *Either/Or*, vol. 1, trans. David F. Swenson and Lillian Marvin Swenson (Garden City, N.Y.: Doubleday Anchor, 1969), 37.

11. The original German reads *"Was vernünftig ist, das ist wirklich; und was wirklich ist, das ist vernünftig"* (*Grundlinien der Philosophie des Rechts*, in *Sämtliche Werke*, vol. 7, ed. Hermann Glockner [Stuttgart: Fr. Frommanns Verlag, 1952], 33). My translation is the traditional one, but I should add that Hegelian scholars now tend to prefer: "What is rational is actual and what is actual is rational," because Hegel used *Wirklichkeit* as a technical term meaning a synthesis of essence and existence. This scholarly translation avoids the mistaken impression that Hegel's view is that whatever is, is right—which would be a tacit approval of all sorts of vicious political regimes. See, for example, G. W. F. Hegel, *Philosophy of Right*, trans. T. M. Knox (Oxford: Clarendon Press, 1949), 10.

12. Søren Kierkegaard, *Concluding Unscientific Postscript*, trans. Walter Lowrie and David F. Swenson (Princeton, N.J.: Princeton University Press, 1960), 315, 387.

13. Ibid., 81.

14. Søren Kierkegaard, *Fear and Trembling*, in *Fear and Trembling* and *The Sickness unto Death*, trans. Walter Lowrie (Garden City, N.Y.: Doubleday Anchor, 1954), 31.

15. Ibid.

16. Karl Marx, "Theses on Feuerbach," in *Marx and Engels: Basic Writings on Politics and Philosophy*, ed. Lewis S. Feuer (Garden City, N.Y.: Doubleday Anchor, 1989), 244.

17. Ibid.

18. Karl Marx, *Toward the Critique of Hegel's "Philosophy of Right,"* in Feuer, 263.

19. Marx writes: "the production of too many useful things results in too many useless people" (Karl Marx, *Economic and Philosophical Manuscripts*, in *Marx's Concept of Man*, ed. Erich Fromm [New York: Ungar, 1969], 145).

20. Karl Marx, *A Contribution to the Critique of Political Economy*, in Feuer, 43.

21. Karl Marx and Friedrich Engels, "Manifesto of the Communist Party," in Feuer, 26.

22. Ibid., 7.

23. Friedrich Engels, "Letters on Historical Materialism: Engels to Franz Mehring," in Feuer, 408.

24. Karl Marx and Friedrich Engels, *The German Ideology,* in Feuer, 254.

25. Friedrich Nietzsche, *The Will to Power,* trans. Walter Kaufmann and R. J. Hollingdale (New York: Vintage Books, 1968), 535.

26. Friedrich Nietzsche, "On Truth and Lie in an Extra-Moral Sense," in *The Portable Nietzsche,* ed. and trans. Walter Kaufmann (New York: Viking Press, 1954), 46–47.

27. Friedrich Nietzsche, *Beyond Good and Evil,* trans. Walter Kaufmann (New York: Vintage Books, 1966), 203.

28. Ibid., 30–31.

29. Ibid., 3.

30. Ibid., 68.

31. Nietzsche, *The Will to Power,* 35.

32. Jeremy Bentham, "A Fragment on Government," in *A Bentham Reader,* ed. Mary Peter Mack (New York: Pegasus, 1969), 45.

33. John Stuart Mill, *Utilitarianism* (New York: E. P. Dutton, 1951), 10.

34. John Stuart Mill, *On Liberty,* in *Utilitarianism, Liberty, and Representative Government* (New York: E. P. Dutton, 1950), 95–96.

35. John Stuart Mill, *Principles of Political Economy,* ed. J. M. Robson, in *Collected Works: John Stuart Mill,* vol. 3 (Toronto: University of Toronto Press/Routledge and Kegan Paul, 1965), 945.

36. Ibid., 947.

37. Rüdiger Safranski, *Schopenhauer and the Wild Years of Philosophy* (Cambridge, Mass.: Harvard University Press, 1990).

38. *Begriffschrift* means roughly "conceptual writings." The German title was retained in the section of the book translated by Peter Geach in *Translations from the Philosophical Writings of Gottlob Frege* (Oxford: Oxford University Press, 1952).

7

Pragmatism, the Analytic Tradition, and the Phenomenological Tradition and Its Aftermath
The Twentieth Century

Pragmatism

Let us cross at last from old Europe to the New World and visit the pragmatists—a school that makes the first truly American contribution to the history of philosophy and one that also provides a bridge between the nineteenth and twentieth centuries. The logician and **semiologist** Charles Peirce (1839–1914) invented the term "pragmatism" and meant it to be the name of a method whose primary goal was the clarification of thought. Perhaps pragmatism was conceived in Peirce's mind when he read the definition of "belief" offered by the psychologist Alexander Bain. Belief is "that upon which a man is prepared to act," said Bain. Peirce agreed and decided that it followed from this definition that beliefs produce habits and that the way to distinguish between beliefs is to compare the habits they produce. *Beliefs*, then, are *rules for action*, and they get their meaning from the action for which they are rules. With this definition, Peirce had bypassed the privacy and secrecy of the Cartesian mind and had provided a direct access to mental processes (because a person's belief could be established by observing that person's actions).

In its inventor's hands, pragmatism was a form of radical empiricism, and some of Peirce's claims are reminiscent of Berkeley's. For example, what Berkeley said about ideas ("our idea of anything is our idea of its sensible effects") is not unlike what Peirce said about belief.

James

Providing Direct Access to the Cartesian Mind

Peirce's essay "How to Make Our Ideas Clear," published in 1878, was generally ignored until interpreted by William James (1842–1910) some twenty-five years later. James swore allegiance to what he took to be Peircean principles and set out to promote the doctrine of pragmatism. But Peirce was so chagrined at what James was doing to pragmatism that he changed its name to "pragmaticism," which he said was "ugly enough to be safe enough from kidnappers."[1]

William James was born into a wealthy New England family. (His Irish grandfather, after whom he was named, had wisely invested in the Erie Canal and established his family's fortune.) His father was a theologian with somewhat eccentric religious ideas, but he encouraged the development of his son's independent thought. William and his eventually equally famous brother, Henry—who became one of America's most revered novelists—were schooled in France, Germany, Switzerland, and England before William finally attached himself to Harvard Uni-

Ugly Enough to Be Safe from Kidnappers

versity, first as a student of science and medicine and then as a professor of medicine, psychology, and, ultimately, philosophy. The philosophy that James taught was influenced by his study of psychology and evolutionary theory, but his philosophy was also in many ways a response to personal psychological, moral, and religious crises that he experienced throughout his life, Peirce's pragmatism, as James interpreted it, provided an objective way to address these crises.

Where Peirce had meant for pragmatism merely to provide a formula for making ordinary thought more scientific, James saw it as a philosophy capable of resolving metaphysical and religious dilemmas. Furthermore, he saw it as both a theory of meaning and a theory of truth. Let us first look at James's pragmatic theory of meaning. In *Pragmatism,* he wrote:

> Is the world one or many?—fated or free?—material or spiritual?—here are notions either of which may or may not hold good of the world; and disputes over such notions are unending. The pragmatic method in such cases is to try to interpret each notion by tracing its respective practical consequences. What difference would it practically make to anyone if this notion rather than that notion were true? If no practical difference whatever can be traced, then the alternatives mean practically the same thing, and all dispute is idle.[2]

James concluded from this thought process the following principle: "There can be no difference anywhere that doesn't make a difference elsewhere."[3]

To clarify James's point, we will take three sentences, each quite different from the others, and test them for pragmatic meaning:

   A. Steel is harder than flesh.
   B. There is a Bengal tiger loose outside.
   C. God exists.

From a pragmatic point of view, the meanings of sentences A and B are unproblematic. We know exactly what it would be like to believe them, as opposed to believing their opposites. If we believed an alternative to A, it is clear that in many cases we would behave very differently than we do behave now. And what we believe about B will also have an immediate impact on our behavior. What about sentence C? Here we see what James himself would admit to be the subjective feature of his theory of meaning. If certain people believed that God existed, they would conceive of the world very differently than they would conceive of it if they believed God did not exist.

I now believe that steel is harder than flesh.

However, there are other people whose conceptions of the world would be practically identical (i.e., identical in practice) whether they believed that God did or did not exist. For these people, the propositions "God exists" and "God does not exist" would mean (practically) the same thing. For certain other people who find themselves somewhere between these two extremes, the proposition "God exists" means something like, "On Sunday, I put on nice clothes and go to church," because, for them, engaging in this activity is the only practical outcome of their belief (and a belief is just a rule for action, as Peirce had said).

So much for the pragmatic theory of meaning. Now for the pragmatic theory of truth. James had this to say about truth: "ideas (which themselves are but parts of our experience) become true just insofar as they help us to get into satisfactory

I am dressed up, therefore God exists.

A Pragmatic Proof of God's Existence

relation with other parts of our experience, . . . Truth in our ideas means their power to 'work.'"[4] James also said (perhaps less felicitously) that the issue was that of the "cash value" of ideas.[5]

It is interesting to compare the pragmatic theory of truth with the other two theories of truth that have competed with each other throughout the history of Western philosophy: the *correspondence* theory and the *coherence* theory. The correspondence theory has been the dominant one and has been especially favored by empiricists. It says simply that a proposition is true if it corresponds with the facts. The sentence "The cat is on the mat" is true if and only if the cat is in fact on the mat. The main attractions of this theory are its simplicity and its appeal to common sense. The main weaknesses are (1) the difficulties in explaining how linguistic entities (words, sentences) can *correspond* to things that are nothing like language, (2) the difficulty in stating exactly what it is that sentences are supposed to correspond to (facts? What is a "fact" if not that which a true sentence asserts?), and (3) a particular awkwardness in its application to mathematics (what is it to which the proposition "$5 + 2 = 7$" corresponds?). The coherence theory of truth asserts that a proposition is true if it coheres with all the other propositions taken to be true. This theory has been preferred by rationalists. Its greatest strength is that it makes sense out of the idea of mathematical truth ("$5 + 2 = 7$" is true because it is entailed by "$7 = 7$," and by "$1 + 6 = 7$," and by "$21 \div 3 = 2 \times 3 + 1$," etc., etc.). Its greatest weakness is its vicious circularity. Proposition A is true by virtue of its coherence with propositions B, C, and D. Proposition B is true by virtue of its coherence with propositions A, C, and D. Proposition C is true by virtue of its coherence with A, B, and D, and so forth. (Think of the belief system of a paranoid. All his beliefs cohere perfectly with one another. Everything that happens to him is evidence that everybody is out to get him.)

Now, the pragmatist says that the test of correspondence and the test of coherence are not competing theories, but simply different tools to be applied to beliefs to see if those beliefs "work."

The Paranoid Theory of Truth

Sometimes one test is a satisfactory tool, sometimes the other, but neither is the sole criterion of truth. James's most extended account of truth is this:

> True ideas are those that we can assimilate, validate, corroborate and verify. False ideas are those that we cannot. . . . The truth of an idea is not a stagnant property inherent in it. Truth *happens* to an idea. It *becomes* true, is *made* true by events.[6]

If we return to our three model sentences, we see that A certainly *works*. Believing that steel is harder than flesh definitely puts us in a much more satisfactory relation to the rest of our experience than does believing the opposite. For most of us, B usually does *not* work. Under typical conditions, believing that there is a Bengal tiger loose outside the room we now occupy would put us in a paranoid relation with the rest of our experience. Of course, sometimes believing it to be true *would* work. (Namely, we are tempted to say, when there really is a tiger outside.)

What about the third example? Obviously, the truth or falsity of the claim that *God exists* cannot even come up for those people for whom there is no practical difference whether they believe it or not. But for those people for whom the distinction is meaningful, the pragmatic test of truth is available. Unlike for the propositions in sentences *A* and *B*, there is no *direct* pragmatic test of the proposition "God exists." In fact, the empirical evidence, according to James, is equally indecisive for or against *God's* existence. About this and similar cases, James said, "Our passional nature not only lawfully may, but must, decide an option between propositions, whenever it is a genuine option that cannot by its nature be decided on intellectual grounds."[7] (In asserting this, James sounded very much like Kant.) James went on to say that for many people, the belief in *God* does work, though he was prepared to admit that for a few it does not work. Rather, a belief in *God* puts some people in a state of paranoic fear vis-à-vis the rest of their experiences. So, for the first group, the proposition "God exists" is true, and for the second group, it is false.

It was this subjective side of James's theory of truth that displeased many philosophers, including Peirce. This feature of pragmatism was somewhat ameliorated by the work of John Dewey. First, one last point about James: The allusion earlier to the similarity between him and Kant was not gratuitous. Both Kant and James tried to justify on prac-

For Some, a Belief in God Definitely Has Cash Value

tical grounds our right to hold certain moral and religious values that cannot be justified on purely intellectual grounds. Furthermore, just as Kant had seen himself as trying to mediate between the rationalists and the empiricists, so did James see himself as mediating between what he called the "tender-minded" and the "tough-minded" philosophers:

The Tender-Minded	The Tough-Minded
Rationalistic (going by "principles")	Empiricist (going by "facts")
Intellectualistic	Sensationalistic
Idealistic	Materialistic
Optimistic	Pessimistic
Religious	Irreligious
Free-willist	Fatalistic
Monistic	Pluralistic
Dogmatical	Skeptical

The trouble with these alternatives, said James, was that "you find an empirical philosophy that is not religious enough, and a religious philosophy that is not empirical enough."[8] Obviously, James thought that his pragmatism offered a third, more satisfying, alternative.

Dewey

John Dewey (1859–1952) was perhaps the most influential of the pragmatists—if for no other reason than that he outlived them by so many years.

He was actually schooled in Hegelian idealism (which in the second half of the nineteenth century had a great impact on American and British philosophy, as we will see), and it left a permanent dent in Dewey's way of thinking, contextualizing as it did all philosophy in

terms of history, society, and culture.

But under the influence of James as well as Charles Darwin's theory of evolution, Dewey drifted away from Hegelianism. Where Hegel found humanity progressing by resolving certain logical contradictions in the ideational sphere, Dewey found progress in the resolution of certain organic conflicts between individuals and their social and natural environments. From Darwin, Dewey learned that consciousness, mind, and intellect were not something different from nature, opposed to it and standing in splendid aloofness above it; rather, they were adaptations to nature,

Hegel Putting a Permanent Dent in Dewey's Thought

continuous with it, and, like other appendages of plants, insects, and animals, functioned best when used to solve problems posed to them by the natural world.

Such an idea fit easily into the schema of the pragmatism of Peirce and James. For James, however, pragmatism had been a therapeutic tool for dealing primarily with certain religious and metaphysical conflicts, and with individual psychology. Dewey was more concerned with social psychology. His basic philosophical interests were in politics, education, and morality.

According to Dewey, higher organisms develop as problem-solving mechanisms learned routines that transcend purely instinctual responses. We call these routines "habits." As the organism's environment becomes more ambiguous and the organism itself becomes more complex, its re-

Jamesian Therapy

sponses become more "mental." Intelligence evolves when habit fails to perform efficiently. Intelligence interrupts and delays a response to the environment when a problematic situation is recognized as problematic. Thought is, in fact, a "response to the doubtful as such." The function of reflective thought is to turn obscurity into clarity. Such a transformation is called "knowledge." The move from ignorance to knowledge is the transition from "a perplexed, troubled, or confused situation at the beginning [to] a cleared-up, unified, resolved situation at the close."[9] Ideas are plans for action. They are "designations of operations to be performed"; they are hypotheses. Thinking

Ideas Are Deferred Actions

is simply "deferred action." Thoughts that do not pass into actions that rearrange experience are useless thoughts. (The same is true of philosophies.)

> There is [a] first-rate test of the value of any philosophy which is offered us: Does it end in conclusions which, when they are referred back to ordinary life-experiences and their predicaments, render them more significant, more luminous to us, and make our dealing with them more fruitful? Or does it terminate in rendering the things of ordinary experience more opaque than they were before and depriving them of having in "reality" even the significance that they seemed to have?[10]

Traditional epistemologists, whether rationalist or empiricist, have erred. They believed that what was to be known was some reality preexisting the act of knowing. For them, the mind is the mirror of reality, or what Dewey called "the spectator theory of knowledge." It sought to find certainty, either in universals (rationalism) or in sense data (empiricism). But universals and sense data are not the *objects* of knowledge; rather, they are the *instruments* of knowledge. One of the consequences of Dewey's revision is that philosophy must abandon what hitherto had been considered as "ultimate questions" about Being and Knowledge. Knowledge must be instrumental. Its function is to solve problems.

Strictly speaking, then, the object of knowledge is constructed by the inquiring mind. Knowledge changes the world that existed prior to its being known, but not in the Kantian sense in which it *distorts* reality (the noumenal world); rather, knowledge changes the world in the sense that it imposes new traits on the world, for example, by clarifying that which was inherently unclear.

> The function of reflective thought is to transform a situation in which there is experienced obscurity, doubt, conflict, disturbances of some sort, into a situation that is clear, coherent, settled, harmonious.[11]

According to Dewey, the definition of the world as the totality of substances (things) was abandoned with the advent of modern science, which revealed not "objects" but relationships. In abandoning that definition, science also dissolved the distinction between *knowing* and *doing*. Galileo is credited by Dewey for initiating this revolution, a revolution that all but philosophers have accepted. Science allows us to escape from the tyranny of the past and allows us to exert some control over our natural and social environment. And yet, it is not only scientists who know. Poets, farmers, teachers, statespeople, and dramatists *know*. Nevertheless, ultimately all must look to the scientists for a methodology. In fact, science is just a sophisticated form of common sense. Science, or its strategies, should play the role in the contemporary world that the Church played in the medieval world. Scientific techniques must be applied to the development of both values and social reform.

For Dewey, there is no dichotomy between scientific facts and values. Values are a certain kind of facts found in experience, facts such as beauty, splendor, and humor. But like the products of every other intervention into reality, they reveal themselves relative to the interests of the inquirer. But Dewey's "pragmatic instrumentalism" is *not* just a form of utilitarianism. The error of utilitarianism is to define value in terms of objects antecedently enjoyed; but for Dewey, just because something *has* been enjoyed does not make that thing *worthy* of enjoyment. Without the intervention of thought, enjoyments are not values. To call something valuable is to say that it

**Science Must Take Over the Role
Played by the Medieval Church**

fulfills certain conditions—namely, that it directs conduct well. There is a difference between the loved and the lovable, the blamed and the blamable, the admired and the admirable. What is needed is an active and cultivated appreciation of value. Its development is a supreme goal, whether the problem confronted is intellectual, aesthetic, or moral.

In fact, the ultimate goal of action should be the full development of individuals as human beings. Therefore, democracy and education have the same goal. Each individual has something to contribute to the construction of social institutions, and the test of value of all institutions will be the contributions they make back to the individual in terms of creating the conditions for the all-around growth of every member of society. Such growth involves achieving certain kinds of experiences that are *final*, in that they do not provoke the search for some other experience. These are aesthetic experiences. Sometimes, according to Dewey, these experiences are so intense that they are designated as "religious."

The Analytic Tradition

Shortly before the turn of the century, an amazing phenomenon occurred in Britain, and the ripple effect brought it to America. The British discovered Hegel! This discovery took place long after Hegelianism had been declared dead on the Continent. Neo-Hegelianism found some able defenders in men like F. H. Bradley at Oxford, J. E. McTaggart at Cambridge, and Josiah Royce at the University of California. But the Anglo-American national characters (if there are such things) could not have been very comfortable with

The British Discover Hegel

Hegelian idealism, and it is not surprising that a realist reaction was soon provoked. (Notice that "realism" is used here in the Lockean sense of naming a *real* external world and not in the medieval sense of naming the reality of Platonic Forms.) This revolt was led by G. E. Moore and Bertrand Russell.

Moore

George Edward Moore (1873–1958) had come to Cambridge to study classical literature ("the Greats," as it is known there), and part of his program involved taking philosophy classes, where, according to him, he heard the most astonishing things asserted—things to which he could attach no precise meaning. It seemed to him that the lectures were full of denials of things that every sane human knew to be true. Moore must have been an annoying under-graduate. If McTaggart asserted that space was unreal, Moore would ask if that meant that the wall next to him was *not* nearer than the library building; if McTaggart asserted that time was unreal, Moore wanted to know if that meant that the class would *not* end at noon. Russell found Moore's "naive" questions to be very exciting. Years later Russell wrote of Moore:

Young George Moore and Bertie Russell Discover That the Grass Is Green

> He took the lead in rebellion, and I followed, with a sense of emancipa-tion. Bradley argued that everything common sense believes in is mere appearance; we reverted to the opposite extreme, and thought that *everything* is real that common sense, uninfluenced by philosophy or theology, supposes real. With a sense of escaping from prison we

allowed ourselves to think that grass is green, that the sun and stars would exist if no one was aware of them.[12]

Moore continued to defend common sense throughout his life, even though Russell would later find his own reasons for doubting it. (Russell: "Science itself has shown that none of these common-sense notions will quite serve for the explanation of the world.")[13] Indeed, Moore came to be known as the "philosopher of common sense." Common sense became for him what sense data had been for the empiricists and what reason had been for the rationalists—namely, the foundation of certainty. In one of his most famous essays, "A Defence of Common Sense," Moore listed a series of propositions that he claimed *to know with certainty to be true*, including these:

A. There exists at present a living human body, which is my body.
B. This body was much smaller when it was born than it is now.
C. Ever since it was born it has been in contact with, or not far from, the surface of the earth.
D. Ever since it was born it has been at various distances from a great number of physical objects.

**G. E. Moore Reads to His Students the List
of Things He Knows for Certain**

E. The earth had existed many years before my body was born.
F. Many other human bodies had existed before my body was born, and many of them had already died before my birth.

This list goes on and on. It is a rather boring list, but Moore knew full well that his list was tedious. The point is that, according to him, every one of these propositions has been denied by some philosopher, somewhere, sometime. The truth usually *is* boring, and we should get suspicious when we hear dramatic metaphysical theses that deny commonplace beliefs, such as the Hegelian claims: Time and space have no objective reality; the individual is an abstraction; mathematics is only a stage in the dialectic; the Absolute is expressed, but not revealed, in the world. Moore did not necessarily want to claim that these assertions were untrue, only that they were strange and that no obvious meaning could be attached to them. As Moore's student and friend John Maynard Keynes said, the question most frequently on Moore's lips was, "What *exactly* do you mean?" And, said Keynes, "If it appeared under cross-examination that you did not mean exactly anything, you lay under a strong suspicion of meaning nothing whatever."

The Hegelian philosophers at Cambridge and Oxford in the 1880s and 1890s had spent a lot of time inventing new philosophical terminology in order to devise novel ways of talking, because they all seemed to agree that there was something defective about our ordinary discourse concerning the world. Moore was not a bit convinced that these new ways of speaking were really necessary. He wanted to know *exactly*

what was wrong with ordinary language. Moore's commitment to our normal way of thinking and talking about the world is seen very clearly in this passage from "A Defence of Common Sense":

> I [assume] that there is some meaning which is *the* ordinary . . . meaning of such expressions as "The earth has existed for many years past." And this, I am afraid is an assumption which some philosophers are capable of disputing. They seem to think that the question "Do you believe that the earth has existed for many years past?" is not a plain question, such as should be met either by a plain "Yes" or "No," or by a plain "I can't make up my mind," but is the sort of question which can be properly met by: "It all depends on what you mean by 'the earth' and 'exists' and 'years': If you mean so and so, and so and so, and so and so, then I do; but if you mean so and so, and so and so, and so and so, or so and so, and so and so, and so and so, or so and so, and so and so, and so and so, then I don't, or at least I think it is extremely doubtful." It seems to me that such a view is as profoundly mistaken as any view can be.[14]

It is very clear that, with Moore, the aim of philosophy is not that of generating grandiose metaphysical schemes, nor is it even that of arriving at the truth (much less, the Truth); rather, its goal is the clarification of meaning. This goal puts Moore squarely in the camp of the analytic philosophy that Frege had pioneered—a kind of philosophy that, for better or for worse, was to dominate a great part of the twentieth century. Moore was the initiator of what might almost be called a *movement*: one that was antimetaphysical, concerned with detailed analysis, obsessed with the problem of meaning, and far removed from the social, political, and personal problems that afflicted people of his day. Furthermore, with his concern with precise language, Moore took the first step in the direction that has since been called the "linguistic turn." We will see all these features again in Russell, in the logical positivists, and in Wittgenstein.

For all his virtues, Moore seems a bit too complacent to many philosophers today. His perhaps overly satisfied attitude toward the world can be easily detected in the following passage:

> I do not think that the world or the sciences would ever have suggested to me any philosophical problems. What has suggested philosophical problems to me is things which other philosophers have said about the world and the sciences.[15]

Russell

Moore's friend at Cambridge, Bertrand Russell (1872–1970), was born into a prominent noble family. His grandfather, Lord John Russell, was a British prime minister. Bertrand himself inherited an earldom. He was privately educated, and he early demonstrated unusual mathematical skills. His temporary flirtation with Hegelianism must have gone against all his native instincts and abilities. The philosophy of McTaggart and Bradley had no use for the mathematical and scientific precision for which Russell had a natural affinity. As we saw, Moore helped Russell break away from Hegelianism's fatal attraction,

Hegelianism's Fatal Attraction

and for a brief period Moore and Russell thought alike. But Moore did not know mathematics and was uninterested in science; so even though Moore and Russell always agreed that the main job of the philosopher was that of analysis, they soon went their separate philosophical ways.

In 1900 Russell went to the International Congress of Philosophy in Paris and met the great mathematician and logician Guiseppe Peano. Conversations with him and other mathematical luminaries such as Gottlob Frege set Russell on a path that led to one of his major works, *Principia Mathematica*, written in collaboration with Alfred North Whitehead in 1910–1913. This work was a protracted defense of Frege's thesis that all of arithmetic is an extension of the basic principles of logic. Probably Russell's major contribution to the history of philosophy was his demonstration of the power of symbolic logic as a tool of philosophical analysis.

Reading *Principia Mathematica*

A key feature of Russell's overall view was his belief in philosophy's subordination to science. Russell thought that philosophy should be built on science rather than the other way around because there was less risk of error in science than in philosophy. He was one of many analytical philosophers who assumed that "science is innocent unless proved guilty, while philosophy is guilty unless proved innocent."[16] The fact that Russell saw philosophy as ancillary to science, along with the fact that science was changing so rapidly during the period in which Russell wrote, partially explains why Russell's philosophy evolved so much over the many years that he developed it. His most uncharitable critics claimed that Russell made a philosophical career for himself by writing a book every year in which he refuted his book of the previous year. And, indeed, it is difficult to state exactly what Russell's philosophy *is*, precisely because of its many transformations over the years. But there were certain common denominators that survived and unified his views despite all the changes. One constant in his thought was his view of philosophy as essentially analytical. In 1924 he wrote:

> Although . . . comprehensive construction is part of the business of philosophy, I do not believe it is the most important part. The most important part, to my mind, consists in criticizing and clarifying notions which are apt to be regarded as fundamental and accepted uncritically. As instances I might mention: mind, matter, conscious-ness, knowledge, experience, causality, will, time. I believe all these notions to be inexact and approximate, essentially infected with vagueness, incapable of forming part of any exact science.[17]

Another constant in Russell's philosophy was his commitment to Ockham's razor, which, as we have seen, is a plea for theoretical simplicity, an injunction not to "multiply entities beyond necessity."

Russell formulated it thus: "Wherever pos-sible, substitute constructions out of known entities for inferences to unknown entities."[18] He thought we should try to account for the world in terms of those features of it with which we have direct acquaintance and we should avoid the temptation of positing the existence of anything with which we cannot be acquainted, unless we are forced to do so by undeniable facts or by a compelling logical argument.

I will let Russell's "Theory of Descrip-tions," which he took to be one of his major contributions to philosophy, represent his views: From Plato forward, philosophers had struggled with the logic of the con-cept of existence, and many of them, including Plato, were driven to create grandiose metaphysical schemes to accommodate the prob-

Lord Russell with Razor

lems caused by that concept. Russell found most of these schemes to be *too* metaphysical (i.e., too much in violation of the strictures of Ockham's razor) or to be simply too paradoxical. Let us look at three such problems dealing with the question of existence.

1. I say, "The golden mountain does not exist." You ask, "What is it that does not exist?" I answer, "The golden mountain." By doing so, I seem to be attributing a kind of existence to the very thing whose existence I just denied. (And what *thing* is that?) Furthermore, if I say, "Unicorns do not exist" and "Round squares do not exist," I seem to be saying that golden mountains, unicorns, and round squares are three different things, and none of them exists! The Platonists' solution to this problem was to say that terms like "the golden mountain" designate ideals that exist in a realm of pure being, but not in the physical world. Clearly, such a view would be too metaphysical for Russell and would cry out for the application of Ockham's razor.

The Golden Mountain— Which (Unfortunately) Does Not Exist

2. Consider the sentence "Scott is the author of *Waverley*." Logicians have held that if two terms denote the same object, these terms could be interchanged without changing the meaning or truth of the proposition being expressed by the sentence. (If A = B, then [A = B] = [B = A] = [A = A] = [B = B].) Now, the novel *Waverley* was published anonymously, and many people wanted to know who wrote it. King George IV was particularly interested to know because he wanted to find out who was maligning his

ancestors. The king did *not* want to know whether the sentence "The author of *Waverley* is the author of *Waverley*" was true, nor if the sentence "Sir Walter Scott is Sir Walter Scott" was true. (Though a Platonic/Leibnizian solution to the problem would be that, indeed, *all* sentences are versions of the proposition "Everything is everything," or "A = A." But such a meta-

Majesty! We have discovered that Scott is Scott.

Oh Goody!

physical "solution" could never satisfy a Bertrand Russell.)

3. Consider this sentence: "The present king of France is bald." This assertion seems false (because there is no such person), but, according to the law of the excluded middle, the negation of any false proposition must be true, so it follows that there must be truth to the claim "The present king of France is not bald." Yet surely that sentence is false too. Must we once again accept some kind of metaphysical solution to the dilemma by consigning to an ideal realm of being the object designated by the term "the present king of France," along with the ideal characteristics "bald" and "hairy"? The Platonic logicians thought so. Russell thought not. (Russell said that the Hegelians would find the solution in a synthesis: "The present king of France wears a toupee.")

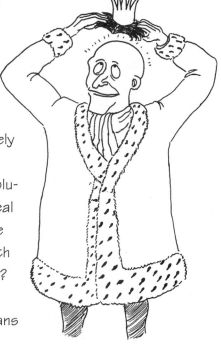

The Hegelian Solution

So here we have three different logical problems concerning the concept of being or existence. The goal of Russell's Theory of Descriptions was to unveil the true logical structure of propositions about existence in order to eliminate paradoxes and metaphysical obfuscations. Russell discovered a formula that he thought could perform this job:

> There is an entity $\underline{C}$, such that the sentence "$\underline{X}$ is $\underline{Y}$" is true if and only if $\underline{X} = \underline{C}$.

In this formula, C is an entity, Y is a characteristic written in the form of an adjective, and X is the subject to which the adjective is attributed. For example, the sentence "The golden mountain does not exist" is rendered by Russell as: "There's no entity C, such that the sentence 'X is golden and mountainous' is true if and only if X = C." In other words, the offending term, "the golden mountain" (offending because it seems to denote an entity, that is, name a thing) has been transformed into a description (golden and mountainous), and the real assertion of the proposition is that there is no existing object that could be correctly characterized using that description. Notice that the notion of "existence" has been analyzed out of the term "the golden mountain."

Concerning the second problem, the sentence "Scott is the author of Waverley" becomes "There is an entity C, such that 'X wrote Waverley' is true if and only if X is C; moreover, C is Scott." So the characteristic "authorly" properly describes an existing entity (Scott) and does so in a way that is not merely tautological. Notice once again that the notion of existence has been analyzed out of the description "the author of Waverley."

Finally, the sentence "The present king of France is bald" means "There is an entity C, such that 'X is kingly, French, and bald' is true if and only if X = C." But there is no entity to which such a description correctly applies, so the sentence is false; and so is its negation because there is also no entity that is correctly described as being "kingly, French, and hairy." So we can assert that both sentences are false without violating the law of the excluded middle.

In each of these three cases, Russell applied Ockham's razor and excised the concept of existence. Russell rather immodestly said of his solution, "This clears up two millennia of muddle-headedness about 'existence,' beginning with Plato's *Theaetetus*."[19]

The exposition of the Theory of Descriptions has probably been the most technical presentation in this book, and even then, it has been greatly simplified. Much of Russell's philosophy was highly specialized, but Russell the technical philosopher contrasted greatly with Russell the social critic and activist. He spent part of World War I in jail as a pacifist. (He was disappointed that Moore joined the war effort as a British officer; and he was even more disappointed that his student Ludwig Wittgenstein returned to the Continent to join the Austrian army as a private.) Russell was a harsh critic of the social policies of both the United States and the Soviet Union, and after World War II, he became an active protester against nuclear weapons. (He was jailed when he was eighty-nine years old for inciting

> True Being exists only in the realm of Being: *Plato*
>
> Being truly exists as an actuality of a potentiality: *Aristotle*
>
> True Being is Perfection, and Perfection is True Being: *Anselm*
>
> There is no True Being. Being is a mere word, naming nothing: *William of Ockham*
>
> Being is truly a characteristic of either of two substances: *Descartes*
>
> True Being is monadic: *Leibniz*
>
> Being? Beats me! Truly, *Hume*
>
> Being is not a predicate: *Kant*
>
> Being is the Rational, and the Rational is ($\underline{Bes}$?): *Hegel*
>
> Being is the manifestation of the Will: *Schopenhauer*
>
> Being does not exist; only Will to Power is: *Nietzsche*
>
> Being cannot be thought: *Kierkegaard*
>
> There is an entity c, such that "x is y" is true if and only if x = c.

the public to civil disobedience after an illegal rally in Hyde Park to protest the presence of American atomic weapons in Britain; in his nineties, he was actively engaged in preaching against the American involvement in Vietnam.) In this respect, Russell was the very opposite of G. E. Moore, who, as we've seen, never found anything to engage his intellect and passions except things said by other philosophers. In 1960 when the journalist Ved Mehta went to Russell's home to interview him about his philosophy, Mehta was met by Russell at the door and was asked by Russell if he had not heard about The Bomb. Russell told Mehta that in the face of the implications of the nuclear crisis, there was no time to discuss philosophy.

Logical Positivism

The paradigmatic case of the view that philosophy's job is that of logical analysis came from a group of European philosophers who are known as the **logical positivists.** Their movement grew out of some seminars in the philosophy of science offered at the University of Vienna in the early 1920s by Professor Moritz Schlick. The original group, which called itself the "Vienna Circle," was composed mostly of scientists with a flair for philosophy and a desire to render philosophy respectable by making it scientific. Their technical inspiration came primarily from the work of Ernst Mach, Jules Poincaré, and Albert Einstein. The models for their idea of logical analysis came from *Principia Mathematica,* by Russell and Whitehead, and from *Tractatus Logico-Philosophicus,* recently published by Wittgenstein. (Much to the great annoyance of its members, Wittgenstein stayed aloof from the Vienna Circle—you will read a lot more about Wittgenstein shortly.)

The Vienna Circle was positively antagonistic toward most of the history of philosophy, finding only Hume's empiricism and Kant's antimetaphysical stance worthy of respect.

Besides Schlick (who was murdered in 1936 by an insane student on the steps of the University of Vienna), other people associated

**Wittgenstein Aloof
from the Vienna Circle**

with the movement were Otto Neurath, Hans Reichenbach, A. J. Ayer, and Rudolf Carnap. By the early 1930s, their passion for scientific truth was well known, so they were not much liked by the Nazis (whose views did not fare well in the light of scientific scrutiny); nor did the members of the Circle like the Nazis much, and the advent of Hitler's regime scattered the group throughout British and American universities, where they exerted even more influence than perhaps they might have done had they remained in Austria and Germany.

At the risk of oversimplifying the platform of logical positivism (but only slightly), I can say that the main project of the Vienna Circle was the resurrection and updating of Hume's Fork. All putative propositions would be shown to be either *analytic* (tautologies whose negation leads to self-contradiction), *synthetic* (propositions whose confirmation depends on observation and experimentation), or *nonsense*. The positivists' conclusions were therefore like Hume's in many respects. For example, Carnap wrote, "In the domain of *metaphysics*, including all philosophy of value and normative theory, logical analysis yields the negative result that *the alleged statements in this domain are entirely meaningless.*" Take a look at Carnap's analysis of the function of language:[20]

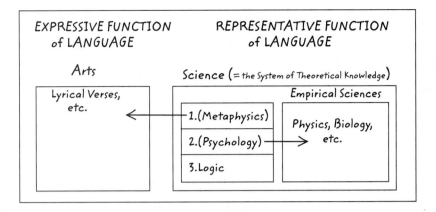

We see that language has only two duties: expression and representation. Once psychology has been correctly established as an empirical science and metaphysics correctly recognized as an art form, philosophy is seen to be nothing but logic. According to Carnap, there is nothing wrong with the poetic function of metaphysics as long as it is identified and treated as such. Carnap wrote,

> The non-theoretical character of metaphysics would not be in itself a defect; all arts have this non-theoretical character without thereby losing their high value for personal as well as social life. The danger lies in the *deceptive* character of metaphysics; it gives the illusion of knowledge without actually giving any knowledge.[21]

Even some of Hume's skeptical musings were too metaphysical for the positivists. Hume had claimed that there was no good reason to believe that any event ever caused another event because there was no sense datum representing any *cause*, only sense data representing series of events. But for Schlick, Hume's search for an entity to correspond to the name "cause" was itself suspect. Schlick said, "The word cause, as used in everyday life, implies *nothing but* regularity of sequence because *nothing else* is used to verify the propositions in which it occurs. . . . The criterion of causality is successful prediction. That is all we can say."[22]

Schlick's comments about causality reveal another feature of the positivistic view, namely, that (in the case of synthetic claims) *the meaning of a proposition is its method of verification.* Furthermore, the language of verification would have to be reduced to what were called "protocol sentences." Protocol sentences were to be assertions that expressed the raw verifiable facts with complete simplicity. These sentences would be "the absolutely indubitable starting points of all knowledge," according to Schlick. An example would be "Moritz Schlick perceived red on the 6th of May, 1934, at 3:03 P.M. in the room numbered 301 in the Philosophy Hall at the University of Vienna." The logical positivists, looking for **incorrigibility** as the foundation of science, decided that even protocol sentences were not certain enough because they did not designate the simplest facts, so they tried to reduce protocol sentences yet further to what they called "confirmation sentences," an example of which would be "Red here now." These sentences were more certain because they were less complex than protocol sentences; but the trouble with them turned out to be that the act of writing down the phrase "here now" produced a meaning not identical to the actual pointing that took place when the confirmation sentence was uttered. Not only that, but to name the experience as "red" seemed to transcend the perceptual event by categorizing it as a member of the class of red experiences, thereby referring to more than what was actually present in the experience. Ultimately, it was suggested that certainty could be found only in an act of *pointing* and *grunting*.

"I saw a book."

The person whose acquaintances call him M.S., and whose passport No. 13456 is registered with the Austrian government, and who is myself, could correctly have said on May 6th, 1934, at 3:03 P.M. in room 301 of the University of Vienna, "I perceive red."

Red here now

 GRUNT!

By now it was beginning to become obvious that something had gone very wrong and that this part of the positivist program was hopeless. The logical positivists had tried to find the foundations of science, and instead they had reverted to the cave dweller mentality. They fell to squabbling over this problem, and it was never resolved to anyone's satisfaction, including their own.

Logical Positivists Arguing

We have seen Carnap's demonstration that metaphysics is only an expressive, not representative, form of language. The positivists performed a similar outrage on moral language, claiming that it was simply a disguised display of emotion, often coupled with "commands in a misleading grammatical form," according to Carnap.[23] So the sentence "Stealing is immoral" really means something like this:

Therefore, the so-called sentence "Stealing is immoral" is really only the expression of emotion and can be neither true nor false. It expresses what Ayer called a "pseudo-concept."[24] Such were the moral consequences of the positivists' radical application of Hume's Fork.

Needless to say, most philosophers were not very satisfied with this account of ethics. Furthermore, as has been indicated, logical positivism began to come undone over its failure to find the much-heralded incorrigibility in protocol sentences and confirmation sentences. (As one commentator put it, the positivists set out to sea unfurling the sails of what they took to be a water-tight "man-o'-war," only to find that it leaked badly. They began patching the leaks and discovered that the patches leaked. By the time the ship sank, they were patching patches on patches.) Logical

positivism came to its final grief over another internal question: If all propositions are either analytic, synthetic, or nonsense, what is the status of the proposition "All propositions are either analytic, synthetic, or nonsense"? It too must be either analytic, synthetic, or nonsense. If it is analytic (Ayer's view), it is a mere tautology and tells us nothing about the world. Furthermore, in this case, we should be able to look up the word "proposition" in the dictionary and discover it to be defined in terms of analyticity and syntheticity. But it's not. If the proposition is synthetic (Carnap's view), then we should be able to verify it empirically. But verification isn't possible either. So it looks as though the key principle of positivism is neither analytic nor synthetic. Wittgenstein, whose *Tractatus Logico-Philosophicus* had been the main inspiration of positivism, took the heroic step of claiming that it was nonsense (though, as we will see, he thought *some* nonsense was better than other nonsense). This

Some Nonsense Is Better Than Other Nonsense (after Sir John Tenniel)

quandary pretty much spelled the end of logical positivism. Perhaps Professor Jon Wheatley was writing its obituary when he said, "Logical positivism is one of the very few philosophical positions which can be easily shown to be dead wrong, and that is its principal claim to fame."[25]

Wittgenstein

The author of the *Tractatus Logico-Philosophicus*, the book that so inspired the logical positivists, was Ludwig Wittgenstein (1889–1951).

He has earned himself a longer discussion in this overview than have most philosophers because he has the unusual distinction of having inspired two philosophical movements: logical positivism and what came to be known as "ordinary language philosophy." Each of these movements dominated a portion of the analytic tradition in this century, and, ironically, in many respects the later movement refutes the earlier movement.

Was sich überhaupt sagen lässt, lässt sich klar sagen; und wovon man nicht reden kann, darüber muss man schweigen.

Wittgenstein was born into a wealthy, refined, Viennese family. Uninterested in material riches, he gave away his entire inheritance.

In 1911 he went to Manchester, England, to study aeronautical engineering. His genius for mathematical thinking was soon recognized, and he was directed to Cambridge to study with Bertrand Russell. When Wittgenstein returned to Austria to enlist in the army during World War I, one story has it that he put a ream of paper in his backpack and went into the trenches with it. He was soon taken captive by the Italians and, as a prisoner of war, set about writing the *Tractatus* (which puts that work in the category of "great books written in jail," along with Boethius's *The Consolations of Philosophy* and part of Cervantes' *Don Quixote*).

Proposition 1: The World Is All That Is the Case

The *Tractatus*, which is barely 100 pages long, is set up as a series of seven propositions. Each proposition is followed by a sequence of numbered observations about each proposition, or observations about the observations, or observations about the observations about the observations. For instance, the first page begins thus:

1.   The world is all that is the case.

1.1   The world is the totality of facts, not of things.

1.11   The world is determined by the facts, and by their being all the facts.

1.12   For the totality of facts determines what is the case, and also whatever is not the case.

1.13   The facts in logical space are the world.

1.2   The world divides into facts.

1.21 Each item can be the case or not the case while everything else remains the same.

2. What is the case—a fact—is the existence of states of affairs.[26]

Wittgenstein held the view that, because we can say true things about the world, the structure of language must somehow reflect the structure of the world. That is part of what he means in paragraph 1.1, "The world is the totality of facts, not of things." Now, what are the facts of which the world consists? They are, to use Russell's term, **"atomic facts."** They are the simplest facts that can be asserted and are the simple truths into which all other more complex truths can be analyzed. In the *Tractatus*, Wittgenstein did not say exactly what these facts were, and it was these facts that the positivists were seeking with their attempts to construct protocol sentences and confirmation sentences.

The positivists liked other features of the *Tractatus* as well. They particularly approved of the conception of philosophy that Wittgenstein put forth:

> Most of the propositions and questions to be found in philosophical works are not false but nonsensical. Consequently we cannot give any answer to questions of this kind, but can only establish that they are nonsensical. (4.003)

> The correct method in philosophy would really be the following: to say nothing except what can be said, i.e., the propositions of natural science—i.e., something that has nothing to do with philosophy—and then, whenever someone else wanted to say something metaphysical, to demonstrate to him that he had failed to give a meaning to certain signs in his propositions . . . this method would be the only strictly correct one. (6.53)

It Cannot Be Said

These paragraphs seem to express perfectly the hard-liner

position of logical positivists. No surprise that the latter thought of Wittgenstein as one of their own. However, certain puzzling statements in the *Tractatus* created quite a bit of discomfort for the members of the Vienna Circle. For example, Wittgenstein wrote, "The whole sense of this book might be summed up in the following words: what can be said at all can be said clearly and what we cannot talk about we must consign to silence." Now, the positivists wanted to interpret Wittgenstein as saying here, "Metaphysicians, shut up!" But Wittgenstein himself seemed curiously attracted to what he called "the silence" and made further enigmatic allusions to it. In paragraph 6.54 he wrote,

> My propositions serve as elucidations in the following way: anyone who understands me eventually recognizes them as nonsensical, when he has used them—as steps—to climb up beyond them. (He must, so to speak, throw away the ladder after he has climbed up it.) He must transcend these propositions and then he will see the world aright.

It was here that Wittgenstein was admitting that his own propositions were nonsense, but apparently a special kind of *higher* nonsense. What would higher nonsense be like? Wittgenstein continued:

> *How* things are in the world is a matter of complete indifference for what is higher. God does not reveal himself in the world. (6.432)

> It is not *how* things are in the world that is mystical, but *that* it exists. (6.44)

The solution to the enigma of life in space and time lies *outside* space and time. (6.4312)

Slowly and in horror the truth dawned on the Vienna Circle. Wittgenstein was a mystic! He was *worse* than the metaphysicians.

For a while, Wittgenstein seemed satisfied with the *Tractatus*. It had answered all the philosophy questions that could be sensibly asked.

As he had written: "When the answer cannot be put into words, neither can the question be put into words. The *riddle does not exist*. If a question can be framed at all, it is possible to answer it" (6.5).

Wittgenstein dropped out of philosophy. He went off into the villages of the Austrian Alps as a primary schoolteacher. But he was not completely happy in his new work, and his mind was not at rest. Russell spearheaded a move to get Wittgenstein to return to Cambridge and to have the *Tractatus* accepted as Wittgenstein's doctoral dissertation. Wittgenstein was given the professional chair of the retiring G. E. Moore, and much excitement was generated over the fact that Wittgenstein had returned to philosophy.

However, word soon got around that what Wittgenstein was now saying about philosophy was not what had been expected of him. It was not easy to know exactly what *was* going on, however, because the eccentric Wittgenstein was very secretive about his new views and he insisted that his students be so too. Nevertheless, some mimeographed copies of notes from his lectures began to circulate. It was not until after his death that his work from this period was published as *Philosophical Investigations*. But long before the appearance of that book, it had become clear that a major shift had taken place in Wittgenstein's thinking. Both the positivism and the mysticism of the *Tractatus* were gone, for better or for worse. Yet there continued to be some common denominators between the two works. Philosophy was still seen as essentially the concern with meaning, and it was still very much language-oriented. In the *Tractatus*, Wittgenstein had written, "*The limits of my language are the limits of my world*" (5.6). That view continued to hold in the *Investigations*, but language itself now seemed much less limited than it had been in the earlier book.

Let us start our discussion of the *Investigations* with a look at the problem of meaning. Throughout the history of philosophy, from Plato to the *Tractatus*, the key model of meaning was that of *denotation*, that is, of *naming*. Even where philosophers like Frege, Russell, and the author of the *Tractatus* had distinguished between "reference" (denotation) and "sense," the former was given priority. According to Wittgenstein, the historical prioritizing of naming as the key feature of meaning had generated a certain kind of metaphysical picture that was pervasive in Western thought and that was in error. Plato thought that words had to be names of things that existed unchanging and eternally, and because there was no such thing in the observable world, he developed his theory of the other-worldly Forms. Aristotle thought words named something unchanging *in* the world, namely, substances. In the medieval period, the nominalists also thought of words as names but thought that they named *nothing*. Their conclusion therefore was like that of the last sentence of Eco's novel *The Name of the Rose*, namely, "we have only names." The empiri-

cists held that words named sense data and that any word not doing so was suspect. The pragmatists thought that words named actions, and the positivists, Russell, and the early Wittgenstein thought they named atomic facts.

The later Wittgenstein broke completely with this tradition, claiming that *the meaning of a word is its use in the language.*"[27] He wrote,

Think of the tools in a tool box: there is a hammer, pliers, a saw, a screwdriver, a rule, a glue pot, glue, nails and screws.—The functions of words are as diverse as the functions of these objects. (And in both cases there are similarities.) . . . It is like looking into the cabin of a locomotive. We see handles all

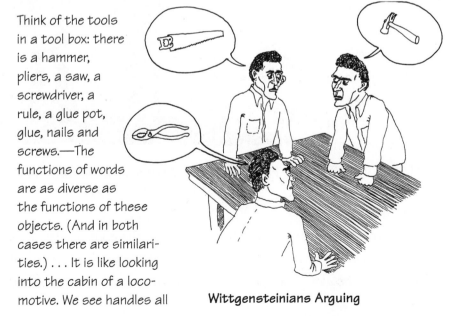

Wittgensteinians Arguing

looking more or less alike. (Naturally, since they are supposed to be handled.) But one is the handle of a crank which can be moved continuously (it regulates the opening of a valve); another is the handle of a switch, which has only two effective positions, it is either off or on; a third is the handle of a brake-lever, the harder one pulls on it, the harder it brakes; a fourth, the handle of a pump: it has an effect only so long as it is moved to and fro. (11, 12)

So language, like tools or like the gadgets in the cabin of a locomotive, can get jobs done, and its meaning is found in the work it accomplishes. Suppose two people are driving rapidly toward a certain destination, trying to arrive before sunset because the headlights are broken, and suppose the driver says, "Well, bad luck! The sun just went down." Now, what if the passenger says, with a look of superiority, "We now know that the sun does not 'go down,' and that the illusion that it does is the result of the earth turning on its axis." Does what he said *mean* anything? No, because in that context, it gets no job done (even though in another context that same sentence would get a job done). In fact, there is something mad about inserting this scientific fact into the context described. There would also be something mad if the passenger, having found a hammer in the glove compartment, began hitting the driver with it

From *Rosencrantz and Guildenstern Are Dead*, a Play by Tom Stoppard and explained the action by saying "Hammers are for hitting." Yes, but not for hitting just anything, anytime, any place. And the same is the case with language.

Still, a tool can serve a number of functions. In some contexts, a hammer can serve as a weapon or as a paperweight. How about language? Does it have only two uses, as the logical positivists suggested (an expressive function and a representative function)? Wittgenstein asked:

> But how many kinds of sentence are there? Say assertion, question, and command?—There are *countless* kinds: countless different kinds of use of what we call "symbols," "words," "sentences." And this multiplicity is not something fixed, given once for all; but new types of language, new language-games, as we may say, come into existence, and others become obsolete and get forgotten. (23)

This comment brings up another feature of Wittgenstein's theory of meaning related to his claim that "the meaning is the use." He wrote, "The question 'What is a word really?' is analogous to 'what is a piece in chess?' . . . Let us say that the meaning of a piece is its role in the game" (108). Wittgenstein generalized his claim when he called any language a "language-game." Let's consider this point. All games are rule-governed. The meaning of a piece (or a chip, or card, or mitt) in the game is derived from its use according to the rules. What is a pawn? A pawn is a piece that moves one square forward, except on its first move, when it may move two squares. It may take the opponent's piece laterally and is converted to a queen if it reaches the opposite side of the board. Similarly with words, phrases, and expressions— they are rule-governed, and their meaning is derived from the use to which they may be put according to the rules of the language game. There are lots of kinds of rules determining language use: grammatical rules, semantical rules, syntactical rules, and what could generally be called rules of context. Some of these rules are very rigid, some are very flexible, and some are negotiable. These variations are true in a comparison of different games (the rules of chess are more rigid than those of ring-around-the-rosy), or even in a comparison *within* a game (rules governing the pawn's moves are rigid, but those governing the pawn's size are flexible). But even flexible rules are rules, and they can't be broken without certain consequences. When some of the rules of a given language game are broken in subtle ways, "language goes on holiday" (38), as Wittgenstein said,

Right! Then it's my move.

and one result is a certain kind of *philosophy* (as in the case of metaphysicians), and another result is a certain kind of *madness* (as in the case of Alice in Wonderland). The allusion to *Alice* is not gratuitous. The Alice books were among Wittgenstein's favorites, no doubt because they are compendiums of linguistic jokes showing the lunacy that results when the function of certain features of language are misunderstood. Think of the episode when the White King tells Alice to look down the road and asks her if she sees anyone there. "I see nobody on the road," said Alice. "I only wish *I* had such eyes," responds the king. "To be able to see Nobody! And at that distance too!" What has gone wrong here? The joke is based on what some of Wittgenstein's followers called a "category mistake"—the miscategorization of certain linguistic facts and the drawing of absurd conclusions from the miscategorization. (According to the "ordinary language philosopher" Gilbert Ryle, this miscategorization was the error made by Descartes that resulted in the mind-body problem. He had placed "minds" in a similar category with bodies, making them "thinking things"—ghostly, spiritual *beings* that somehow cohabitated with physical beings, but no one could figure out how.)

Or consider the case of the White Queen, who promises to pay her lady's maid "Twopence a week, and jam every other day" but then refuses to provide the jam on the grounds that it never *is* any other day. Surely this is language gone on holiday.

The Elusiveness of Jam

What about the positivists' search for the simplest constituents of reality on which to base the scientific edifice? Wittgenstein asked,

> But what are the simple constituent parts of which reality is composed?—What are the simple constituent parts of a chair?—The bits of wood of which it is made? or the molecules, or the atoms?—"Simple" means: not composite. And here the point is: In what sense "composite"? It makes no sense at all to speak absolutely of the "simple parts of a chair." (47)

So much for the search for atomic facts.

In the *Tractatus*, Wittgenstein had written, "Most of the propositions and questions of philosophy arise from our failure to understand the logic of our language" (4.003). He still held more or less the same view in the *Investigations*, but by then his conception of "the logic of our language" had changed radically. It was no longer the philosopher's job to reveal the hidden logic *behind* language; rather, it was to reveal the implicit logic of ordinary language (hence the term "ordinary language philosophy"). Philosophers were to show that a failure to grasp that implicit logic could result in "a bewitchment of our intelligence by means of language" (109), and they were to show that unwarranted tampering with our ordinary way of thinking and talking about the world could produce a "linguistic holiday," which generates the jokes that make up much of the history of philosophy. Wittgenstein said, "[My aim in philosophy is] to show the fly the way out of the fly bottle" (309). Apparently in Wittgenstein's native Vienna, a common flytrap was made by putting some honey in a vinegar bottle.

The fly, traveling on its merry way, would smell the honey, deviate from its path into the bottle, and either drown in the sticky, sweet stuff or buzz to death. For Wittgenstein, much of philosophy was like that buzzing. To "show the fly the way out of the fly bottle" was not to *solve* philosophical problems but to *dissolve* them by showing that they are the result of deviating from the path of everyday language. This analogy illustrates the conservative side of Wittgenstein's thought. According to him, "Philosophy can in no way interfere with the actual use of language; it can in the end only describe it.

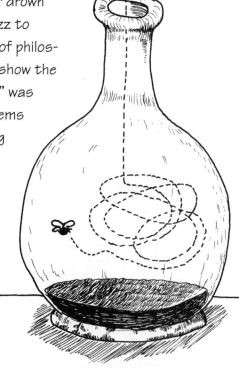

The Fly in the Fly Bottle

For it cannot give it any foundation either. It leaves everything just as it is" (124).

The apparent complacency here is reminiscent of G. E. Moore, but the comparison, though good in some respects, is bad in others. Wittgenstein's mind was in constant turmoil and perplexity. There was a brooding disquietude about the man and his thought that belied the Vermeer-like bourgeois self-satisfaction of passages like the one I just quoted.

Quine

The most important representative of the analytic tradition in the second half of the twentieth century is probably Willard Van Orman Quine, who was born in Akron, Ohio, in 1908. He went to Oberlin Col-lege for a degree in mathematics, and there he became fascinated with Bertrand Russell's mathematical philosophy. He pursued the topic in his doctoral dissertation at Harvard under the direction of Alfred North Whitehead. After receiving his Ph.D., he visited Vienna, Prague, and Warsaw on a fellowship awarded him by the university and was able to talk with philosophers of the Vienna Circle and with leading Eastern European logicians. He returned to Harvard and took up his career there as a professor of philosophy. Even after

W. V. Quine

his retirement from Harvard at seventy years of age, he continued for the next twenty years to give lectures and otherwise participate in the philosophical profession.

Quine's two most important books are *From a Logical Point of View* (1953) and *Word and Object* (1960). Throughout most of the rest of his work, he has taken the ideas presented in these two books and tinkered with them, elaborating, modifying, and defending them. In *From a Logical Point of View* Quine calls himself a pragmatist, so some have placed him in the tradition of Peirce, James, and Dewey, but it is more generally agreed that he is best understood as responding to the logical positivists with whom he had conversed in Europe and, in his unique way, carrying out their program.

This categorization is in some ways surprising, because by 1960 most philosophers believed that logical positivism had bitten the dust, in no small part due to Quine's pair of silver bullets as represented by his 1951 article titled "Two Dogmas of Empiricism" (included in *From a Logical Point of View*). The dogmas he attacks are two of the positivists' most dangerous weapons. The first dogma Quine challenges is reductionism, the positivists' attempt to reduce each putative synthetic proposition (check the Glossary if you don't recall this phrase) to protocol sentences or confirmation sentences and then to correlate these basic propositions with even more basic,

Quine's in Town

incorrigible sense-data experiences. Reductionism is a main feature of the program of empiricism initiated by Locke, refined by Berkeley and Hume, and touted triumphantly by the positivists as the final nails in the coffin of religious, moral, and metaphysical discourse. Instead, this form of reductionism itself seems to have been vanquished, at least in part because of Quine's critique.

The second dogma that Quine targets is the analytic-synthetic distinction (see pp. 179–180 and pp. 197–200 and p. 322). Quine does not claim that there are no such things as analytic sentences ("All bachelors are male" is a clear example of one) or synthetic sentences ("Some dogs are spotted" is one such); rather, he tries to demonstrate that ultimately the boundary between the two supposed types cannot be drawn except arbitrarily. Take this sentence: "Owls hoot." Is it synthetic or analytic? It ought to be synthetic because its negation does not lead to a self-contradiction. Yet our certainty of the sentence "Owls hoot" seems greater than that of the sentence "Owls are members of the order Strigiformes," which proves to be analytic. Similarly, sentences like "Strawberries are red when ripe" or "Heavy objects fall when unsupported" seem to have at least as much certainty as "Tomatoes are fruits, not vegetables" (they are, you know!). Yet the first two examples would normally be classified as synthetic and the third as analytic. Quine is not saying that it is impossible to categorize these kinds of sentences one way or the other, but that ultimately we do so only arbitrarily and that this arbitrariness rules out the analytic-synthetic distinction as one on which we could rest much philosophical

weight—certainly not the amount that the logical positivists thought it could bear.

In fact, the real object of Quine's attack is to demonstrate the circularity of a whole cluster of philosophical views sacrosanct to analytical philosophers. Characterizations of *meaning* were made in terms of *analyticity* (that is, the nature of an analytic proposition), analyticity in terms of *synonymy*, and synonymy in terms of *meaning*, and so on forever, without managing to anchor any part of this system outside the vicious circle that had been produced.[28]

One motive for Quine's revision is his dislike of the positivists' claim that mathematics is *necessarily true* but *empty*. He believes that math has content and is not "necessarily" necessary. He does not want to revert to Kant's synthetic a priori to explain this content nor to Mill's view of math as empirical generalization. Instead, Quine develops a type of epistemological **holism** according to which all parts of our system of knowledge are interrelated rather than fragmented into different categories (categories like "the certainty of sense data," "the certainty but emptiness of analytic propositions," "the uncertainty and probabilistic nature of synthetic propositions," "the meaningfulness guaranteed by verifiability," "the nonsense of metaphysics," etc.). Quine defends the power of mathematics in our systems of knowledge by saying that its strength lies simply in "our determination to make revisions elsewhere instead."[29] If something went wrong with an experiment of ours, math would be the last thing we would give up. Yet an extreme discrepancy between our expectations and the data might make us more willing to consider even the abandonment of math. After all, some features of **quantum mechanics,** the most advanced stage of physical theory, have suggested that we might have to abandon the law of the excluded middle in logic.

Much to the horror of the few remaining logical positivists, Quine admits that the dissolution of the synthetic-analytic distinction and the abandonment of reductionism produce "a blurring of the supposed boundary between speculative metaphysics and natural science."[30] You might think that this admission and Quine's attack on the two dogmas of positivism would establish him as an enemy of logical positivism. But, in fact, Quine has remained sympathetic to the spirit of the positivist program all his professional life. He believes that responsible philosophy must be a form of empiricism, that it must be scientific, and that it must defend materialism (or "physicalism," as he calls it). From the latter point of view he concludes that a form of behaviorism must be the correct answer to the mind-body problem.

Quine's theory of meaning follows the lead of Frege and Russell in redirecting attention from *words* to *sentences* as the true units of meaning. Hume's empiricism was flawed because it made the mistake of trying to correlate individual words with individual experiences. (Take an idea like "God," "cause," or "self." Hume asked: "From what impression is that idea derived?" If he could find no sense datum corresponding to the idea, then the word naming the idea was meaningless.) On the contrary, by taking the sentence rather than the word as the unit of meaning, Quine avoids Hume's excessive reductionism, and he escapes the opposite extreme, Platonism, as well. For Plato, a word like "green" must name an essence, "greenness," that is more real than individual instantiations of greenness. This move violates Ockham's razor because items like "essences," "meanings," and "Forms" become real things that must be accounted for ontologically. Meanings become *things* that mediate between words and objects. Quine writes, "The explanatory value of special and irreducible intermediary entities called meanings is surely illusory."[31]

Quine makes great use of a technique that is now generally recognized as a hallmark of analytic philosophy—what he calls *contextual definition*. It is a form of paraphrase in which sentences that seem to provoke philosophical puzzles (for example, "Greenness is a color") are restated in ways that delete the offending terms (for example, "Anything green is colored"). We have already seen this technique used to great effect in Russell's Theory of Descriptions, whose function was to deal with the verb "to be" in ways that relieved us of the need to posit some metaphysical object called "being." This method of contextual definition reveals a suspicion on the part of the philosophers who use it that ordinary language cannot represent ideas in a successful manner and that therefore the philosopher must be constantly alert against language's deceptive snares. (In this respect Quine is something like Wittgenstein, who wrote in *Philosophical Investigations*, "Philosophy is the battle against the bewitchment of our intelligence by means of language" [109]. The difference is that Wittgenstein did not suspect that ordinary language itself is the culprit, rather, that the fault lies with our propensity to saddle ordinary language with monolithic philosophical assumptions.) Unlike Russell or the positivists, however, Quine uses contextual definition pragmatically. He does not claim that it reveals the true, hidden logical structure of thought disguised and burdened by ordinary language. Rather, the convenience of contextual definition is that it provides a way of bypassing certain features of ordinary expression that appear to lead us into an overpopulated metaphysical landscape. It also provides a language that can adequately represent all scientific theorizing.

I should mention as an aside a common objection raised against the method of paraphrasing in terms of contextual definition by opponents of the type of analytic philosophy employed by Quine and his tradition. They ask, how do we know that the elimination of the metaphysical problem in the sentence replaced by the paraphrase is not illusory? Perhaps the contextual definition simply disguises a genuine philosophical truth about reality. Generally, philosophers who raise this objection trust ordinary language more than does Quine. Wittgenstein would probably be in this camp.

Despite Quine's admission that the sometimes stilted language of logical analysis could never replace ordinary discourse, for him only the language of physics is capable of making literally true statements about reality. This belief signals Quine's physicalism—his updated version of the old materialist thesis that there is only matter in motion, a view that we ran into first in Democritus and then

New Age Analytic Philosophy

later in Hobbes. Ordinary language has *instrumental* value—it helps us muddle our way through life—but it is not equipped to express truths about reality, except sometimes in a metaphorical way. Quine even seems suspicious of the status of the sciences other than physics. Biology and psychology only give us another form of metaphorical truth about what's really there.

You might be surprised to discover that despite Quine's physicalism, he is not a reductionist. He is unconvinced that sciences like chemistry or biology can be reduced to physics or that all mental states can be translated into neurological events. He is satisfied to assert that "there is no mental difference without a physical difference."[32] Apparently the ultimate facts about mental life are the kind of facts that physics talks about, but at least for now—and perhaps forever—there is no way of reducing descriptions of mental events to descriptions of the most basic physical particles. Between these two levels there seems to be a space that only metaphorical language can fill. Yet Quine apparently thinks that this large space is of no interest to philosophy.

It is not surprising that many contemporary analytic philosophers who otherwise respect Quine for his rigor do not agree with him
on this topic. Some of them believe that this space to which Quine
is philosophically indifferent is the space of greatest interest to
thoughtful people, including philosophers, because it is constitutive
of human experience. It is in this space, for instance, where we find
activities and institutions like art, economics, morality, politics, linguistics, and the experience of selfhood.

Related to Quine's physicalism is a bold theory he produced in
1960 that he calls the "indeterminacy of translation" thesis. This
has proved to be one of his most controversial themes. Imagine a
team of field linguists trying to formulate manuals to allow them to
translate into English the unknown language of the subjects among
which they find themselves. We are to suppose that these linguists
have no access to any knowledge about the culture and institutions
that have produced the language in question. The linguists must concentrate on the relation between the verbal and bodily behavior of
the speakers and the physical stimuli that provoke these behaviors.
Quine believes that if these linguists work independently of each

other they will come up with a number of divergent manuals, each of which will be incompatible with the other manuals, but all of which could be compatible with the native speaker's behavior—linguistic and bodily—and the physical stimuli in the environment. Because all these imaginary manuals are compatible with the physical facts (Quine's main concern), there are no physical facts that can determine which of the manuals is the *correct* manual. A manual that facilitates conversation and cooperation is as correct as all others that *do* the same thing. This conclusion constitutes a form of radical behaviorism. If the same physical stimuli provoke the same responses, these responses are equivalent to one another.

Quine imagines that the linguists are trying to decipher the expression "*gavagai*," which the natives utter whenever a rabbit runs by.[33] Furthermore, whenever the linguists point to a rabbit while asking the question, "*Gavagai?*" the natives always make affirmative gestures and sounds. According to Quine, in this case we can conclude that a correct translation of *gavagai* would be, "There is a rabbit over there." But he also thinks numerous other translations would be equally correct. In fact, Quine argues that in the situation described, all these sentences are equivalent:

1. There is a rabbit over there.
2. A stage in the development of a rabbit is over there.
3. There are undetached rabbit parts over there.
4. There is rabbit-parts fusion over there.
5. There is an instantiation of rabbithood over there.

Contrary to most theories of meaning, which would say that sentences 1 through 5 are not at all synonymous, Quine concludes that because they are all systematically compatible with the same set of physical stimuli, they *are* synonymous and that therefore an indeterminacy of translation is revealed.

Quine admits that translation 1 is the most likely way of reading *gavagai*, but only for reasons of convenience, not reasons of "truth." His point is that from the perspective of bare physical fact (especially elementary physical particles, etc.), each of these translations is as good as the others. According to Quine, if this indeterminacy thesis rejects not only most philosophical accounts of language and mind as well as our ordinary everyday conceptions of them, so be it. Let the chips fall where they may. And certainly Quine's theory does wreak havoc with our normal ways of thinking about these topics, so much so that his theory is vulnerable to the charge of being outlandish. For example, a critic has pointed out that if you buy a rabbit as a pet, Quine's indeterminacy thesis turns your perfectly acceptable wish to cuddle such a pet into the perverse desire to fondle undetached rabbit parts.[34] (I would add that the translation of gavagai as "rabbit-parts fusion" would make the culinary term "rabbit stew" a tautology.) Another critic suggests:

Many readers may feel that this consequence of the indeterminacy thesis—apparently, the overthrow of our everyday conception of mind—shows that something has gone wrong. It may reinforce the feeling that the focus on stimulus meanings was unduly self-denying and was bound to yield a distorted and impoverished picture of meaning and mind.[35]

Quine's theory of the indeterminacy of translation has attracted much critical attention. This attention is not because philosophers feel that the issue of translation itself is necessarily of central importance; rather, they believe that Quine is right to see his thesis as the logical extension of radical physicalism, and by contesting the indeterminacy thesis they may be contesting physicalism itself.

At any rate, even philosophers who are opposed to Quine's overall views find themselves influenced by a variety of arguments in his widely read writings. There are probably few important analytic philosophers on the contemporary scene who have not found themselves incorporating Quinean ideas into their own systems, or at least feeling the need to respond publicly to his views. This list includes names like Donald Davidson, Hilary Putnam, Noam Chomsky, Jerry Fodor, Jerold Katz, Nelson Goodman, Wilfrid Sellars, Ian Hacking, and John Searle, just to name a few. Also, the younger generation of analytic philosophers has felt Quine's continuing influence. Among this group are some outstanding women philosophers, including Lynn Hankinson Nelson and Louise Antony, who have argued that Quine's philosophy should be attractive to feminists.[36]

The Phenomenological Tradition and Its Aftermath

Husserl

A number of European thinkers had continued to work well within the Continental philosophical tradition inaugurated by Descartes despite the unrelenting attack on that tradition by the logical positivists. Primary among them was Edmund Husserl (1859–1938), the founder of a philosophy that he called "phenomenology" (from the Greek *phainómenon*, meaning "appearance"—hence, the study of appearances). He traced the roots of his view to the work of Descartes. Like Descartes, Husserl placed consciousness at the center of all philosophizing, but Husserl had learned from Kant that a theory of consciousness must be as concerned with the *form* of consciousness as with its *content* (Descartes had failed to realize this), so he developed a method that would demonstrate both the structure and the content of the mind. This method would be purely *descriptive* and not *theoretical*. That is, it would describe the way the world actually reveals itself to consciousness without the aid of any theoretical constructs from either philosophy or science. This method laid bare the world of what Husserl called "the natural standpoint," which is pretty much the everyday world as experienced unencumbered by the claims of philosophy and science. Writing about the natural standpoint in *Ideas: General Introduction to Pure Phenomenology*, Husserl said,

> I am aware of a world, spread out in space endlessly, and in time becoming and become, without end. I am aware of it, that means, first of all, I discover it immediately, intuitively, I experience it. Through sight, touch, hearing, etc., . . . corporeal things . . . are for me simply there, . . . "present," whether or not I pay them special attention.[37]

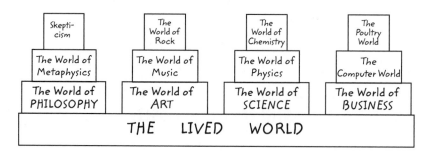

Worlds upon Worlds

This world of the natural standpoint is the absolute beginning of all philosophy and science. It is the world as actually *lived*. Other worlds can be built upon the *lived world* but can never replace it or undermine it. For human beings ultimately there is only the lived world of the natural standpoint. But Husserl wanted to "get behind" the content of the natural standpoint to reveal its structure. To do so, he employed a method like Descartes's radical doubt, a method that Husserl called "phenomenological reduction" (or *epochê*, a Greek word meaning "suspension of belief"). This method brackets any experience whatsoever and describes it while suspending all presuppositions and assumptions normally made about that experience. Bracketing the experience of looking at a coffee cup, for instance, requires suspending the belief that the cup is *for* holding coffee and that its handle is for grasping. Bracketing reveals the way the cup presents itself to consciousness as a number of possible structures. (I can't see the front and the back at the same time, nor the top and the bottom, nor see more than one of its possible presentations at any given moment.)

If we apply the *epochê* to the more philosophically significant example of the experience of *time*, we must suspend all belief in clocks, train schedules, and calendars. Then we will discover that *lived time*

Prof. Edmund Husserl Performs an *Epochê* on a Coffee Cup

is always experienced as an eternal *now*, which is tempered by a memory of earlier nows (the thenness of the past) and is always rushing into the semiexperienceable but ultimately nonexperienceable thenness of the future. Phenomenologically speaking, the time is always "now." To do anything is to do something now. You can never act then.

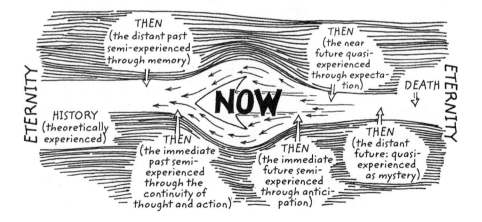

Similarly, a phenomenological reduction of the experience of space reveals the difference between *lived space* and *mapped space*. Lived space is always experienced in terms of a here-there dichotomy, in which I am always here and everything else is always at different intensities of thereness. (Jean-Paul Sartre, Husserl's errant disciple,

**From the Natural
Standpoint**

**From the Standpoint
of the Epochê**

would later draw very pessimistic conclusions from this discovery.)
So the here-now experience is the ground zero of the experience of
space and time. It is somehow the locus of the self.

One of Husserl's main insights (actually derived from the work of
his teacher Franz von Brentano) and one that was to be incorporated
into both the later phenomenological tradition and, in some cases,
the analytic tradition,[38] was his treatment of the *intentionality* of all
consciousness (i.e., its referentiality). The Husserlian motto here is
"All consciousness is consciousness of . . ." (This motto means there
is no such thing as self-enclosed thought; one thinks *about* something. You can't be just aware—you have to be aware *of* something,
and afraid *of* something, and concerned *about* something. There are
no intransitive mental states, not even Kierkegaard's "dread"—the
fear of absolutely nothing. It is still the fear *of* nothing.) It is this
intentionality (or referentiality) that distinguishes consciousness
from everything else in the universe.

Husserl claimed that the phenomenological suspension could be
performed on the *object* of intentionality (e.g., the coffee cup) or on

the act of conscious-
ness itself.
Therefore, he
believed it was
possible to step
back from normal
consciousness into a
kind of pure conscious-
ness, a transcendental
ego, a self-behind-the-self,
which, like Descartes's "I am"
(but more deeply real), would be
the starting point of all knowledge. Husserl's ideas get very
complex here, and few of his disci-

**The Self behind the Self
(But Is There a Self behind
the Self behind the Self?)**

ples have chosen to follow him into these ethereal regions.

Today, Husserl is most admired for his *method*. This method has
had a number of outstanding adherents, including Martin Heidegger,
Maurice Merleau-Ponty, and Sartre. Shortly, we will review the philosophies of Heidegger and Sartre, Husserl's best-known, if most wayward, disciples, and we will let them represent the outcome of the
evolution of phenomenology into existentialism.

Heidegger

Martin Heidegger (1889–1976) was an early colleague of Husserl and
a student of his phenomenology, but it soon became clear that his
philosophical concerns were quite different from Husserl's. The latter's phenomenological reduction claimed to discover certain essential features of objects like coffee cups and matchboxes and to provide an account of our knowledge of these kinds of beings. Heidegger,
however, was interested in applying the method to a deeper question—that of Being itself. He was not concerned with questions
about the nature of individual "beings" (questions that he called

"ontic" questions); rather, he was interested in the Being of beings—the fact that individual beings are at all (what he called "ontological" concerns). We saw that Gottfried Leibniz in the seventeenth century had asked the primary ontological question, "Why is there something rather than nothing?" but he had asked it only as a theological query in order to prove the existence of God. Furthermore, by Leibniz's time it was already too late to ask the question correctly,

Martin Heidegger

according to Heidegger, for Being had already been concealed in the Western tradition by one thousand philosophical and scientific misconceptions. But it had not always been so. The pre-Socratics had been astounded in the presence of Being and had asked truly ontological questions.

But these *true thinkers* (thinkers are better than mere philosophers, for Heidegger) were followed by Plato, who distracted thought away from Being and into an artificial idealistic world of Forms, and by Aristotle, who concentrated on "beings" and provoked a technological tradition in which Being itself would be forgotten. Heidegger wanted

A Pre-Socratic Philosopher Finds the Being of His Own Thumb (And Is Duly Impressed!)

to "call us back to a remembrance of Being"—to return us to our primordial astonishment in its presence. We must come home to Being—stand in its presence and establish a harmonic concordance with it rather than merely intellectualize it.

One thing that prevents us from returning home to Being is the language we employ to do it. It has become encrusted with the fragments and dust of a ruined past, and it must be cleansed and purged if it is to become a viable path to Being. Luckily (and quite

Being Speaks

conveniently, if you are German, as was Heidegger), of the modern languages, German is the closest to the truth, because it's less bespattered with lies and because it's more powerful and more spiritual than other languages—though ancient Greek, the language of the pre-Socratics themselves, remains the most powerful. The Greek of those first thinkers comes to us from a time when its speakers were direct witnesses to Being.

Heidegger mined this language, going into its deepest **etymologies.** For instance, he discovered that the Greek word for "being," *Parousia*, designates something that "stands firmly by itself and thus manifests and declares itself"[39] and that the Greek word for "truth," *aletheia*, means "uncoveredness."[40] But simply studying Greek or being able to speak German is not enough. A new beginning must be found that will be radically innovative and return us to origins at the same time. To this end, Heidegger generated a flood of technical vocabulary, to the delight of some and the annoyance of others.

Heidegger Mining Language

Take a look, for example, at one of his characterizations of the meaning of the word "care": "ahead-of-itself-Being-already-in-(the-world) as Being-alongside (entities encountered within-the-world)."[41] (ten dashes already!)

It is not easy to see that these clumsy neologisms restore lost meanings—that Heidegger's artificial language is closer to the truth than is the language of everyday life. It is ironic that Heidegger's reasons for rewriting ordinary language are in some ways similar to those of Russell and the logical positivists. The latter created an artificial syntax because they believed it was closer to the hidden truth of language; Heidegger did so because he believed that it was closer to the hidden truth of Being.

Humans have certain attitudes toward beings. In this respect, we are like other animals. But unlike other animals, humans also have an attitude toward Being itself. We "comport" ourselves toward it. We are unique not simply because only we can question Being, but also in that, in questioning Being, we put our own Being in question. We are the only being whose own Being is a question for itself. Therefore, our being is different. Heidegger designated that difference by saying that other beings *are*; we *ex-ist*. He named human existence *Dasein* (being there). Unlike other beings, which are merely *in* the world, *Dasein has* a world. Heidegger rejected the intellectualism of most philosophers who have seen the world as primarily the object of human knowledge. For him, knowing was just one way of being-in-the-world. Furthermore, knowing is itself not just an intellectual act.

To "understand" something is to understand it in the context of usage, to understand it as something serviceable or dangerous. Things are not just "present-at-hand"; they are not just objects for disinterested scientific investigation; they are "ready-to-hand." The there of our being-there (Dasein) is filled with objects that are there for us, ready-to-hand. We have *care* or *concern* for them. This "care" (*Sorge*) is one of the main characteristics of human existence; we care for the world around us, both the natural and the human world. And when we express care not just for beings but for Being itself, we are our most authentic selves as humans.

Being-within-the-world entails being-with-others. The there of Dasein is populated not only with objects for our use but also with the Dasein of others. Our relationship to others is neither that of presence-at-hand nor readiness-to-hand, for we must acknowledge that others make the same demands on us that we make on them. There is a danger, however, of giving in too much to their demands. We can "come not to be ourselves." We can be sucked into the third-person theyness of others. This form of inauthentic existence in which we live in the opinions and desires of the anonymous they is a form of fear that produces a hollowness. "Fallenness" is Heidegger's term for succumbing to this fear. Unfortunately, fallenness is not just a side effect of bad choices. It is of the essence of human existence. We have "fallen" into a world of others. But it is possible to come out of inauthenticity through *Sorge*: care for Being and care for beings, care for the future, for the past, and for the community.

We are also rescued from inauthenticity through *Angst*, anxiety. We experience anxiety in the recognition of death. This anxiety is not the same as the simple fear of death. Anxiety is cognitive. It produces knowledge that we are going to die. It reveals to us that Dasein is being-toward-death. We discover the meaning of our being as Dasein in the possibility of not-being Dasein, that is, in death. It is also this discovery that reveals to us our own freedom, for in the face of our imminent annihila-

We Have Fallen into a World of Others

tion we must choose a life that justifies its own worth despite its necessary termination.

Most of these ideas were developed in Heidegger's major work *Being and Time*, published in 1927. It contained two parts and ended

Human Existence Is Being-toward-Death

with a series of questions that Heidegger promised to answer in a third part. But Part 3 was never written. One critic says that Heidegger himself felt that the path to Being had "come to a dead end."[42]

After 1927, rather than returning to the unfinished section of *Being and Time*, Heidegger wrote a number of shorter works, some of

The Phenomenological Tradition and Its Aftermath • **359**

A Dead End?

which still have not been released in an English translation. These writings have provoked a great debate among both Heideggerians and his critics as to whether Heidegger changed his mind after 1927 concerning the key philosophical questions. There seems to be at least a change of emphasis, in which *language* (the new path to Being) almost eclipses Being, including the human being, as language swallows up the individual. "Language is the house of Being in which man ek-sists by dwelling."[43] It is not that humans speak language but that language speaks itself through humans. It follows therefore that poets rather than philosophers are the true custodians of Being—and particularly the German poet Friedrich Hölderlin, who conveniently happened to be from Heidegger's neck of the woods but who inconveniently ended up in an asylum. The key feature of poetry is a

kind of naming, nomi-
nation, an act that
"realizes" in the sense
of making real. As in
Nietzsche, the Pla-
tonic hierarchy has
been inverted. It is the
artists and not the
scientists who speak
Truth. Eventually, in
Heidegger's final
works, poetic language
itself seems to give
way to the poetic

silence between words. Truth would have to be "silence about silence."

Despite the enormous influence of Heidegger's philosophy, a
shadow has been cast over his life and his work. In 1933, as rector of
the University of Freiburg, Heidegger had joined the Nazi party and
had given speeches praising Adolf Hitler. Within a year, he resigned his
post and issued no more praise of the Führer. In fact, Heidegger himself came under the scrutiny of the Nazis. Yet he never publicly apolo-
gized for his support of a party that was soon to commit unimagin-
able atrocities, and he remained silent about the Holocaust. What is
the connection between his silence and the Silence that speaks
Truth? Apparently none. His critics say that his silence conceals a
sinister truth. They also claim to find a concordance between his
bombastic pseudointellectual German diction and his obsession with
death and land, on the one hand, and the ghoulish and vacuous ideas
of Nazism on the other. His defenders say that Heidegger was a
politically naive philosophical genius who made a political mistake and,
when he realized it was a mistake, made another by not publicly
denouncing his first mistake. They say this major personal flaw does
not detract from the value of his work.

Sartre

Another of Edmund Husserl's erstwhile disciples was Jean-Paul Sartre (1905–1980). Besides being one of the most important philosophers of the twentieth century, Sartre was also an essayist, novelist, and playwright.

His early philosophical ideas are developed in his novel *Nausea* (1938); in his treatises, *Transcendence of the Ego* (1936) and *Being and Nothingness* (1943); and in his essay "Existentialism Is a Humanism" (1946). In these works, we see the influence not only of Husserl but also of Heidegger and Kierkegaard.

Jean-Paul Sartre

First, let us look at Sartre's theory of consciousness. From Husserl, Sartre had learned that consciousness is always referential, in that it always refers beyond itself to an *object*. "Unreflected consciousness" is consciousness before it is reflected upon or philoso-

Consciousness always refers

Unreflected consciousness

phized about. When I read a novel, the object of the unreflected consciousness is the hero of the novel. When I run to catch a trolley, the object of the unreflected consciousness is "streetcar-to-be-caught."

In unreflected consciousness, there is no self, no "I" to be found; only its objects exist—Don Quixote or the streetcar. Reflective consciousness is consciousness that reflects on itself. According to Sartre (and contrary to Descartes),

Reflective consciousness — consciousness reflecting on consciousness

the ego, or the I, is to be discovered only in reflected consciousness. Not only is it *discovered* there, but it also is actually partially created there.

Once we study consciousness phenomenologically (bracket it, make it the object of reflective consciousness), we discover that it is

"a monstrous . . . impersonal spontaneity"[44] in which thoughts come and go at *their* will, not ours. This spontaneity is a form of dizzying freedom, according to Sartre, and contemplation of it leads to anguish. We actively struggle to impose order on this free spontaneity, and when we fail, neurosis and psychosis ensue.

Sartre mentioned the case of a woman who dreaded her husband's leaving for work because she feared that upon his departure she would sit nude in the window like a prostitute. Because she knew she was *free* to do so, she feared she *would* do so. (This theme was inspired by Kierkegaard's account of dread. When God told Adam not to eat the apple, Adam then knew that he *could* eat it—that he was *free* to do so—and he knew that if he could, he *might*. That is, he experienced his freedom as dread.)

In our own case, as in the case of that woman, sometimes the order we impose upon consciousness breaks down, and consciousness is revealed to us as the monstrous spontaneity that it is. As a philosophical exercise, Husserl had suspended all beliefs and all "normality" in the *epoché*, but Sartre discovered that an *epoché* can break in on us when we least expect it, not as a philosophical exercise but as a crisis of consciousness, as when we look into a chasm and suddenly feel the urge to throw ourselves in.

This crisis of consciousness is what happens to Roquentin, the "hero" of Sartre's novel *Nausea*, as he sits on a park bench looking at the knotted roots of a chestnut tree.

Suddenly, all the old assumptions break down, and he sees the tree not as a tree but as a "black, knotty, raw, doughy, melted, soft, monstrous, naked, obscene, frightening lump of existence."[45] Suddenly, the tree's Being has presented itself to him. Roquentin discovers that that Being, as it reveals itself in the crisis of consciousness, is pure superfluity, pure excess.

The rationalists Spinoza and Leibniz were badly mistaken. Not only is Being not necessary, but it also is *absurd*. Far from there existing a "sufficient reason" for the being of Being, there is no reason for it to exist at all. So the Sartrean existentialist finds his or her own existence as a superfluity in an absurd world. Yet human beings do exist. They have been thrown into a meaningless world without

their permission. What is the relation between human beings and the world?

The most significant form of this relationship is that of "the question." By questioning the world, I reveal a *nothingness* in Being. When I seek Pierre in a café and discover that Pierre is *not* there, I reveal a nothingness in reality. (Pierre's absence is *real*.)

In the same way, I discover that a nothingness separates me from myself. There is a nothingness between me and my past (I am *not* who I was) and between me and my future (the person I will be is *not* who I am).

I Await Myself in the Future

This realization again makes me aware that "I await myself in the future. Anguish is the fear of not finding myself there, of no longer even wishing to be there."[46] This anguish stems from my discovery that my self is not a stable, solid entity that lasts through time; rather, it is a *creation* that I must make and remake from moment to moment.

Not only must I create myself, but I must also create my world. I do so by bestowing values on the world. According to the pre-Sartrean view of freedom, values preexist my freedom. I am placed between these values, and my freedom consists in my ability to choose between these preexisting values. According to the Sartrean view, through freedom, I bestow value on the world by choosing aspects of it. Freedom preexists values. Life has no meaning or value except that which I give to it. Ultimately, my choice of values

The Old View of Freedom

cannot be justified because there are no eternal (Platonic) values, no stone tablets, no Scriptures to which I can appeal to justify my choices. In the final analysis, no set of values is objectively any more valuable than any other set. This discovery leads to more anguish (of course!).

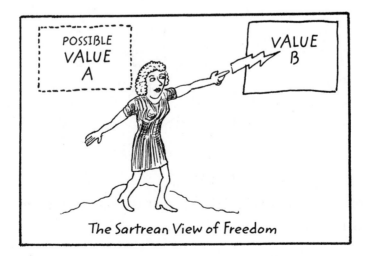

The Sartrean View of Freedom

"My freedom is anguished at being the foundation of values while being itself without foundation."[47]

Certainly my freedom is not absolute. Consciousness runs up against "facticity" in existence (i.e., that which cannot be changed). If a boulder falls in my path, I cannot change the fact that it is there or that it is impenetrable. But I am free to interpret the meaning of

its "thereness" for me. It may mean an obstacle to be conquered, or it may mean that my goal of reaching the mountain top is defeated, or I may interpret it as an object of aesthetic contemplation or as a scientific specimen. "Situation" is what Sartre called the interpretation of facticity. To interpret facticity is to create a world for me to inhabit. I am always "in situation" and am always freely creating worlds. In fact, in this respect . . .

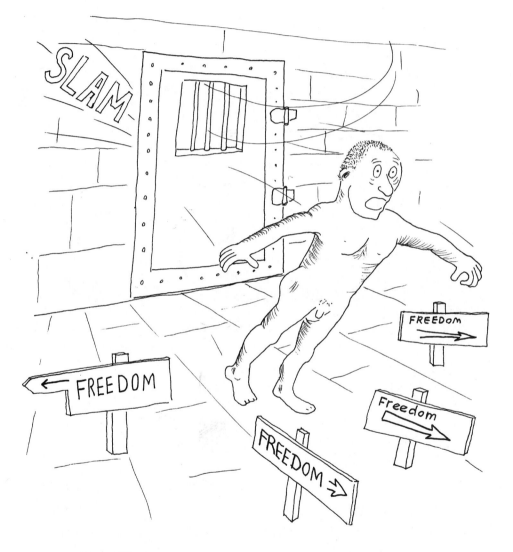

". . . I am condemned to be free."[48]

Most people create worlds in "bad faith." That is, rather than facing up to their responsibility and freedom, people flee from them by denying them or by blaming them on others, on fate, or on "the Establishment."

But there can be no blaming in good faith. We cannot blame our upbringing, our parents, our poverty (or our wealth), or the "hard times" because we alone determine the *meaning* that these things have for us.

We are always free because there are always alternative choices—the ultimate alternative is death. If I do not shoot myself, then I have chosen whatever is the alternative to death.

A major complication in the experience of our freedom is that we must encounter other free beings. The unity that I have imposed on my consciousness is momentarily shattered when the Other *looks* at me and transforms me into the *object* of his gaze. I can recover my own selfhood only by looking at him and transforming him into my object. (This is like Hegel's master-slave relation, except that no synthesis is possible.) "Hell," said Sartre, "is other people."[49]

Sartre's philosophy ends with what many philosophers take to be a pessimism that reflects the plight of the human in the modern world. Sartre denied that he was a pessimist. Instead, he made heroes of us all. The authentic human being knows that all her acts are ultimately futile in the face of death and the absurdity of existence, yet she chooses to persevere. In God-like fashion, she creates worlds upon worlds. Like Sisyphus, she pushes her boulder daily up the steep incline of existence, without excuse and without complaint. It is, after all, *her* boulder. She created it.

Structuralism and Poststructuralism

Beginning in the 1960s, Europe's fascination with phenomenology and existentialism gave way to an interest in a new movement called structuralism. This movement was in its inception a reaction against phenomenology and existentialism; nevertheless, its members kept returning to the themes raised by existential phenomenology.

Saussure

Although structuralism had a major influence on philosophy, it actually began in the social sciences and found its inspiration in the turn-of-the-century work of the Swiss linguist Ferdinand de Saussure (1857–1913). In his posthumously published *Course of General Linguistics*, agreeing with his contemporaries the pragmatists and anticipating the view of the later Wittgenstein, Saussure argued that "meanings" are neither names of fixed essences (as in rationalism) nor names of sensorial experiences (as in empiricism). Rather, the meaning of a linguistic phenomenon is a function of its location in an underlying linguistic structure. This linguistic object is not defined by some positive feature inherent to it, but rather in terms of the negative relations in which it stands to other objects in the system. (Both in terms of its sound [phonic value] and its meaning [semantic value], the word "bed" is what it is by *not* being "bad," "bid," "bod," or "bud.")

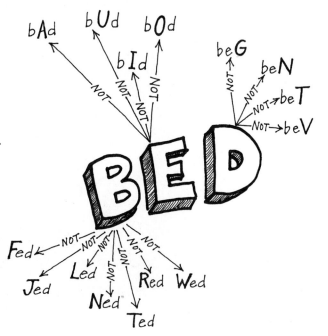

According to Saus-
sure, a language is a system of *signs*. A sign is a
combination of a *sound*
(or an audio-image) and
an *idea* (or concept). The
former is called a "signifier," the latter a "signified." (This terminological
distinction is germinal for
all structuralist thinkers.)
A sound can only be a sign
if it is related to a con-

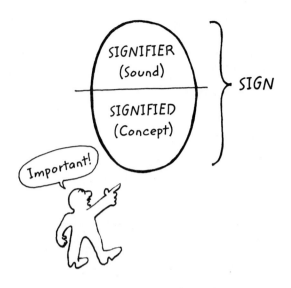

cept. Therefore, there must be a *system of conventions* that relates
sounds to concepts. Saussure's linguistics studies this system.

A major emphasis of Saussurean theory is on the *arbitrary*
nature of the sign. That is to say, the relation between the signifier
and the signified is a purely conventional one, not one based in
nature. The sound "cat" *could* have denoted the idea "dog," but it just
didn't turn out that way. There is no natural connection between the

sound "cat" and the
ideas we have of that
particular feline.

There are excep-
tions—so-called ono-
matopoeia. But even
these are usually more
arbitrary than they
seem. Dogs in California
say, "Bow-Wow"; but in
France they say, "Ouâ-
Ouâ"; and in Germany,
"Wau-Wau"; and in Italy,
"Bau-Bau."

There is an anti-Platonic philosophical implication in this aspect of Saussurean theory. The sign is arbitrary at both ends. That is, there are no absolutes at either end. Both the signifier and the signified evolve in relation to other entities within their audio-conceptual system and in relation to other such systems, which means that there are no fixed universal

WHAT? No Absolutes?

concepts. In that case, the Platonic ideal of absolute knowledge is a myth.

So the signifier and the signified are both purely *relational* entities. They exist only insofar as they relate to other entities, and the relationship is mainly a *negative* one. Saussure said of signs, "Their most precise characteristic is being what the others are not."[50]

As Wittgenstein was to do later, Saussure drew an analogy between language and chess. The shape of the chess piece is arbitrary. Any shape will do as long as the piece can be distinguished

from other pieces with different functions. The identity of a chess piece (or of a signifier, or of a signified, or of a sign) is not dependent on some inherent essence that it has but is totally a function of differences within the system to which it belongs. As Saussure said, "there are only differences, without positive terms."[51]

Lévi-Strauss

At the end of his work, Saussure called for a new science, *the general science of signs*, which he named **semiology**, with linguistics as its model, even though linguistics would be only *part* of this science. In semiology, human conventions, rituals, and acts would be studied as signs (combinations of signifiers and signifieds). These behavioral signs would be demonstrated to be as arbitrary as linguistic signs and would be shown to stand in the same relationship to other parts of the behavioral system that linguistic signs do to language.

It is only a slight exaggeration to say that **structuralism** is the science that Saussure called for, a science whose specific formulation is the creation of the French anthropologist Claude Lévi-Strauss (b. 1908).

Most contemporary anthropology is concerned with the organization of specific societies. It tends to correspond to a form of **functionalism** in that it often explains social institutions and

Claude Lévi-Strauss

phenomena in terms of their utilitarian value within the culture. (E.g., any nomadic desert tribes that became dependent on swine herding would not survive. Therefore, the prohibition against eating the flesh

of pigs will become insti-
tutionalized in such societies. Hence "Jehovah's"
and "Allah's" prohibition
against pork.)

Lévi-Strauss rejects
the functionalist inter-
pretation of social phe-
nomena. Many social
institutions have no utility at all in and of themselves but take on mean-
ing when related to all
the other institutions
within the society. Fur-
thermore, rather than
concerning himself exclu-
sively with the organiza-
tion of particular soci-

eties, Lévi-Strauss looks for *universal* characteristics of all societies.
All cultures, despite their many differences, are products of the
human brain. Therefore, "there must be somewhere beneath the surface features common to all."[52]

The search for universals distinguishes Lévi-Strauss from the
mainstream functionalist movement and puts him in a philosophical
tradition that originated with Socrates and Plato (so Plato isn't
completely dead after all!) and that is most clearly expressed in the
modern period by Kant's search for synthetic a priori truths. What is
new in Lévi-Strauss is the claim that the human universals exist only
latently at the level of *structure* and not at the level of manifest
fact. (Though, of course, Marx and Freud said something similar. And,
indeed, Marx and Freud, as well as Saussure, have influenced structuralism deeply.) When we look at Lévi-Strauss's statement of his

method, we see the impact of Saussurean linguistics on his thought because he treats cultural phenomena the way Saussure treated signifiers.

1. "Define the phenomenon under study as a relation between two or more terms, real or supposed."
2. "Construct a table of possible permutations between these terms."
3. Treat the table as the structure of necessary logical connections ("a sort of periodic chart of chemical elements"), which will demonstrate that the empirical phenomenon under study "is only one possible combination among others."[53]

Periodic Chart of Possible Social Relations

Chart #72—Mother

Mother to Son	Mother to Daughter	Mother to Husband	Mother to Her Father
Mother to Her Mother	Mother to Nephew	Mother to Niece	Mother to Sister
Mother to Brother	Mother to Uncle	Mother to Aunt	Mother to Grandmother
Mother to Grandfather	Mother to Female Cousin	Mother to Male Cousin	Mother to Godmother

Notice two things here. First, Lévi-Strauss's method is a rationalistic method (rationalistic because its goal is the discovery of necessary logical relations, which are in fact a priori) in which empirical phenomena themselves are "demoted" and empiricism goes by the board. Second, there is offered here a kind of halfway house between freedom and determinism. There are choices, but they are severely restricted for both individuals and cultures. These choices are at the same time created and limited by the structural system of which they are a part. Lévi-Strauss says, "human societies, like individual human beings . . . never create absolutely; all they do is choose certain combinations from a repertory of ideas."[54]

In *The Savage Mind* (*La pensée sauvage*, 1962), Lévi-Strauss tries to demonstrate the essentially *logical* nature of all human thought, including that of so-called primitives. The logical foundation of all mental activity is the recognition of opposites, contrasts, and similarities. In this sense, the "savage mind" (really, "thinking in the raw") is as rational as any other mind. Furthermore, it demonstrates an exceptional awareness of the crude sensory data of nature and an intuitive ability to detect analogous systems within the sensual vocabulary of colors, sounds, smells, and tastes.

Lévi-Strauss, in *The Savage Mind*, tries to destroy once and for all the myth ingrained in popular prejudice and supported by Lévi-Strauss's anthropological predecessors that primitives are like children and think in some pre-adult manner. He accomplishes this goal with a two-edged argument. First, he demonstrates areas of typical primitive thinking that are far more sophisticated than our own. Second,

he demonstrates examples of cultured thought that are in fact quite primitive.

As an example of sophisticated thought among the primitives, Lévi-Strauss tells us, concerning a tribe in the Philippines, that

> Ninety-three percent of the total number of native plants are recognized by the Hanunóo as culturally significant. . . . The Hanunóo classify all forms of the local avifauna into seventy-five categories. . . . They distinguish about a dozen kinds of snakes . . . sixty-odd types of fish . . . insect forms are grouped by the Hanunóo into a hundred and eight name categories, including thirteen for ants and termites.[55]

As an example of primitive thought among the "sophisticated," we need only consider our attitude toward such cultural icons as "the bed in which George Washington slept," or perhaps toward Madonna's bra, or the parchment that claims to be the U.S. Constitution. (It is

not. We would still have a constitution even if the parchment were destroyed.) Many people treat these articles like primitive fetishes.

In summary, according to Lévi-Strauss, universally valid principles of human thought hold for all peoples at all times. Historical and cultural contingencies can overlay these principles with levels of abstractions and technical obfuscations, but these contingencies never replace that which they disguise. To observe this universal logic in its purest form, we should study the "unpolluted" mind of pretechnical peoples. In such a way, we will discover the unity of the human race.

Lacan

By the end of the 1970s, structuralism itself began to give way to a series of splinter groups that, opposed as they often were to one another, can all be designated by the term "poststructuralism."

This "movement" is not really an outright rejection of structuralism. It is, rather, a radicalization and intensification of some of its themes. Like structuralism, it found its home not only in philosophy but also in the social sciences, in **psychoanalysis,** and in literary criticism. The bridge between structuralism and poststructuralism was constructed by the French psychoanalyst Jacques Lacan (1901–1981), as seen in his dense and often perversely obscure book

Écrits. Yet Lacan claimed not to be inventing a new theory or even reinterpreting the theories of Sigmund Freud, the founder of psychoanalysis, but simply to be *reading* Freud's text carefully (something he apparently thought others had failed to do). Undaunted by the fact that neurology had failed to produce the empirical evidence for psychoanalysis that Freud had anticipated, Lacan claimed to find its justification in linguistics. Psychoanalysis is, after all, "the talking cure." It is

**Jacques Lacan
Reads Sigmund Freud**

essentially about language. According to Lacan, "the unconscious is structured like a language."[56] This epigram is an invitation to apply the insights of linguistics to the study of the human mind.

There is, of course, such a thing as prelinguistic experience. It gives the infant access to the Real, in all its Nietzschean disorder. The Real is experienced as pain and joy, but the child's access to language alienates it from the Real. Organic need (what Freud called "instinct," or *Trieb*) is experienced as an aboriginal *lack*. As organic need is translated into language, it becomes *desire*, and the original experience of lack is cast into the unconscious. Human existence is so hopelessly insatiable because underneath desire is a radical lack of being. But desire cannot address it directly because desire is language-bound.

Desire takes a metonymical course ("metonymy" refers to the displacement of meaning from one signifier to another signifier that is contiguous to the first, in terms of either meaning or sound; e.g.,

Metonymical Reasoning

"He takes too much to the bottle," or any rhyme: "cat, fat, mat"); it moves from sign to tangential sign without ever being able to grasp the absolute lack that it conceals. Lacan's "desire is a metonymy"[57] refers to this process. Desire is translated into *demand*, but demand is not really concerned with any particular object because no particular object can replace the forever-lost object.

If we retrace the metonymical wanderings of true need (which has been caught in the nets of the signifier), we find that desire, in its labyrinthine course, ends up with itself as its own object. Desire desires desire. This is one meaning of Lacan's infamous phrase, "Desire is the desire of the Other."[58] Every desire is, finally, the desire to be desired by the Other, a desire

to impose oneself upon the Other. Ultimately, then, every demand is a demand for love.

What have been repressed into the unconscious are not biological instincts because these have already been translated into words. It is *words*—signifiers—that have been consigned to the unconscious. "The unconscious [is] a chain of signifiers."[59] In conscious language and thought, the emphasis is on the objectivity of the signified (i.e., the objectivity of meaning). This emphasis disguises the creativity of the signifier (the word). It obscures and even denies the

The rigidity here →

$$\frac{\text{Signifier}}{\text{signified}}$$

← ... disguises the creative possibility here.

fact that the signifier can slide easily past its normal frontiers to reveal amazing new relations between itself and its possible signifieds. Unconscious language and thought know this truth, but the institutional strictures of conscious thought and language ("the discourse of reason," or Logos) ignore this scandalous wisdom. Conscious language uses conventional signs associated with fixed meanings. It *must* do so; otherwise we wouldn't understand each other. But the unconscious is freed from the necessity of public understanding. It can *play* with the signifier without regard for its real meaning. It can produce its own private "meanings." However, there is a bridge between consciousness and the unconscious. That bridge is *poetry*. Poetic language is close to a form of unconscious language. It constitutes a kind of intermediary level between conscious and unconscious discourse. ("I should have been a pair of ragged claws scuttling across the floors of silent seas.")[60]

The poet hovers somewhere between the expressly public and the intensely private. According to Lacan, the difference between the patient and the poet is that the former's poetic play with the relationships among signifiers is strictly private. The psychotic who feared birds because he knew that, in French slang, police officers on bicycles are referred to as "swallows," lives in a purely private poetic world. He does so because of an incommunicable personal experience that he has suffered, an experience that can be traced in the unconscious by following the network of signifiers in which his mind is enmeshed.

Silence: Poet at Work   Silence: Lunatic at Work

What Lacan called the Imaginary designates the world of the infant (and the world of some psychotics), a world in which the subject is lost in its own imagery, in its own fantasy. The "images" of the Imaginary are representations of lived experience before that experience is alienated into language. We deliver ourselves from the entrapment of the Imaginary by entering into the fullness of language, which is to say, by entering into the Symbolic. By naming a thing, the subject distances herself from it. When she names it, she denies that she *is* it. Access to the Symbolic fixates the mind and rescues it

from the undifferentiated flux of the Imaginary. It mediates between self and self, between self and thing. If there were no possibility of "registering oneself in the Symbolic," there would be no possibility of individuality because individuality requires differentiation.

Lacan was ambivalent concerning the worth of the entry into the symbolic order. On the positive side, it is this access that makes individuality possible and that has given the human its superiority over nature. On the negative side, precisely by alienating himself from nature and creating an unconscious into which he can suppress his own natural self, the individual becomes more artificial, distancing himself from the truth of

his own reality, and enters into a system of rigid determinism. It is in Lacan's determinism that we see him at his most pessimistic.

When the subject gains access to the Symbolic, that individual enters into a preestablished system with its own rules and structures. The self is assimilated into a network of relations in which the self is always an effect and never a cause. The subject becomes fashioned by the structure of language. The logic of the relations between signs replaces the lived experience of the Real. The individual becomes a prisoner of the autonomous order of signs. As in the later Heidegger, it is not the subject but the language that speaks.

Derrida

Another important theorist in the Continental poststructuralist movement (and one who has come to teach philosophy in southern California) is the French philosopher Jacques Derrida (b. 1930). Well, at least he was *trained* in philosophy, but one of the hallmarks of his view is the demotion of philosophy from the privileged status it has always claimed for itself as arbiter of Reason. Traditional philosophy, which Derrida derides as logocentrism, has devalued other forms of writing, especially poetic, metaphorical, and literary writing, as being further from the Truth than is philosophical discourse. Philosophy only grudgingly uses language to express its insights into meaning and reality. Yet, according to Derrida, philosophical discourse suffers from the same

**The Parisian Philosopher
at Disneyland**

vicissitudes as every other form of speech and writing, and every attempt even to say what one means by "meaning" and "reality" must necessarily self-destruct.

So Derrida willingly plays twentieth-century Sophist to would-be twentieth-century Platos. His version of relativism derives from a radicalization of Saussure's linguistics. If, as Saussure had argued, every sign is what it is by not being the others, then every sign involves every other sign. Therefore, there is never any "meaning" fully present; rather, all meaning is infinitely deferred. (Derrida recognizes that this conclusion is true of his own meaning as well—that his discourse is parasitical on the discourse that he criticizes—but he accepts this paradox playfully, albeit a little *too* playfully for some of his critics.)

Every presence of meaning or of being (because "being" can only present itself in the context of "meaning") is an absence, and every absence is a presence. Derrida designates this fact of "surplus meaning" as "*différance*," wittingly misspelling the French word *différence*, punning on the fact that the French verb *différer* means both "to differ" and "to defer."[61]

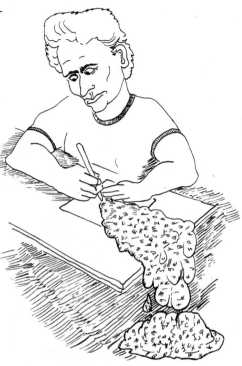

An Excess of Meaning

In fact, punning is very much to the point here. Derrida's idea can be partially understood by thinking of how almost all words have multiple meanings. "Dog," for instance, according to the *Random House Dictionary*, can be correctly used to distinguish between domestic canines, on the one hand, and wolves, jackals, and foxes on the other, *or* it can include all these animals. It can designate the male canine, as opposed to the bitch, *or* can include both. It can also refer to "any of various animals resembling a dog." It can designate "a despicable man or youth," an "ugly, boring, or crude girl or woman," or anybody in general, as in "a gay dog," can refer to feet, or to "something worthless or of extremely poor quality." It's also the name of "any of various mechanical devices for gripping or holding something," or it is a sausage, or the object of ruin (to go to the dogs), or of unhappiness (a dog's life), or, as a verb, to track with hostile intent, or to put on airs, and so on and so on.

If Derrida is right, the word "dog" cannot help but carry with it some, or most, of these meanings in any of its uses. Every meaning is, to use Freud's language, "over-determined" (overloaded with significance). If we say, "but the context determines the meaning," we forget that the meaning also determines the context. (The English literary critic Terry Eagleton reminds us of the sign in the London subway: "Dogs must be carried on the escalator." And if I don't own a dog, may I not use the escalator?)

Getting Caught on the Escalator without a Dog

Because of this constant excess and slippage of meaning, every text, philosophical or otherwise, ends up defeating the first principles of its own logic, as Derrida tries to demonstrate: The key philosophical dichotomies collapse in upon themselves, for example, reality-appearance, being-nothingness, knowledge-ignorance,

certainty-doubt, theism-atheism, noumenon-phenomenon, fact-value, reason-unreason, waking-dreaming. Or, to use Derrida's language, they "deconstruct" themselves. (His form of analysis is known as **deconstruction.**) According to Derrida, the fact that all texts self-destruct is really a fact about language, hence about human thought. Yet every attempt to escape from "the prison-house of language" is an avenue leading back to it. And because, as Heidegger and Lacan pointed out, language creates the self (and not the other way around, as was traditionally supposed), the self itself is decentered and demoted under Derrida's deconstructive gaze.

Structuralism and Poststructuralism ◆ **393**

Irigaray

There are other important figures in the poststructuralist philosophical movement, such as Michel Foucault, Gilles Deleuze, and Félix Guattari in France and Richard Rorty in America, but perhaps the interest in the relation between language and selfhood has been most doggedly pursued by certain women philosophers in France, notably Hélène Cixous, Julia Kristeva, and Luce Irigaray. These are important, but not easy, writers to read. Understanding them requires a familiarity not just with philosophy but also with linguistics and psychoanalysis. And readers must be prepared to decode dense texts that are jungles of double meaning and eccentric syntax. Yet these difficult texts are in fact examples of the kind of feminine writing their authors recommend as a way of deconstructing the Cartesian logos, which, according to them, is part of the mechanism of the oppression of women. For that oppression is not merely to be found empirically in

Deconstructing the Cartesian Logos

the day-to-day workings of society, politics, and economics, but it is manifested in the logos of social organization itself, in the very act of producing *meaning*. That which is understood as "real" is a social product resultant from a "symbolic order" (to use the Lacanian phrase), and that order is "phallocentric," that is to say, constructed by men for their pleasure and advantage. If the perception of reality is to be transformed in a liberating manner, **phallocentrism** itself must be deconstructed. This negative act of deconstruction must be accompanied by a positive act of creation—Cixous and Irigaray call in various ways for the creation of a peculiarly feminine form of language and writing. Despite this common goal, there are significant divergences among these philosophers. Here I concentrate on a summary of some of the ideas of Luce Irigaray, whose background is in psycholinguistics and who is a practicing psychoanalyst, yet who presented herself for the prestigious *doctorat d'État* in philosophy because she felt that philosophy's role as master discourse needed to be questioned and disturbed precisely because of its claim to be the pursuit of Truth.

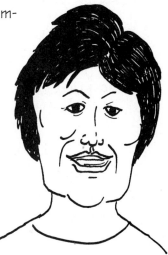

Luce Irigaray

As a psychoanalyst, Irigaray has been deeply influenced by Freud and by the Lacanian reading of Freud. But although she finds ammunition in Freudian theory for her attempt to destabilize the logos of **patriarchal** discourse, she is devastatingly critical of Freud's own surrender to that same **misogynistic** logic when it comes to his account of female sexuality. For Freud, oddly, a person's sexual history turns on an act of visual perception. When the little girl sees that the naked little boy has an organ that is missing to her, she believes that hers has been taken from her, and she envies the boy that addition (penis envy). Because sexual difference depends on visibility and because in women there is nothing to

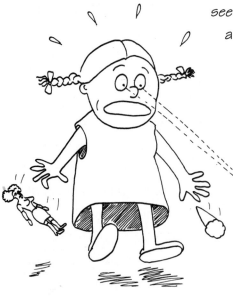

The Little Girl Sees the Naked Little Boy

see (*rien à voir*), woman is defined as a *lack* and is therefore outside representation. Women are seen as incomplete and inadequate males. In her book *Speculum of the Other Woman* (1974), Irigaray sets out to disrupt this absurd logic. The meaning of the word "speculum" is itself of interest. It originally meant "mirror," but it also refers to the medical instrument used by gynecologists to examine the womb (and hence alludes to a "spectator"). Furthermore, it is associated with the term "speculate" and is therefore related to the philosophical enterprise itself.

Irigaray applies the first definition of the word "speculum" when she points out that Descartes's philosophy (whose analysis occupies the middle of her book) shows the mind reflecting (and reflecting on) its own being—a hollow, autistic echo chamber of sameness. Descartes's narcissistic speculations purport to be meditations on the human condition but in fact are only meditations on the masculine (phallic) thought process—one that is incapable of representing woman as anything but the negative of its own reflection. In Irigaray's second definition, the (male) gynecologist's speculum allows him to gaze into the nothingness that is female sexuality, yet that instrument is necessarily shaped like the vaginal passage itself. Hence, the male gaze is after all determined by the feminine. Again, male philosophers *speculate,* that is, they gaze—yet they are unable to represent that which determines their gaze, the feminine other. (A woman privileges not vision but touch, but because touch cannot be seen, it cannot be reflected in the [male] mirroring mind.)

In Irigaray's influential essay "This Sex Which Is Not One," woman is characterized as indefinable because she is "decentered" and "multiple." Like Cixous and Kristeva, Irigaray believes that an account of woman's "difference" must involve an investigation of the feminine unconscious. She does not use Lacan's phallic symbolic realm as her key category in this analysis; rather, she employs the Imaginary—

Woman as the Reflection of the Cartesian Self

connected with the Freudian **pre-oedipal** relationship between mother and daughter (usually marginalized in Freudian and Lacanian theory)—where she finds a "difference" that is not simply the negative mirror image of the male.

Irigaray's account of *le parler femme*, or "womanspeak," shows it deriving from this pre-oedipal domain. Her first book, *The Language of Dementia* (1973) is an investigation of the relation between the demented speakers and the words they speak. This relationship is one of alienation—a passive repetition of words and phrases that speak themselves through the demented person, rather than that person being a true speaker. Yet, according to Irigaray, this relationship is very much the one that women find themselves in vis-à-vis phallocentric discourse. So far, woman has needed either to remain silent or to reenact the representation of herself as (literally) *seen* through men's eyes, that is to say, replicate a language that *erases* her. Irigaray seeks a form of creative language, writing, and thought that is truly woman's—one that allows woman to represent herself, one that, like the fluid elements of water and air that Irigaray equates with woman, is "continuous, dilatable, viscous, conductive, diffusible, . . . [changing] in volume or strength . . . according to the degree of heat."[62] That is, one that is very much like the writing of Irigaray herself.

Quo Vadis, Philosophia?

Topics for Consideration

1. Analyze the three following assertions, first from the perspective of William James's pragmatic theory of *meaning* and then from his theory of *truth:*

   A. The world is flat.

   B. Reality is only a dream.

   C. After your death, your soul will be directed to either heaven or hell, depending on God's judgment of your life.

2. What in general is the pragmatists' idea of *useless thought?* What kind of thinking is useful?

3. Write an essay in which you imagine G. E. Moore's response to Descartes's claim that, in the absence of a proof of God's existence, Descartes cannot be certain that he has a body (see page 162).

4. In your own words, describe what you take to be the point of Russell's Theory of Descriptions. What philosophical problems does he hope to clear up with that theory?

5. According to the logical positivists, all assertions are either analytic, synthetic, or nonsense. What function does this thesis have for the logical positivists?

6. According to the text, what is the main weakness of the thesis of the logical positivists that all assertions are either analytic, synthetic, or nonsense?

7. What features of Wittgenstein's *Tractatus* did the logical positivists like, and what features did they dislike?

8. Contrast the later Wittgenstein (in *Philosophical Investigations*) with the earlier Wittgenstein (in *Tractatus Logico-Philosophicus*) on the topic of "nonsense."

9. Explain what features of Quine's philosophy would be repugnant to the logical positivists and what features would be attractive to them.

10. Paraphrase Quine's "indeterminacy of translation" thesis as clearly as you can, and then either defend it or attack it.

11. Choose an object, event, or experience on which you can perform a phenomenological reduction (i.e., an *epochê*). First, write a description of that object, event, or experience from the perspective of everyday life. Then, after performing the *epochê*, write a report describing the same object, event, or experience from the perspective of the phenomenological reduction.

12. What do you suppose Heidegger means when he "calls us back to a remembrance of Being"? What obstacles stand in the way of our responding to this call, according to him?

13. Compare Heidegger and Sartre on the topic of our relations to other people.

14. Kierkegaard has been called "the father of existentialism." Write an essay explaining how Kierkegaard, who is a radical Christian, and Sartre, who is a radical atheist, can both be called existentialists.

15. Compare and contrast Lévi-Strauss's theory of how the human mind functions with the theory of mind developed by any other philosopher who appeared in this book (e.g., Descartes, Locke, Kant).

16. Show the extent to which Saussure's linguistic theory has influenced Lacan's version of psychoanalysis and Derrida's deconstruction.

Notes

1. Quoted in Morton White, *The Age of Analysis* (New York and Toronto: New American Library, 1955), 158.

2. William James, *Pragmatism and the Meaning of Truth* (Cambridge, Mass.: Harvard University Press, 1979), 28.

3. Ibid., 30.

4. Ibid., 34.

5. Ibid., 32.

6. Ibid., 97.

7. William James, *The Will to Believe* (Cambridge, Mass.: Harvard University Press, 1979), 20.

8. James, *Pragmatism*, 15.

9. John Dewey, *How We Think*, in *John Dewey: The Later Works, 1925–1953*, vol. 8, ed. Jo Ann Boydston (Carbondale and Edwardsville, Ill.: Southern Illinois University Press, 1986), 199–200.

10. John Dewey, *Experience and Nature* (New York: Dover Publications, 1958), 7.

11. Dewey, *How We Think*, 195.

12. Bertrand Russell, "My Mental Development," in *The Philosophy of Bertrand Russell*, ed. Paul Arthur Schilpp (Evanston, Ill.: Library of Living Philosophers, 1946), 12.

13. Bertrand Russell, *Philosophy* (New York: W. W. Norton, 1927), 2.

14. G. E. Moore, "A Defence of Common Sense," in *G. E. Moore: Selected Writings*, ed. Thomas Baldwin (London and New York: Routledge, 1993), 111.

15. G. E. Moore, "An Autobiography," in *The Philosophy of G. E. Moore*, ed. Paul Arthur Schilpp (La Salle, Ill.: Open Court, 1968), 14.

16. Christopher Hookway, *Quine: Language, Experience, and Reality* (Stanford, Calif.: Stanford University Press, 1988), 198. Hookway is speaking about W. V. Quine in this passage, but it applies to Russell as well.

17. Bertrand Russell, "Logical Atomism," in *Logic and Knowledge: Essays 1901–1950*, ed. Robert Charles Marsh (London: George Allen & Unwin, 1956), 341.

18. Ibid., 326.

19. Bertrand Russell, *A History of Western Philosophy* (New York and London: Simon & Schuster, 1972), 831.

20. Rudolf Carnap, *Philosophy and Logical Syntax* (London: Kegan Paul, Trench, Trubner, & Co., 1935), 32.

21. Ibid., 31.

22. Moritz Schlick, "Causality in Everyday Life and in Recent Science," in *Knowledge and Value: Introductory Readings in Philosophy*, ed. Elmer Sprague and Paul W. Taylor (New York: Harcourt, Brace, 1959), 195, 206.

23. Carnap, 24.

24. Alfred Jules Ayer, *Language, Truth, and Logic* (New York: Dover, 1952), 113.

25. Jon Wheatley, *Prolegomena to Philosophy* (Belmont, Calif.: Wadsworth, 1970), 103.

26. Ludwig Wittgenstein, *Tractatus Logico-Philosophicus*, trans. D. F. Pears and B. F. McGuinness (London and New York: Routledge, 1994), 5. Subsequent references to this book appear in parentheses in the text, using Wittgenstein's paragraph numbering system rather than page numbers.

27. Ludwig Wittgenstein, *Philosophical Investigations*, trans. G. E. M. Anscombe (New York: Macmillan, 1964), 6–7, par. 43. Subsequent references to this book appear in parentheses in the text, using Wittgenstein's paragraph numbering system rather than page numbers.

28. Not all analytic philosophers agree that Quine has defused the synthetic-analytic distinction. See H. P. Grice and P. F. Strawson, "In Defense of a Dogma," *Philosophical Review* 65 (1956): 141–58.

29. W. V. Quine, "Two Dogmas in Retrospect," *Canadian Journal of Philosophy* 21 (1991): 270.

30. W. V. Quine, "Two Dogmas of Empiricism," in *From a Logical Point of View*, 2d ed., rev. (Cambridge, Mass.: Harvard University Press, 1961), 20.

31. Ibid., 12.

32. W. V. Quine, "Facts of the Matter," in *Essays on the Philosophy of W. V. Quine*, ed. R. W. Shahan and C. V. Swoyer (Hassocks: Harvester, 1979), 163.

33. W. V. Quine, *Word and Object* (New York and London: John Wiley & Sons, 1960), 51 ff.

34. Peter Unger, *Philosophical Relativity* (Oxford: Blackwell, 1984), 18.

35. Hookway, 141.

36. Lynn Hankinson Nelson, *Who Knows? From Quine to a Feminist Empiricism* (Philadelphia: Temple University Press, 1990); and Louise M. Antony, "Quine as Feminist: The Radical Import of Naturalized Epistemology," in *A Mind of One's Own: Feminist Essays on Reason and Objectivity*, ed. Louise M. Antony and Charlotte Witt (Boulder, Colo.: Westview Press, 1993).

37. Edmund Husserl, *Ideas: General Introduction to Pure Phenomenology*, trans. W. R. Boyce Gibson (London: Collier-Macmillan, 1969), 91.

38. For a good example of treatment of intentionality by an analytic philosopher, see John Searle, *Intentionality: An Essay in the Philosophy of Mind* (New York: Cambridge University Press, 1983).

39. Martin Heidegger, quoted in George Steiner, *Martin Heidegger* (New York: Viking, 1979), 46.

40. Martin Heidegger, *Being and Time*, trans. John Macquarrie and Edward Robinson (New York: Harper & Brothers, 1962), 265.

41. Ibid., 237.

42. Steiner, 114.

43. Martin Heidegger, "Letter on Humanism," trans. Frank A. Capuzzi and J. Glenn Gray, in *Martin Heidegger: Basic Writings*, ed. David Farrell Krell (New York: Harper & Row, 1977), 213. The word "ek-sistence" is Heidegger's revision of the word "existence" in which he stresses the Greek etymology of standing out and relating existence to ecstasy ("ek-stasy," stepping out of oneself).

44. Jean-Paul Sartre, *The Transcendence of the Ego*, trans. Forrest Williams and Robert Kirkpatrick (New York: Noonday Press, 1957), 98–99.

45. Jean-Paul Sartre, *Nausea*, trans. Lloyd Alexander (New York: New Directions, 1964), 127.

46. Jean-Paul Sartre, *Being and Nothingness*, trans. Hazel Barnes (New York: Washington Square Press, 1992), 73.

47. Ibid., 76.

48. Jean-Paul Sartre, "Existentialism Is a Humanism," trans. Bernard Frechtman, in *Existentialism and Human Emotions* (New York: Citadel Press, 1990), 23.

49. Jean-Paul Sartre, *No Exit*, trans. Stuart Gilbert (New York: Alfred A. Knopf, 1948), 61.

50. Ferdinand de Saussure, *Course in General Linguistics*, trans. Wade Baskin (New York: Philosophical Library, 1959), 117.

51. Ibid., 120.

52. Edmund Leach, *Lévi-Strauss* (London: Fontana, 1970), 26.

53. Claude Lévi-Strauss, *Totemism*, trans. Rodney Neeham (Boston: Beacon Press, 1963), 16.

54. Claude Lévi-Strauss, *Tristes Tropiques*, trans. John Russell (New York: Atheneum, 1964), 160.

55. Claude Lévi-Strauss, *The Savage Mind*, trans. George Weidenfeld and Nicolson, Ltd. (Chicago: University of Chicago Press, 1966), 4. In this passage Lévi-Strauss is quoting with approval a Yale University doctoral dissertation by H. C. Conklin.

56. Jacques Lacan, *The Four Fundamental Concepts of Psycho-Analysis*, trans. Alan Sheridan (New York: W. W. Norton, 1978), 20.

57. Jacques Lacan, *Écrits: A Selection*, trans. Alan Sheridan (New York: W. W. Norton, 1982), 175.

58. Ibid., 264.

59. Ibid., 297.

60. T. S. Eliot, "The Love Song of J. Alfred Prufrock," in *The Waste Land and Other Poems* (New York and London: Harcourt, Brace, Jovanovich, 1962), 6.

61. See Gayatri Chakravorty Spivak's explanation of the term "différance" in the Translator's Preface to Jacques Derrida, *Of Grammatology*, trans. G. C. Spivak (Baltimore and London: Johns Hopkins University Press, 1976), xliii–xliv.

62. Luce Irigaray, *Ce sexe qui n'en est pas un* [The sex which is not one] (Paris: Minuit, 1977), 109. Translated by Toril Moi for inclusion in her *Sexual/Textual Politics: Feminist Literary Theory* (London and New York: Routledge, 1993), 142.

Glossary of Philosophical Terms

Boldfaced type indicates terms that are cross-referenced within the glossary.

accident In Greek and medieval logic, a characteristic of a **substance** that is not essential to the substance. Rationality is part of the **essence** of human beings, but being bald or hairy is accidental.

aesthetics The philosophy of art. The branch of philosophy that investigates questions such as, What makes something a work of art? Are there absolute values in art, or are aesthetic values always relative? Can there be aesthetic arguments, or are aesthetic judgments based only on preference? What is the status of art among other human intellectual and creative endeavors?

alienation A term usually associated with Hegelian or Marxian philosophy, designating the estrangement of a subject from its own **essence** or the rupture between a subject and its natural object.

analogy The assertion of similarity between two otherwise differing objects. Analogy was claimed by many **Platonic** medieval philosophers as one of the main sources of our knowledge of God. For example, although we do not know God directly, we know something about his mind based on an analogy between human and divine wisdom.

analytic philosophy The view that the main function of philosophy is the analysis of meaning rather than the construction of philosophical theories about the world. Analytical philosophers believe that certain key concepts in ordinary language and in scientific, moral, and religious discourse are philosophically vague or misleading. Philosophical problems can be solved and pseudophilosophical problems can be dispelled through the clarification of these concepts. The theories that analytic philosophers do generate tend to be demonstrations of the logical relationships among these different realms of discourse rather than grandiose **metaphysical** schemes. Although many of the pioneers of this school at the end of the nineteenth century and beginning of the twentieth century were Continental Europeans, the movement has become primarily an Anglo-American one.

analytic proposition A **proposition** whose predicate is contained in its subject (for example, "A triangle has three angles"; here the subject, "triangle," already entails the notions of "three" and of "angles"). The negation of an analytic proposition always produces a self-contradiction. Analytic propositions are contrasted with **synthetic propositions.** The idea of analyticity plays a major role in the philosophies of Leibniz, Hume, Kant, and the **logical positivists.** Quine's philosophy attempts to demote its significance.

anthropomorphism The projection of human qualities onto the nonhuman world.

a posteriori A belief, **proposition,** or argument is said to be a posteriori if its truth can be established only through observation. Classical **empiricism** was an attempt to show that all significant knowledge about the world is based on a posteriori truths.

a priori A belief, **proposition,** or argument is said to be a priori if its truth can be known independently of observation. Definitions, arithmetic, and the principles of logic are usually held to be a priori. Classical **rationalism** was an attempt to show that all significant knowledge of the world is based on a priori truths, which most of the rationalists associated with innate ideas.

Arianism A fourth-century heresy named after its leader, Arius, who denied the **doctrine of the Trinity,** holding that Christ had his own **essence,** which was divine, but which was independent of God's essence.

asceticism The religious or moral theory and its practice involving the requirement that one eschew all luxuries and any material goods other than the bare essentials.

atheism The claim that there is no God, or that there are no gods.

atomic facts A term of Bertrand Russell's used by him and other **analytic philosophers** to designate the most basic, simple facts out of which all other facts could be constructed. These facts were "atomic" in the original sense of the word, that is, indivisible. There was never consensus over what "atomic facts" are exactly. Some analytic philosophers decided that they were facts about **sense data;** others, that they were literally physical facts.

atomism The view of Leucippus and Democritus that the whole of reality is constructed out of invisible, indivisible, ultimate particles of being that they called atoms. The splitting of the "atom" in the twentieth century ended atomism. (The current atomic theory is not really a form of atomism.)

axiology The general term for the theory of values. It incorporates **aesthetics** and **moral philosophy.**

beatific vision, the A vision that bestows bliss, or extreme happiness, on the individual who has the vision.

canon The documents or books declared to be central to the beliefs of any religious, philosophical, or literary tradition by the authorities of that tradition. For instance, the book of Genesis is canonical to Judaism and to Christianity. The Gospel of Mark is canonical to Christians but rejected by Jews.

Cartesian The adjectival form of René Descartes's name. For example, "Cartesian philosophy" is the philosophy of Descartes.

catharsis The purgation of dangerous emotions. In Aristotle's philosophy this act is accomplished through the active engagement with dramatic art; in other theories it is accomplished by a cold shower.

causality The supposed relationship of **necessity** among events such that whenever event X happens, event Y cannot fail to follow. In that case, it is said that X causes Y.

conceptual analysis The logical and semantic analysis carried out by **analytic philosophers** of concepts deemed to be philosophically problematical in order to resolve or dissolve the philosophical problems that these concepts seem to entail.

conceptualism Abelard's theory of **universals,** located somewhere between **nominalism** and **moderate realism,** according to which concepts in the mind are abstractions that the human mind makes from similarities really existing in the natural world. As such, concepts are accurate but not perfect representations of universals.

contingency Used in philosophy to designate the opposite of **necessity.** In the sentence "This square is large," the word "large" stands in a contingent relation to the word "square," while the word "angles" in the sentence "This square has four right angles" stands in a necessary relation to the word "square."

cosmogony Theories or stories about the origins of the universe.

cosmological argument An **a posteriori** attempt to prove that God exists by showing that his existence can be deduced from certain observable facts in the universe. It was put forth by Maimonides and defended by St. Thomas Aquinas, Descartes, Leibniz, Locke, and Berkeley, among others. It was rejected by Hume, Kant, and Kierkegaard.

cosmology Theories about the nature of the universe.

deconstruction The creation of the contemporary French philosopher Jacques Derrida, based on his eccentric but provocative reading of the linguistic theory of Ferdinand de Saussure. Deconstruction is a theory of texts (philosophical, fictional, legal, scientific), according to which, because of the very nature of thought and language, almost all traditional texts can be shown to "deconstruct" themselves, that is, to undermine and refute their own theses.

deduction A form of argument in which the conclusion follows necessarily from the premises.

determinism The view that every event that occurs, occurs necessarily. Every event follows inevitably from the events that preceded it. There is no **randomness** in reality; rather, all is law-governed. **Freedom** either does not exist (hard determinism) or exists in such a way as to be compatible with **necessity** (soft determinism).

deus ex machina A phoney solution. Literally "god from a machine." Greek dramatists of inferior quality would create complex plots loaded with difficult problems, and then, with the use of a machine, drop a god onto the stage (played by an actor on a cable) who solved the problems supernaturally.

dialectic In the philosophies of Hegel and Marx, the dialectic is a mechanism of change and progress in which every possible situation exists only in relation to its own opposite. This relationship is one of both antagonism and mutual dependency, but the antagonism (a form of violence) eventually undermines the relationship and overthrows it. (However, sometimes the term "dialectical" is used only to emphasize a relationship of reciprocity between two entities or processes.)

doctrine of the double truth A medieval theory attributed to Averroës and developed by the Latin Averroists, according to which there exist side by side two categories of truth: revealed (religious) truth and philosophical (scientific) truth. These two kinds of truth do not compete with each other even where they appear to contradict each other; they simply offer discrepant perspectives on the same object. Whether a cynical theory, as some believed, or an insight into the nature of truth, as others believed, for a short time it allowed progress in the investigation of topics that otherwise might have been banned by religious authorities.

doctrine of the Trinity An official Christian **dogma** asserting the unity of the Father (God), the Son (Jesus), and the Holy Ghost (or Holy Spirit) in one divine Godhead.

dogma The principal tenets of a religious system as determined and enforced by the authorities. The word has also acquired a pejorative sense, referring to fossilized beliefs held tenaciously and uncritically.

Donatism A fourth-century heresy named after its founder, Donatus, who held that sacraments were invalid if the ministering priest was in a serious state of sin.

dualism The **ontological** view that reality is composed of two distinct kinds of beings, usually (as in Descartes) minds and bodies.

empiricism The **epistemological** view that true knowledge is derived primarily from sense experience (or, in "purer" strains of empiricism, exclusively from sense experience). For empiricist philosophers, all significant knowledge is **a posteriori,** and **a priori** knowledge is either nonexistent or tautological. The "classical" empiricists were the seventeenth- and eighteenth-century Britons—Locke, Berkeley, and Hume—all of whom denied the existence of innate ideas and conceived of the human mind as a "blank slate" at birth.

entropy The hypothetical tendency for systems to achieve a state of maximum equilibrium through reduction of tension.

epistemology Theory of knowledge; answering questions such as, What is knowledge? What, if anything, can we know? What is the difference between opinion and knowledge?

eschatology The study of last, or final, things. In theology, the study of death, or of the Last Judgment, or of the end of the world.

essence That feature of an object or concept that establishes the nature and definition of the object or concept. For example, Aristotle said that rationality is the essence of human beings, and even though the ability to laugh or to blush is unique among humans, neither ability is part of the human essence.

ethics Moral philosophy; the branch of philosophy that answers questions such as, Is there such a thing as the Good? What is "the good life"? Is there such a thing as absolute duty? Are valid moral arguments possible? Are moral judgments based only on preference?

etymology The study of the origins and histories of words.

evolution As used here, the transformation over time of one species of natural living being into another species.

existentialism A twentieth-century philosophy associated principally with Jean-Paul Sartre but also thought to encompass the work of Karl Jaspers, Martin Heidegger, Gabriel Marcel, Albert Camus, Simone de Beauvoir, and Miguel de Unamuno, among others. More of a shared attitude than a school of thought, it can nevertheless be roughly defined by saying with Sartre that existentialists are those who believe that, in the case of humans, "existence precedes essence." This is the thesis that there is no human nature that precedes our presence in the world. All humans individually create humanity at every moment through their free acts.

false consciousness A term in Marxian philosophy, originating with Friedrich Engels, designating the psychological state of mind of members of a society dominated by **ideology.**

forms Usually associated with the philosophies of Plato or Aristotle. For Plato (in whose philosophy the word "Form" is capitalized in this text), everything that exists in the physical or conceptual world is in some way dependent on Forms, which exist independently of the world but are the models (**essences, universals,** archetypes) of all reality. Forms are eternal and unchangeable and the ultimate object of all true philosophizing. For Aristotle, forms are also the essences of things, but they exist *in* things and are not independent of them. The form of an object and its function are ultimately related.

freedom Freedom exists if there are such things as free acts and free agents, that is, if some acts are performed in such a way that the authors of those acts could be held responsible for them. Some philosophers (called libertarians) say that these acts *do* exist, that some acts are freely chosen from among genuine alternatives, and that therefore **determinism** is false. ("I did X, but under exactly the same circumstances, I could have done Y instead. Therefore, X was a free act.") Other philosophers (called soft determinists) also say that free acts exist but define "free acts" not in terms of genuine alternative choices but in terms of voluntary acts. ("I wanted to do X, and I did do X; therefore X was a free act.") Still other philosophers (called hard determinists), while agreeing with the definition of "free act" given by libertarians, deny that any such free acts or agents exist.

functionalism The view in anthropology that socially acceptable behaviors and institutions can be explained by showing that they have survival value for their society.

hedonism Either the view that pleasure and pain *should* be the only motives for correct action (called moral hedonism, defended by Epicurus and Bentham) or the view that pleasure and pain *are* the only motives for voluntary action (called psychological hedonism, or **psychological egoism,** defended by Hobbes).

holism The view that the parts of a system are not independent, discrete units; rather, they are what they are by virtue of their relationship to one another and to the whole system.

idealism The **ontological** view that, ultimately, every existing thing can be shown to be spiritual, mental, or otherwise incorporeal (hence, a version of **monism**); usually associated in Western philosophy with Berkeley and Hegel.

ideology A term in Marxian philosophy designating the status of cultural phenomena (such as art, religion, morality, and philosophy) as systems of propaganda supporting a specific socioeconomic system and its beneficiaries.

incorrigibility An empirical statement has incorrigibility if a person who believes it could not be wrong. An example might be, "I feel pain now," uttered in a case where one in fact does feel intense pain. Whether such statements actually exist is controversial, but **empiricism** in its classical form (Locke) and modern form (**logical positivism**) put great stock in them.

induction A form of argument in which the premises are descriptions derived from empirical observations; generalizations are made from these observations. In induction, the conclusion stands in only a probabilistic relation to the observations on which it is based.

law of identity *See* **principle of identity.**

law of noncontradiction *See* **principle of noncontradiction.**

law of the excluded middle *See* **principle of the excluded middle.**

logic The branch of philosophy that studies the structure of valid inference; a purely *formal* discipline, interested in the structure of argumentation rather than in its content.

logical positivism A development within **analytical philosophy** initiated in Austria and Germany between the two World Wars by scientifically minded philosophers and philosophically minded scientists as a reaction against what they took to be the overblown **metaphysical** grandstanding of European philosophers in the nineteenth century. Their goal was to make philosophy respectable by making it scientific. Philosophy would be restricted to logical analysis whose outcome would be the demonstration that the only truly meaningful **propositions** are those of mathematics, logic, and science. All others would be shown to be merely poetic, emotive, **analogical,** or nonsense.

Manicheanism A religious system asserting the domination of reality by two opposing irreducible supernatural forces, Good and Evil.

materialism The **ontological** view that, in the final analysis, all phenomena can be demonstrated to be material in nature and that mental and spiritual phenomena are either nonexistent or have no existence independent of matter (e.g., as in Democritus, Hobbes, Marx, and Quine).

mechanism A theory claiming that the whole of reality is like a machine. Reality is made up of material objects in motion or at rest, standing in direct **causal** relationships with one another, requiring no explanation other than the laws of Newtonian physics.

metaphysics The branch of philosophy that attempts to construct a general, speculative worldview; a complete, systematic account of all reality and experience, usually involving an **epistemology,** an **ontology,** an **ethics,** and an **aesthetics.** (The adjective "metaphysical" is often employed to stress the speculative, as opposed to the scientific, or commonsensical, features of the theory or proposition it describes.)

metempsychosis The passage of the soul at the death of the body into the newly born body of another creature, human or animal. The belief in such a transmigration of souls is held in several philosophical and religious systems.

misogyny The hatred of women.

moderate realism An aspect of Thomas Aquinas's theory of mind and language, related to Abelard's **conceptualism,** espousing the Aristotelian view that **essences** are not separate from the physical world—as in Plato and **Platonic realism**—rather, they are embedded in natural objects. The human mind is capable of abstracting these essences from the natural world, along with other general characteristics, thereby forming the **universals,** which are accurate representations of these similarities that exist in the real world.

monad Term from Leibnizian **metaphysics** designating the simplest, most basic **substance,** which Leibniz took to be a unit of psychical energy that is both nonphysical and nonspatial, yet from which all physical and spatial objects are derived—perhaps in the way that neither hydrogen nor oxygen is liquid, yet two parts of hydrogen and one part of oxygen produce liquid.

monism The **ontological** view that only one entity exists (e.g., as in Spinoza) or that only one *kind* of entity exists (e.g., as in Hobbes and Berkeley).

moral philosophy See **ethics.**

mysticism The view that reality reveals its true nature only in a superrational ecstatic vision.

naive realism The view, attributed both to unsophisticated persons and to certain philosophers who defend a commonsense picture of the world, that reality is pretty much the way it appears to our senses.

naturalism As employed in this text, naturalism is the **epistemological** view that a natural phenomenon can be explained only by references to other natural phenomena; or **ontological** view that all is nature, that there are no supernatural or unnatural phenomena, and that there is no natural hierarchy of value. For example, humans are no more valuable per se than coyotes.

necessary condition A component, feature, or state of any object or idea X that must be present before the object or idea can correctly be designated as X, and whose absence guarantees that an object or idea is not an X. For example, oxygen is a necessary condition of combustion. Some necessary conditions are also **sufficient conditions.** Life is both a necessary and a sufficient condition of any organic system. Divisibility by two is a necessary and sufficient condition of an even number. Divisibility by four is a sufficient but not a necessary condition of evenness.

necessity (1) Logical necessity: There is a relation of logical necessity (or logical entailment) between two **propositions** if the assertion of one of them, together with the denial of the other, results in a contradiction. For example, there is a relation of logical necessity between the sentences "Linda is my sister" and "Linda has at least one brother" because the assertion of the one and the denial of the other would result in a contradiction. (2) Ontological necessity: There is a relation of ontological necessity between two events X and Y if the occurrence of the first event X *must* be followed by the second event Y. (**Determinism** claims that every event is necessary; i.e., every event follows necessarily from the events preceding it. Indeterminism claims that *not all events are necessary.*)

nihilism Either the view that nothing exists or the view that nothing deserves to exist.

nominalism The theory of language and mind claiming that the **universals** do not name independent **Forms, essences,** or general similarities that truly exist in the natural world. Rather, they are mere names designating convenient categorizations of the world for pragmatic human interaction with it. In the medieval world, nominalism (such as that of William of Ockham) was meant as a form of **empiricism.** In the more radical modern versions (such as Nietzsche's and Derrida's), nominalism is a skeptical doctrine, implying that what the human mind knows is not a real, natural world, but rather a world of convention created arbitrarily.

noumenal world Kant's name designating ultimate reality—the forever unknowable but necessarily existent reality behind the phenomenal world, or the world of appearance. Phenomena are in fact appearances of noumena.

numerology The study of numbers in order to reveal their supposed esoteric or mystical meanings.

ontological argument An **a priori** attempt to prove that God exists by showing that, from the very concept of God, his existence can be deduced. This argument has been defended by a number of religious philosophers in the **Platonic** tradition. It was first formulated by St. Anselm and appears in one form or another in the work of Descartes, Spinoza, Leibniz, and Hegel. It has some able contemporary defenders, for example, Charles Hartshorne and Norman Malcolm. But it has been rejected by some notables, too, including St. Thomas, Hume, Kant, and Kierkegaard.

ontology Theory of being; the branch of philosophy pursuing such questions as, What is real? What is the difference between appearance and reality? What is the relation between minds and bodies? Are numbers and concepts real, or are only physical objects real?

pantheism The view that everything is divine, that God's "creation" is in fact identical with God: from the Greek *pan* ("all") and *theos* ("god").

patriarchy Literally, rule by the father. Generally, any system in which political power is essentially in the hands of older males.

Pelagianism A religious view named after its founder, Pelagius, declared heretical by early medieval Christianity. It denied original sin and, according to Church authorities, overemphasized the role of free will in achieving salvation.

phallocentrism In the theory of **psychoanalysis,** the phallus is the symbol of male sexual power. Phallocentrism is the belief that such power should be dominant in culture.

philology The study of ancient written records, usually of "dead" languages.

Platonic realism The medieval **Platonic** theory of language and mind that claimed that the **universals** denote real **essences** and other general characteristics. Indeed, essences (**Forms**) are more real than the physical objects in which they are instantiated.

Platonism A theory basing itself on any of these interrelated ideas in Plato's philosophy: the idea that the intellectual or spiritual world is more real than the physical world, which is a mere copy of that superior world; the idea that **essences** are not merely abstractions but exist eternally as **Forms**; the idea of reality as a hierarchy of dependencies, each less real than that upon which it is dependent.

pluralism The **ontological** view that reality is composed of a plurality of beings rather than just of one kind of being (**monism**) or of two kinds of beings (**dualism**).

polytheism The view that more than one god exists.

pragmatism An American philosophical movement developing around the turn of the nineteenth century whose goal was to show that both meaning and truth should be defined in terms of a practical relation between thought and language on the one hand and the natural and social worlds on the other. Language and thought were conceived as problem-solving devices, and philosophical theories, like other ideas, were evaluated exclusively in terms of their instrumentality.

pre-oedipal A term in **psychoanalysis** referring to the time in the child's life before the oedipal period. The oedipal period is when the child begins to develop an erotic attachment to the parent of the opposite sex and a jealous antagonism to the parent of the same sex.

principle of identity Claimed to be one of the three basic laws of thought, this principle states that everything is identical to itself: Fido is Fido; A = A.

principle of noncontradiction Claimed to be one of the three basic laws of thought, this principle states that it is not the case that something both is and is not A at the same time (where A is any identity or characteristic): it is not the case that Fido is brown all over and not brown all over; $\sim(A . \sim A)$.

principle of the excluded middle Claimed to be one of the three basic laws of thought, this principle states that, given anything in the world, it is either A, or not–A (where A is any identity or characteristic): Either Fido is brown all over or Fido is not brown all over; A v $\sim$A.

Priscillianism A fifth-century heresy concerning the **doctrine of the Trinity**—that is, the relation between God the Father, his son, Jesus, and the Holy Ghost—originated by a Spanish bishop, Priscillian, and attacked by St. Augustine in his book *Ad Orosium, contra Priscillianistas et Origenistas.*

proper name As used in association with Gottlob Frege's theory of meaning, a noun or noun phrase that designates individual people, places, or objects, apparently without regard to any descriptive component, e.g., Sacramento, George Washington, the White House, the Capitol. Proper names are contrasted in grammar with general descriptions and with common names, like "horse" and "triangle," which can designate whole classes of objects. Notice, however, that a noun phrase like "the highest mountain in California" can be a proper name if it serves as a synonym for "Mount Whitney," or it can be a description, as in "Which peak in that mountain range would you say is the highest mountain in California?"

proposition As employed in this text, a proposition is whatever is asserted by a sentence. The sentences "It's raining," "Es regnet," and "Llueve" all assert the same proposition.

psychoanalysis The theory created by Sigmund Freud (1859–1939) concerning the causes of repressed wishes and fantasies in the unconscious mind and the relation of these unconscious motives to the conscious mind and to normal and abnormal behavior in general. Also, the psychotherapy associated with that theory.

psychological atomism The view held by Locke, Berkeley, and Hume (though not named as such by them) that all knowledge is built up from simple, discrete psychological data, such as the primitive sensorial experiences of colors, sounds, and tastes. (See also **sense data.**)

psychological egoism The view that the goal of all motivation is to achieve a benefit for oneself. This doctrine rules out altruism as a possible motivation unless that altruism is conceived by the moral agent as being in his or her own self-interest.

quantum mechanics A theory in advanced physics about the nature of atoms and subatomic particles such as electrons, protons, or neutrons that asserts that the behavior of these entities cannot be explained in terms of nineteenth-century **mechanistic** physics nor in terms of traditional theories of **causality.**

randomness If there are events that are totally uncaused and in principle unpredictable, then those events are random events. If there is randomness (i.e., if random events exist), then **determinism** is false.

rationalism The **epistemological** view that true knowledge is derived primarily from "reason" (or *exclusively* from "reason," in the purer strains of rationalism). Reason is conceived as the working of the mind on material provided by the mind itself. In most versions, this material takes the form of innate ideas. Therefore, for the rationalists, **a priori** knowledge is the most important kind of knowledge. In rationalistic **ontologies,** the mind and the world are seen to be in conformity—the real is the rational. The classical rationalists were the seventeenth- and eighteenth-century Continental philosophers Descartes, Spinoza, and Leibniz, but the concept is broad enough to include such philosophers as Parmenides, Plato, and Hegel.

realism The philosophical doctrine that a real material world exists and is accessible by means of the senses, or that the invisible entities named in physics, such as atoms and electrons, are real and not simply constructs of the human mind.

reductionism The project of trying to demonstrate that all apparently complex levels of reality can be shown to be reducible to simpler, more basic levels, for example, the attempt to show that all physical objects can be explained as atomic structures or that all mental events can be explained as neurological events.

reification The result of illegitimately concretizing that which is abstract, that which is general, or that which defies concretization. From the Latin, *res* (thing), hence, to "thingify."

relativism In **ethics** and **aesthetics,** relativism is the view that there are no absolute values; all values are relative to time, place, and culture. In **epistemology,** relativism is the view that there are no absolute truths; all truths are relative to time, place, and culture.

scholasticism The name given to the philosophy practiced in the "schools" of the medieval universities, where all branches of philosophy, **logic,** and linguistics were developed and systematized according to theological schemata.

semiology (sometimes called **semiotics)** The study of the system of signs. A "sign" is an arbitrary mark or sound that has become imbued with meaning by virtue of its membership in a system of conventionality. Language is the most obvious case of such a system of signs, but behaviors and rituals can also be studied semiologically.

sense data A sense datum is that which is perceived immediately by any one of the senses, prior to interpretation by the mind. Sense data include the perceptions of colors, sounds, tastes, odors, tactile sensations, pleasures, and pains. Classical **empiricism** based itself on the supposedly **epistemologically** foundational nature of sense data.

set theory The branch of mathematics that defines its numerical objects in terms of sets (for example, "even number" as the set of all numbers divisible by two) and establishes the logical relations among sets.

skepticism (or scepticism) A denial of the possibility of knowledge. General skepticism denies the possibility of any knowledge; however, one can be skeptical about specific fields of inquiry (e.g., **metaphysics**) or specific faculties (e.g., sense perception) without denying the possibility of knowledge in general.

solipsism The view that the only true knowledge one can possess is knowledge of one's own consciousness. According to solipsism, there is no good reason to believe that anything exists other than oneself.

sophism (1) The doctrines of a group of teachers in fifth-century-B.C.E. Athenian democracy who espoused **relativism** against **epistemological** and **ethical** absolutism and who emphasized rhetoric over reason in argumentation. (2) Sometimes a derogatory term designating a form of deceptive argumentation.

structuralism Based on the philosophical anthropology of the contemporary French theorist Claude Lévi-Strauss (but also finding followers in all the human sciences), structuralism is the view that the human mind is universal in that, everywhere and in every historical epoch, the mind is structured in such a way as to process its data in terms of certain general formulas that give meaning to those mental data.

subjectivism The view that there are no objective truths or values; all truths and values are relative to the subjectivity of the individual. (Subjectivism is a version of **relativism.**)

sublimation A term usually associated with Freud, but employed earlier by Schopenhauer, Marx, and Nietzsche, naming the process of refinement or of spiritualization whereby the more base and crass elements are transformed into more subtle or sublime elements; for example, the sexual or aggressive drives are transformed into art.

substance In philosophy, "substance" has traditionally been the term naming whatever is thought to be the most basic, independent reality. Aristotle defined a substance as whatever can exist independently of other things, so that a horse or a man (Aristotle's examples) can exist independently, but the color of the horse or the size of the man cannot. The seventeenth- and eighteenth-century rationalists took the idea of substance as independent being so seriously that one of their members, Spinoza, claimed there could be only one substance in the world (i.e., only one thing), namely, God, because only God could exist independently. Under Berkeley's criticism of material substance and Hume's criticism of spiritual substance, the concept of substance was very much eroded away. It turned up again in Kant, but only as a category of knowledge, not as a basic reality itself.

sufficient condition A component, feature, or state of any object or idea X that, if present, guarantees that the object is indeed an X. For example, fire is a sufficient condition for heat, but it is not a **necessary condition.** (Heat can be generated without fire.) Sometimes a condition is both necessary and sufficient. Life is both a necessary and a sufficient condition of any organic system. Divisibility by two is a necessary and sufficient condition of an even number. Divisibility by four is a sufficient but not a necessary condition of evenness.

synthetic proposition A **proposition** that can be either true or false and that asserts factual claims about reality. The negation of synthetic propositions, unlike for **analytic propositions,** does not produce self-contradiction ("The cat is on the mat" and "The cat is *not* on the mat" are both possible factual claims about reality). The **empiricists** hold that synthetic propositions are always **a posteriori;** that is, they can be verified or refuted only through observation. By contrast, Kant held that synthetic **a priori** propositions are possible.

teleology A teleological explanation is an explanation in terms of goals, purposes, or intentions (from the Greek *telos,* meaning "goal"). For example, "John closed the window because he didn't want his budgie to escape" is a teleological explanation because it explains John's behavior in terms of his intentions.

theology The systematic study of God and his properties, from the Greek *theos* ("God") and *logos* ("theory," or "study of").

universals A term in medieval theory of language designating common names like "redness," "quickness," "animality," "mammality," "wealth," and "humanity." The status of the universals was hotly debated throughout the Middle Ages, producing theories such as **Platonic realism, moderate realism, conceptualism,** and **nominalism.**

Selected Bibliography

Includes primary sources (some of the original works of the main philosophers discussed in this book) and secondary sources (some suggestions for further study), as well as a few personal comments concerning some of the books recommended.

Wherever possible, inexpensive paperback editions are cited.

General Histories of Western Philosophy

Copleston, Frederick, S. J. *A History of Western Philosophy*, in nine vols., now gathered in three books (New York: Doubleday, 1985). The author's biases are evident, but this work is a "must" for serious research.

Jones, W. T. *A History of Western Philosophy*, 2d ed., in five vols. (New York: Harcourt Brace Jovanovich, 1969). Many long passages from the philosophers, clear presentation, and reasoned discussion.

Russell, Bertrand. *A History of Western Philosophy* (New York: Simon & Schuster, 1945). This eminent philosopher's biases balance out those of Copleston. Beautifully written.

The Pre-Socratic Philosophers

Primary Sources

Barnes, Jonathan. *Early Greek Philosophy* (New York: Penguin Books, 1987). Pertinent selections with commentary.

Nahm, Milton, ed. *Selections from Early Greek Philosophy* (New York: Appleton-Century-Crofts, 1962).

Wheelwright, Philip, ed. *The Presocratics* (New York: Odyssey Press, 1966). It's good to have several anthologies of the fragments of the pre-Socratic philosophers in order to compare translations.

Secondary Sources

Ring, Merrill. *Beginning with the Pre-Socratics* (Mountain View, CA: Mayfield, 1987). A short, well-written commentary on the fragments.

Taylor, C. C. W., ed. *From the Beginning to Plato.* Vol. 1 of *Routledge History of Philosophy* (London and New York: Routledge, 1977). Composed of chapters on the pre-Socratics, each written by a different expert from the perspective of the most recent scholarship in the field. Not directed primarily to the beginning student, but usually accessible. Get this work and the rest of the *Routledge History of Philosophy* from the library.

The Athenian Period
Primary Sources

Aristotle. *The Basic Work of Aristotle*, edited by Richard McKeon (New York: Random House, 1941). This is the main text for all serious students of Aristotle's philosophy.

Plato. *Great Dialogues of Plato*, translated by W. H. D. Rouse and edited by E. H. Warmington and P. G. Rouse (New York: New American Library, 1956). Contains the *Republic*, "Apology," "Crito," "Meno," and "The Symposium," among others. This is only one of many inexpensive paperback editions now available.

Plato. *The Republic of Plato*, translated by Allan Bloom (New York: Basic Books, 1968). Perhaps the most accurate and literal translation (but therefore not the most readable).

Secondary Sources

Adler, Mortimer J. *Aristotle for Everybody* (New York: Bantam Books, 1985). A readable, enticing defense of Aristotle's views by a real Aristotelian.

Barnes, Jonathan. *Aristotle* (New York: Oxford University Press [Past Masters series], 1982). Almost all the books in this series are good, cheap, short, and readable.

Barrett, Harold. *The Sophists* (Novato, CA: Chandler and Sharp, 1987). A short, spirited defense of the views of the Sophists.

Murdoch, Iris. *The Fire and the Sun: Why Plato Banished the Artists* (New York: Oxford University Press, 1978). The author is both a foremost novelist and a top-rate philosopher.

Pirsig, Robert. *Zen and the Art of Motorcycle Maintenance* (New York: Bantam Books, 1982). A (mostly) fascinating contemporary personal investigation of the problem of value that obsessed the Sophists, Socrates, and Plato. Pirsig sides with the Sophists and repairs his Harley.

Stone, I. F. *The Trial of Socrates* (New York: Doubleday [Anchor Books], 1989). Wonderful depiction of Athenian political life at the time of

Socrates. Annoyingly simplistic criticism of Socratic and Platonic philosophy.

Vlastos, Gregory, ed. *The Philosophy of Socrates: A Collection of Critical Essays* (Garden City, NY: Doubleday, 1971). A fine sampling of scholarly work about Socrates.

The Hellenistic Period
Primary Sources

Hadas, Moses, ed. *Essential Works of Stoicism* (New York: Bantam Books, 1961). Contains Marcus Aurelius's "To Himself," Epictetus's "The Manual," and Seneca's "On Tranquility."

Oats, Whitney J., ed. *The Stoic and Epicurean Philosophers: Epicurus, Epictetus, Lucretius, Marcus Aurelius* (New York: Modern Library, 1940). A standard source book.

Plotinus. *The Six Enneads*, translated by S. MacKenna and B. S. Page (Chicago: Encyclopedia Britannica, 1952).

Medieval Philosophy
Primary Sources

Fremantle, Anne, ed. *The Age of Belief* (New York: New American Library, 1954). This is the first of "The Age of . . ." series. These books are short anthologies of works from the period treated. Each selection is preceded by a brief introductory essay. Very helpful.

Hyman, Arthur, and James T. Walsh, eds. *Philosophy in the Middle Ages: The Christian, Islamic, and Jewish Traditions* (Indianapolis: Hackett, 1974). Excellent samplings of the work of the main medieval philosophers, including selections from Augustine, Eriugena, Anselm, and Thomas Aquinas.

Secondary Sources

Eco, Umberto. *The Name of the Rose*, translated by William Weaver (New York: Warner Books, 1984). A best-selling philosophical novel by a medieval scholar. (You get a mean murder mystery as well.)

Gilson, Etienne. *History of Christian Philosophy in the Middle Ages* (New York: Random House, 1955). By one of the great students of the medieval mind.

Kenny, Anthony. *Aquinas* (New York: Hill and Wang, 1980). This is in the Past Masters series, which are short, usually insightful accounts directed to introductory students.

Luscombe, David. *Medieval Thought* (Oxford and New York: Oxford University Press, 1997). A short, expert, up-to-date discussion of the topic.

Price, Betsy B. *Medieval Thought: An Introduction* (Cambridge, MA: Black-well, 1992). Particularly good in relating philosophy to the rest of culture in the Middle Ages.

Renaissance Philosophy
Primary Sources

Cassirer, Ernst, Paul Oskar Kristeller, and John Herman Randall Jr., eds. *The Renaissance Philosophy of Man* (Chicago: University of Chicago Press, 1948). An excellent selection of works by a number of Renaissance philosophers, with good introductory essays.

Santillana, Giorgio de, ed. *The Age of Adventure: The Renaissance Philosophers* (New York: George Braziller, 1957). The second in the fine "The Age of . . ." series.

Secondary Sources

Parkinson, G. H. R., ed. *The Renaissance and Seventeenth-Century Rationalism*. Vol. 4 of *Routledge History of Philosophy* (London and New York: Routledge, 1993). The first half contains a sampling of contemporary scholarship on the subject.

Schmitt, Charles B., ed. *The Cambridge History of Renaissance Philosophy* (Cambridge and New York: Cambridge University Press, 1988). A large collection of essays by specialists in the field of Renaissance intellectual history. Get this one at the library.

Thomas, Keith, ed. *Renaissance Thinkers* (Oxford and New York: Oxford University Press, 1993). A collection of four short books originally published in the Past Masters series. Includes *Erasmus* by James McConica, *Bacon* by Anthony Quinton, *More* by Anthony Kenny, and *Montaigne* by Peter Burke.

Continental Rationalism and British Empiricism
Primary Sources

Berkeley, George. *Philosophical Works* (London: Dent [Everyman's Library], 1992). See especially *Three Dialogues Between Hylas and Philonous*. Very readable.

Berlin, Isaiah, ed. *The Age of Enlightenment: The Eighteenth-Century Philosophers* (New York: George Braziller, 1957).

Descartes, René. *Discourse on Method and Meditations*, translated by L. J. Lafleur (Indianapolis: Bobbs-Merrill [The Library of Liberal Arts], 1960).

Descartes, René. *A Guided Tour of René Descartes' Meditations on First Philosophy,* edited by Christopher Biffle and translated by Ronald Rubin (Mountain View, CA: Mayfield, 1989). Annotated with questions in the margins for students.

Descartes, R., B. Spinoza, G. Leibniz. *The Rationalists* (New York: Doubleday [Anchor Books], 1960). An excellent anthology selected from the key works of these philosophers.

Hampshire, Stuart, ed. *The Age of Reason: The Seventeenth-Century Philosophers* (New York: George Braziller, 1957).

Hobbes, Thomas. *Leviathan* (New York: Penguin Books, 1982).

Hume, David. *An Inquiry Concerning Human Understanding* (Indianapolis: Hackett, 1993).

Hume, David. *A Treatise of Human Nature* (New York: Penguin Classics, 1984).

Kant, Immanuel. *Critique of Pure Reason,* translated by J. M. D. Meiklejohn (London: Dent [Everyman's Library], 1991).

Kant, Immanuel. *Foundations of the Metaphysics of Morals,* translated by Lewis White Beck (Indianapolis: Bobbs-Merrill, 1976).

Kant, Immanuel. *Prolegomena to Any Future Metaphysics* (Indianapolis: Bobbs-Merrill [The Library of Liberal Arts], 1950). Difficult but much more accessible than *The Critique of Pure Reason.*

Leibniz, Gottfried W. *Philosophical Writings,* edited by G. H. R. Parkinson (London: Dent [Everyman's Library], 1990). See especially "Discourse on Metaphysics" and "Monadology."

Locke, John. *An Essay Concerning Human Understanding* (London: Dent [Everyman's Library], 1991).

Locke, John. *Two Treatises of Government* (New York: Hafner, 1964).

Locke, J., G. Berkeley, D. Hume. *The Empiricists* (New York: Doubleday [Anchor Books], 1961). The companion to *The Rationalists.*

Spinoza, Benedict de. *On the Improvement of the Understanding, The Ethics, and Correspondence,* translated by R. H. M. Elwes (New York: Dover Books, 1955). See especially *The Ethics.* (Benedict is the latinized version of Baruch, his real name.)

Secondary Sources

Ayer, A. J. *Hume* (New York: Hill & Wang [Past Masters series], 1980).

Hampshire, Stuart. *Spinoza: An Introduction to His Philosophical Thought* (New York: Penguin Books, 1992). Very readable; written by an excellent philosopher.

Martin, C. B., and D. M. Armstrong, eds. *Locke and Berkeley: A Collection of Critical Essays* (Garden City, NY: Doubleday [Anchor Books], 1968). A good selection of scholarly studies.

Scruton, Roger. *Kant* (New York: Oxford University Press [Past Masters series], 1989).

Warnock, G. J. *Berkeley* (Baltimore: Penguin Books, 1953). Still one of my favorites.

Post-Kantian British and Continental Philosophy

Primary Sources

Aiken, Henry D., ed. *The Age of Ideology: The Nineteenth-Century Philosophers* (New York: George Braziller, 1957).

Hegel, G. W. F. *The Phenomenology of Mind,* translated by J. B. Baillie (New York: Harper & Row [Torchbooks], 1967). Will look impressive on your shelf, but not recommended for the casual reader.

Kierkegaard, Søren. *Fear and Trembling,* translated by Alastair Hannay (New York: Penguin Books, 1985). A fascinating little book.

Marx, Karl, and Friedrich Engels. *Marx and Engels: Basic Writings on Politics and Philosophy,* edited by Lewis S. Feuer (Garden City, NY: Doubleday [Anchor Books], 1989).

Mill, J. S. *On Liberty and Utilitarianism* (New York: Bantam Books, 1993).

Nietzsche, Friedrich. *Basic Writings of Nietzsche,* translated and edited by Walter Kaufmann (New York: Modern Library, 1968). See especially *The Birth of Tragedy, Beyond Good and Evil,* and *On the Genealogy of Morals.*

Nietzsche, Friedrich. *Thus Spake Zarathustra,* translated by R. J. Hollingdale (New York: Penguin Books, 1969). The students' favorite.

Schopenhauer, Arthur. *The World as Will and Idea,* translated by R. B. Haldane and J. Kemp (London: Routledge and Kegan Paul, 1964). Big and imposing but surprisingly readable.

Secondary Sources

Barrett, William. *Irrational Man* (New York: Doubleday [Anchor Books], 1990). Classical work on existentialism. See chapters on Kierkegaard and Nietzsche. Also good for twentieth-century figures.

Fromm, Erich. *Marx's Concept of Man* (New York: Frederich Ungar, 1969). Contains philosophical essays by the early Marx and a long essay by Fromm. Both very good.

Kojève, Alexander. *Introduction to the Reading of Hegel: Lectures on "The Phenomenology of Spirit,"* translated by James H. Nichols Jr. (Ithaca, NY, and London: Cornell University Press, 1993). A very influential, brilliant, but quirky interpretation of Hegel that makes the connection between him and Marx closer than it is usually thought to be.

Mooney, Edward. *Knights of Faith and Resignation: Reading Kierkegaard's "Fear and Trembling"* (Albany: State University of New York Press, 1991). A fine little book by a friend of mine. Buy it; he can use the money.

Popper, Karl. *The Open Society and Its Enemies*. Vol. 2, *Hegel and Marx* (Princeton, NJ: Princeton University Press, 1966). Sir Karl is a foremost philosopher of science. This book is a very interesting and very biased account of Hegel and Marx, blaming them for just about everything that has gone wrong since their time (except those things that Popper had already blamed on Plato in Volume 1).

Rius. *Marx for Beginners* (New York: Pantheon, 1979). Cartoons and text by Mexico's leading political cartoonist.

Safranski, Rüdiger. *Schopenhauer and the Wild Years of Philosophy* (Cambridge, MA: Harvard University Press, 1990). A good way to break into the strange world of nineteenth-century German philosophy.

Singer, Peter. *Marx* (Oxford, England: Oxford University Press [Past Masters series], 1983).

Westphal, Merold. *History and Truth in Hegel's "Phenomenology"* (Atlantic Highlands, NJ: Humanities Press, 1990). You'll need a guide to Hegel's work. This one's good.

Pragmatism, the Analytic Tradition, and the Phenomenological Tradition and Its Aftermath

Primary Sources

Ayer, A. J. *Language, Truth, and Logic* (New York: Dover Publications, n.d.). This short book is the student's best approach to logical positivism. Be careful Sir Alfred doesn't convert you!

Derrida, Jacques. *Of Grammatology*, translated by Gayatri Chakravorty Spivak (Baltimore: Johns Hopkins University Press, 1976). Not easy!

Dewey, John. *The Quest for Certainty* (New York: Putnam [Capricorn Books], 1960).

Heidegger, Martin. *Being and Time*, translated by John Macquarrie and Edward Robinson (New York: Harper & Row, 1962).

Husserl, Edmund. *Ideas: General Introduction to Pure Phenomenology*, translated by W. R. Boyce Gibson (New York: Collier-Macmillan, 1969).

Irigaray, Luce. *Speculum of the Other Woman*, translated by Gillian C. Gill (New York: Norton, 1977).

James, William. *Pragmatism* (Cleveland: Meridian Books, 1961).

Lacan, Jacques. *Écrits: A Selection*, translated by Alan Sheridan (New York: Norton, 1977). Ouch!

Lévi-Strauss, Claude. *The Savage Mind*, translated by George Wiedenfeld and Nicolson Ltd. (Chicago: University of Chicago Press, 1968).

Lévi-Strauss, Claude. *Triste Tropiques: An Anthropological Study of Primitive Studies in Brazil*, translated by John Russell (New York: Atheneum, 1964).

Moore, George Edward. *G. E. Moore: Selected Writings*, edited by Thomas Baldwin (London and New York: Routledge, 1993). See especially "A Defence of Common Sense."

Quine, W. V. *From a Logical Point of View*, 2d ed., revised (Cambridge, MA: Harvard University Press, 1961).

Quine, W. V. *Word and Object* (New York and London: John Wiley and Sons, 1960).

Russell, Bertrand. *The Problems of Philosophy* (New York: Oxford University Press, 1967).

Sartre, Jean-Paul. *Being and Nothingness*, translated by Hazel Barnes (New York: Washington Square Press, 1992).

Sartre, Jean-Paul. *Existentialism and Human Emotions*, translated by Hazel Barnes and Bernard Frechtman (New York: Citadel Press, 1990). Start here.

Sartre, Jean-Paul. *The Philosophy of Jean-Paul Sartre*, edited by Robert Denoon Cumming (New York: Random House [Vintage Books], 1972).

Saussure, Ferdinand de. *Course in General Linguistics*, translated by Wade Baskin (New York: Philosophical Library, 1959).

Weitz, Morris, ed. *Twentieth-Century Philosophers: The Analytic Tradition* (New York: Free Press, 1966). Representative selections from Moore, Russell, the logical positivists, Wittgenstein, and ordinary language philosophers.

White, Morton, ed. *The Age of Analysis: The Twentieth-Century Philosophers* (New York: George Braziller, 1957).

Wittgenstein, Ludwig. *Philosophical Investigations*, 3d ed., translated by G. E. M. Anscombe (New York: Macmillan, 1968).

Wittgenstein, Ludwig. *Tractatus Logico-Philosophicus*, translated by D. F. Pears and B. F. McGuinness (London and New York: Routledge, 1994).

Secondary Sources

Archard, David. *Consciousness and the Unconscious* (La Salle, IL: Open Court, 1984). This comes as close to an "easy access" to Lacan as I've found.

Castaneda, Carlos. *Journey to Ixtlán* (New York: Pocket Book, 1975). An unusual introduction to the idea of phenomenology. Somewhere between anthropology, philosophy, and fantasy.

Danto, Arthur C. *Jean-Paul Sartre* (New York: Viking Press [Modern Masters series], 1975). Great!

Dreyfus, Hubert. *Being-in-the-World: A Commentary on Heidegger's "Being and Time, Division I"* (Cambridge, MA: MIT Press, 1991). The best guide to *Being and Time*.

Duffy, Bruce. *The World as I Found It* (New York: Ticknor and Fields, 1988). A good novel about G. E. Moore, Bertrand Russell, and Ludwig Wittgenstein.

Hookway, Christopher. *Quine: Language, Experience, and Reality* (Stanford, CA: Stanford University Press, 1988). Quine is tough, but this book is a big help.

Leach, Edmund. *Claude Lévi-Strauss* (Chicago: University of Chicago Press, 1989).

Moi, Toril. *Sexual/Textual Politics: Feminist Literary Theory* (New York: Methuen, 1986). Good chapters on Cixous, Irigaray, and Kristeva.

Monk, Ray. *Ludwig Wittgenstein: The Duty of Genius* (New York: Penguin Books, 1990). An excellent biography with philosophical summaries.

Norris, Christopher. *Derrida* (Cambridge, MA: Harvard University Press, 1987).

Passmore, John. *Recent Philosophers* (La Salle, IL: Open Court, 1985). Good, clear account covering philosophical developments up to the early eighties.

Pears, David. *Wittgenstein* (Cambridge, MA: Harvard University Press [Modern Masters series], 1971).

Steiner, George. *Martin Heidegger* (New York: Viking Press, 1979). A sensible introduction to difficult stuff.

Index